D1496463

Japanese Diplomats and Jewish Refugees

A World War II Dilemma

Pamela Rotner Sakamoto

PRAEGER

Westport, Connecticut
London

DS
135
.J3
S26
1998

Library of Congress Cataloging-in-Publication Data

Sakamoto, Pamela Rotner, 1962–
    Japanese diplomats and Jewish refugees : a World War II dilemma /
Pamela Rotner Sakamoto.
        p.   cm.
    Includes bibliographical references and index.
    ISBN 0–275–96199–0 (alk. paper)
    1. Jews—Japan—History—20th century.   2. Refugees, Jewish—
Japan.   3. Sugihara, Chiune, 1900–1986.   4. World War, 1939–1945—
Jews—Rescue—Japan.   5. Righteous Gentiles in the Holocaust—
Japan—Biography.   6. Japan—Ethnic relations.   I. Title.
DS135.J3S26   1998
952'.004924—dc21   98–6076

British Library Cataloguing in Publication Data is available.

Library of Congress Catalog Card Number: 98–6076
ISBN: 0–275–96199–0

First published in 1998

Praeger Publishers, 88 Post Road West, Westport, CT 06881
An imprint of Greenwood Publishing Group, Inc.

Printed in the United States of America

The paper used in this book complies with the
Permanent Paper Standard issued by the National
Information Standards Organization (Z39.48–1984).

10 9 8 7 6 5 4 3 2 1

Conversation with Mr. M. W. Beckelman, Saturday, March 29, 1941—8 P.M.,"
AR 33/44, #461: China, General, 1941 January-July; "Memorandum," from Inuzuka, handed to Captain Herzberg, 17 September 1941, AR 33/44, #462: China,
General, 1941 August-December; *Letters*: from M. Speelman to M. C. Troper,
AJJDC, 6 April 1940, Shanghai, AR 33/44, #459: China, General, 1940 Janu-
ary-June; from Lew Zikman to Cyrus Adler, 22 February 1939, Harbin, AR 33/
44, #723: Japan, General, Emigration, 1939–1941 (March); from Jakob Berglas
to the Chairman of the AJJDC, 15 June 1939, Shanghai, AR 33/44, #458: China,
General, 1939 July-December; from Alex Frieder to Charles Liebman, 3 July
1939, Manila, AR 33/44, #458: China, General, 1939 July-December; from B.
Kahn to Rabbi Stephen S. Wise, 7 June 1940, New York, AR 33/44, #723: Japan,
General, Emigration, 1939–1941 (March); from A. G. Ponevejsky, president of
the Jewish Community of Kobe, to the Joint Distribution Committee, 18 February 1941, AR 33/44, #723: Japan, General, Emigration, 1939–1941 (March);
from A. Ponevejsky to the Joint, 18 February 1941, AR 33/44, #723: Japan,
General, Emigration, 1939–1941 (March); No. 67, from M. Speelman, CAEJR,
7 February 1941, AR 33/44, #461: China, General, 1941 January-July; from Is.
Jessurun Cardozo, Mikve Israel, to the Joint, 18 November 1941, AR 33/44,
#533: Curaçao File; from Irwin Rosen to Isaac L. Asofsky, HIAS, 17 December
1940, AR 33/44, #533: Curaçao File; from A. Ponevejsky to the Joint, 18 February 1941; from A. Ponevejsky to the Joint, 18 February 1941; from Ernst
Baerwald, Berkeley, to Moses A. Leavitt, New York, 5 May 1941, AR 33/44
#724: Japan, General, Emigration, 1941 April-June. Reprinted by permission
of the American Jewish Joint Distribution Committee.

Every reasonable effort has been made to trace the owners of copyright materials in this book, but in some instances this has proven impossible. The author
and publisher will be glad to receive information leading to more complete
acknowledgments in subsequent printings of the book and in the meantime
extend their apologies for any omissions.

To my mother, Sandra Rotner,

and my husband, Tomiyuki Sakamoto, for their support from beginning to end.

Contents

Photo essay follows p. 100

Preface

IN THE SPRING OF 1940, Vice Consul Sugihara Chiune, Japan's only representative in Lithuania, cabled Foreign Ministry headquarters that he had issued a transit visa to a Polish Jew who wanted to go to the United States.[1] This communication prefigured Sugihara's nonstop activity that summer when he rescued Jews by issuing more than 2,000 transit visas, many of which were provided to those who had no emigration prospects. In 1985, Sugihara was recognized as a "Righteous Gentile"—the only Japanese ever so honored—by Yad Vashem, the Israeli institution charged with studying and commemorating the Holocaust.

Fifty-one years after that fateful spring, in the lovely city of Kaunas, I read a *New York Times* article, "A Yeshiva Honors Japanese Protector."[2] I was intrigued by the unorthodox connection between one of the most renowned European yeshivoth, the Mirrer Yeshiva, and a single Japanese diplomat. The Mirrer had the unusual distinction of being the only European yeshiva to survive the Holocaust in its entirety; its approximately 300 members traversed the Soviet Union and Japan with visas from Sugihara and spent the war years in Shanghai.

With that article, my own journey began through Canada, the United States, and Japan. As I traveled from archives to interviews, I wondered about Sugihara's motivations and about the ministry to which he belonged. I realized that Sugihara had not been placed in the context of the ministry he represented, and the ministry had not been spotlighted as an organization separate from the army and navy. The standard account of his actions is that he deliberately disobeyed orders from the Foreign Ministry in order to save Jews. Yet if Sugihara were a renegade diplomat, why did others comply, such as the Japanese ship captains who transported refugees from Vladivostok and the immigration officials who met the ships at the port of Tsuruga? Neither Sugihara nor many of his peers were alive, but the paper trail of documents remained. The documents would help reveal the chain of events surrounding his decision to issue visas.

The Diplomatic Records Office of the Japanese Ministry of Foreign Affairs holds the "Jewish Problem File." Consisting of fourteen bound folders of thousands of pages of cables and reports, the file includes only approximately a dozen pages of correspondence between Sugihara and the Foreign Ministry headquarters in Tokyo. Clearly, other diplomats were concerned with Jews too. What was the connection between the ministry's Jewish policy and Sugihara's actions? Who were the other Japanese diplomats issuing visas? What were the guiding values of this most cosmopolitan of ministries in a militaristic regime? These are some of the questions that focused a long search through the diplomatic cable traffic between overseas consulates and the Tokyo headquarters from January 1934 until May 1943. No one could guide me, because no author—Japanese or foreign—had ever written comprehensively about these records before.

The first references to groups of Jews seeking refuge in Japan and China did not occur until 1938, but I started earlier since Germany had begun encouraging emigration in 1933. Searching for refugees trying to reach Asia after Germany attacked the Soviet Union in June 1941 was a vain hope, but I wanted to know when Japanese diplomats realized what happened to Jews caught in Europe. I also examined a file concerning the Far Eastern Jewish Conference, an annual convention held in Manchukuo from 1937 to 1939.

Seeking the reactions to historical milestones such as *Kristallnacht* in November 1938 and the invasion of Poland was not enough. Lieutenant General Ōshima, ambassador to Germany, was silent on the turning point of *Kristallnacht*, presumably more concerned with improving Japan-German relations than with the shattered glass of synagogues and storefronts belonging to people in whom he had little interest. There is only one reference on September 9, 1939, to the eruption of war in Europe and its connection to the Jews, although there was a flurry of Japanese cable traffic in general at that time.

Immersion in the material proved worthwhile, because change occurred incrementally. Small adjustments were continually made on the basis of consuls' explanations of gray areas and their requests for instructions. Since diplomatic discourse is often vague by nature, close observation of events was also necessary to determine just how relevant words were. Change occasionally came when least expected, such as that set in motion by Sugihara in the quiet weeks before the Tripartite Pact was concluded and announced.

Then, there is the list recording the names of 2,139 people who received transit visas from Sugihara between July 9 and August 26, 1940. I have met some of the people on the list. At first I had difficulty reconciling my impression of now productive and seemingly happy people with an image of poor and desperate refugees. But the list is tangible evidence of their former status, and they are living proof of the list's significance.

Interviews have enriched this work by adding another dimension to the primary sources. I have talked with former Foreign Ministry officials who could recall the atmosphere within the ministry in the late 1930s and early 1940s; Jews who received visas from Sugihara or took refuge in Shanghai; and friends, relatives, and colleagues of Sugihara. I have taken care in using the interviews, since memories may be colored by a variety of harsh wartime experiences and inevitably become distorted over time.

Since this story concerns the period when Japan occupied Korea and parts of China, it was sobering when former Foreign Ministry people reminded me that as the vanquished, they too had suffered. Some of the more than 600,000 Japanese interned in Siberia after the war were Foreign Ministry staff caught in Europe or Manchukuo. Diplomats who had been posted in Europe were repatriated slowly, subject to dreary house arrest followed by interminable train rides interspersed with stays in cold and forbidding camps. The return journey to Japan took several weeks before the war via the trans-Siberian railway; later it required several exhausting, fearful months.

Some of those who returned to Japan faced investigations from General Headquarters of the Supreme Commander Allied Powers as to whether they would be indicted as war criminals. Even interrogations that ended without incident could result in lifelong enmity between former colleagues who suspected each other of betrayal. Sometimes the inquiries led to a sentence in Sugamo Prison.

Several of the Japanese with whom I spoke were still troubled by their struggles to survive in dire circumstances, although few were willing to share their experiences in detail. While they may express sorrow concerning the Holocaust, they perceive themselves as victims as well.

The perspectives of former refugees may also be skewed. Those who reached Shanghai were the lucky ones, although they had generally lost their entire extended families in the Holocaust. Their having survived tends to soften present perceptions of life in Shanghai, which was often bleak. Those who were young at the time fondly recall one of the world's most exciting and decadent cities. Their parents have darker memories, because they were preoccupied with satisfying their families' basic needs and enabling their children to enjoy as normal a lifestyle as possible in a difficult environment.

Survivor accounts tend to differ dramatically from the documents. Where the survivors are effusive in their praise of the Japanese, the documents suggest officials far from receptive to their guests. Where survivors are detailed in recounting daily routines, standards of living, and ethnic tensions, the documents are detached and clinical. When combined, these sources may represent the most accurate version of Japanese policy in practice.

Who was Sugihara? It is a difficult question to answer. But until speaking with his family and friends, I had only a cardboard image of a noble man, saintly but not very human. Interviews revealed his complexity and layers of his past. Views of Sugihara were affected by the issue of whether friends, relatives, and former colleagues had any interest in being publicly associated with his memory. Despite different perceptions, all agreed that Sugihara was reticent in general and consistently silent regarding his aid to Jews.

Neither Jews nor Japanese could have predicted that Jews would end up in Japan and China in 1940 and 1941. But arrive they did, and in increasing numbers in late 1940 and early 1941. This is their story, as I found it in documents—in relatively untouched Japanese ones and occasionally worn American ones—and in the voices of participants, always memorable, scattered across two continents.

NOTES

1. Please note that the surname precedes the first name in Japanese. I have followed the Japanese order in this book.

2. Ari L. Goldman, "A Yeshiva Honors Japanese Protector," *New York Times*, 21 April 1991, 32.

Acknowledgments

I WOULD LIKE TO THANK a number of people who supported my research and writing at The Fletcher School of Law and Diplomacy. John Curtis Perry deserves special thanks for his strong support. He is a superb mentor. Sol Gittleman inspired me with his combination of wisdom and common sense. Ray Moore led me in new directions, as he has done since I was his student at Amherst College. John P. Roche died before I was finished, but his larger-than-life presence has remained with me.

Among my most rigorous and dedicated professors, Benjamin J. Cohen has my gratitude for continuing to assist me even after he left Fletcher for the University of California, Santa Barbara. I credit my professors for helping me obtain a Charlotte W. Newcombe Fellowship from the Woodrow Wilson National Fellowship Foundation. The fellowship's purpose, recognition, and generosity have motivated me since the beginning and reenergized me throughout. I thank John T. Harney for his thoughtful help in bringing this story to a larger audience. At Praeger, I appreciate Jim Sabin's kind direction.

In Japan, I am especially indebted to Teruhisa Shino and Kiyoshi Suwa. They have shared their avid interest in and knowledge of Sugihara in a most generous manner. I could not ask for finer friends and colleagues.

So many people in Japan have informed this project with their particular expertise. I am thankful to Shinpei Ishii, Ryūichi Kaneko at the Tokyo Metropolitan Museum of Photography, Hideki Kaneda and Tetsuya Enomoto from Chūnichi Shimbun, Shunsuke Katori, Chiaki Kitada, Tōru Kobayashi, Yoichi Mikami, Amy Nishida, Naofumi Otani, Izumi Satō, Masaaki Shiraishi of the Diplomatic Record Office, the Sugihara family, the Takechi family, and Mr. Takigawa at the Israeli Embassy, as well as Jason Hyland and Sumiko Shimkin. Naoki Maruyama and Masanori Miyazawa, leading scholars in their fields, have shared their learned publications and research.

In the United States and Canada, I wish to thank Regina Chimberg, Denise Bernard Gluck, and Sally Berman at the American Jewish Joint Distribution Committee; Ari Goldman for initial leads; and Joshua Fogel, Jonathan Goldstein, Kiyoshi Kawai, Sheryl Narahara, Karen Shopsowitz, and Rabbi Marvin Tokayer. Ben-Ami Shillony's initial comments helped me pursue the project with excitement. Allen H. Meyer introduced me to and welcomed my participation in the "Unlikely Liberators Mission to Japan." Harry Fukuhara, one of the organizers, continues to amaze me with his insight into the American and Japanese cultures.

I appreciate the openness of all I have interviewed. I am particularly grateful to Susan Bluman, Hirsh Kupinsky, and Masha Leon. It has been a privilege to meet Ambassador Harumi Takeuchi and benefit from his kindness. All have entertained my repeated requests with good humor and thoughtfulness.

A number of friends helped me maintain balance, among them Rich Benedict, Andy and Chitose Conrad, Shannon Crittenden, So-il Hong, Blanche Hyodo, Donna and John Marino, Barbara Soojian and Michael Diener, Mark Montgomery and Laura Conti, Mariko Noda, and Shirley Yamada. Theresa Moran, David Bell, and Laura Meislin have cheered me on since the beginning. Steve and Toni Saddler and Sachiko Imamura graciously hosted me during research trips in New York and Tokyo. Marie and Norm Clark, friends who are family, have been with me every step of the way.

My family has provided the greatest support. I appreciate the Sakamotos and Nishimuras. I thank my aunt and uncle, Judy and Earle Leeder, and cousins, Sue and Herb Triedman, for their enthusiasm. To my father Howard Rotner, son Masayuki Adam, siblings Philip and Kim Rotner and Beth and Chip Davis, I am deeply grateful.

1

Introduction

NOW A PROUD CANADIAN, Susan Bluman was once a Polish Jew on the run. On September 1, 1939, the fateful day that Germany attacked Poland, Susan turned nineteen. Little did she know that this was the last birthday she would celebrate in her hometown of Warsaw. Before long, she would leave her family and embark on a treacherous journey from Poland to Lithuania.

Days after the German assault, Susan's boyfriend Nate left Warsaw for eastern Poland. He urged Susan to follow, and in December she convinced her father to allow her to go. "I was in love," said Susan, "and I wanted to be with Nate." Her father stated one condition: she must return in two weeks. Neither she nor her father acknowledged that the trip was not an impromptu holiday but rather the beginning of her escape from Europe. "I did not take any family photos because I was certain I would see my family again."

Susan packed lightly and quickly. The dress and ski boots did not match, but she was grateful for the boots later when pushing through waist-high snow in the countryside. The trip was fraught with difficulties. Susan was detained for several days at the border of Nazi-occupied Poland before reaching the Soviet side and reuniting with Nate. They decided to marry and continue eastward.

"Nate wanted to go to a country where he would have a possibility to go west," said Susan. In January 1940, Susan and Nate reached Lithuania, which was independent until the Soviets occupied it in June of that year. The Blumans felt safe at first, but their mood changed. "Everybody became desperate because we knew the war between Germany and Russia was imminent. We all felt desperate to get somewhere, which was impossible because no one wanted Jews."[1]

Like Susan and Nate Bluman, Sugihara Chiune had recently arrived in Lithuania, where he had opened a consulate in Kaunas. He was officially the acting consul, though his rank was vice consul. In reporting to his superiors in Tokyo, Sugihara mentioned little about Jewish refugees until July 1940, when hundreds congregated before the consulate in Kaunas to request Japanese transit visas. On July 28th, Sugihara cabled the Foreign Ministry in Tokyo that "there are about a hundred Jews daily thronging to this consulate for visas via Japan to the United States."[2]

Less than two weeks later, Susan and Nate Bluman stood before Sugihara in his office. The Blumans did not have an entry visa for another country, and Sugihara was not supposed to issue a transit visa without an entry visa for a destination. Moreover, Susan did not even possess a passport. The British consul in Kaunas, acting as a proxy for the Polish government, had placed a photograph of Susan in Nate's passport and registered her name—just as a child would be registered in a parent's passport. Sugihara said nothing about the Blumans' missing entry visa and Susan's nonexistent passport. He simply handed the Blumans transit visa #1569.[3]

In the following weeks, Susan and Nate journeyed east through the Soviet Union via Siberia to Japan. They disembarked at the port of Tsuruga and received an entry stamp for one month. They stayed for more than four months: they stayed until they could find a country to take them, and it was Canada that came through. When their ship docked in Vancouver in July 1941, almost one year had passed since their encounter with Vice Consul Sugihara in August 1940. As Susan had feared, Germany and the Soviet Union were now at war. But she could never have envisioned that German mobile killing squads would then be murdering 8,000 Jews trapped in Vilna and Kaunas.

Susan and Nate Bluman represent two of more than 24,000 Jews who escaped eastward via Japan and China to reach countries in the West between 1938 and 1941. Their destinations included the United States, Canada, Australia, and Palestine. The lucky ones—more than 3,000—successfully emigrated before the Pacific War began on December 7, 1941.[4] The remaining 21,000 endured the war years as visitors in Shanghai.[5]

Shanghai became a haven for Jewish refugees by accident. A designated "treaty port" since 1843, when Great Britain defeated China in the Opium War, Shanghai was open to foreign trade and administered outside Chinese jurisdiction. Other "treaty ports" along the coast, such as Tientsin and Tsingtao, already had small Jewish populations, but they were less accessible to refugees because the Japanese military maintained a strong grip and prevented entry. In the late 1930s, Shanghai was believed to be the only place in the world where a visa was not necessary.

Passports and visas became matters of life and death for refugees intent on fleeing Europe. These documents serve a straightforward purpose—permission to travel abroad. Passports record the holder's identity and citizenship, allow him or her to leave the country, and request protection abroad. Visas indicate that a representative of a foreign state has endorsed a passport, permitting travel within that particular country. Passports arose from the international sea trade in the 1700s, when vessels used them as safe-conduct documents to enter foreign ports. But they became essential to entering a foreign country—whether by land, sea, or air—as a result of war. In the aftermath of World War I, passports and accompanying visas became universally mandatory, and their importance increased with the approach of another war. By the late 1930s, passports and visas were necessary to escape Europe. When European Jews heard that Shanghai did not require visas, they were relieved: a major bureaucratic hurdle had been eliminated.

But by autumn 1941, Shanghai was virtually closed to refugees. Within hours of the attack on Pearl Harbor the Japanese navy occupied the city, and the refugees fell under Japanese authority. Although the occupation would escalate from distressing to frightening, it was never comparable to the Holocaust. How did Japan, a member of the Axis and a traditionally xenophobic nation, become involved in helping Jews?

With the stroke of a pen and the stamp of an official seal, as far west as Casablanca and as far east as Vladivostok, Japanese diplomats issued transit visas in varying numbers from early 1938 until spring 1941. The transit visas signified a way out of Europe: they allowed those who possessed authentic entry visas to make the trip. Some who held phony entry visas could use Japanese transit visas to apply for genuine entry visas before departing Europe. Sugihara's visas were used to flee Europe first and find a destination country later. Those without any emigration prospects obtained Japanese travel certificates, specifically for Shanghai.

This diplomatic activity occurred when Japan and Germany were fashioning an alliance made official by the Tripartite Pact of September 1940, and it continued until the spread of war to the Soviet Union blocked refugees. The Japan-German alliance was thoroughly hollow from the start, but neither Germany nor Japan expected Japan to issue visas to victims of Nazi persecution.[6] Desperate refugees inquired anyway, and Japanese diplomats were forced to respond. They looked to the Foreign Ministry in Tokyo for advice.

The Foreign Ministry viewed the visa question in terms of its effect on Japanese relations with the United States and Germany. Japan did not want to alienate either nation and assumed that its treatment of Jews could upset its balancing act. The ministry confided to its diplomats that Japan did not want Jews but that it would not persecute them. Transit through Japan was acceptable; entry was not. The ministry's position was clear but delicate.

While the Foreign Ministry reacted to Jewish refugees with caution and concern, the army and navy responded with interest. Several so-called "Jewish experts" stationed in China and Manchukuo were adamant that accepting Jewish refugees could work to Japan's advantage. They believed that Jewish capitalists abroad, particularly in the United States, would contribute to the economic development of the Japanese state of Manchukuo out of gratitude for Japan's benevolence toward Jewish refugees. They conceived elaborate schemes to solicit capital in exchange for refugee settlements.

Japanese diplomats in Europe, China, and Manchukuo were expected to follow the government's overall policy regarding Jews. The policy was decided at a meeting of five cabinet ministers—aptly called the Five Ministers Conference—in December 1938 as the flow of Austrian Jewish refugees to the Far East increased from occasional to steady. Prime Minister Konoe Fumimaro, Army Minister Itagaki Sheishirō, Naval Minister Yonai Mitsumasa, Foreign Minister Arita Hachirō, and Finance Minister Ikeda Shigeaki agreed upon a guideline apparently influenced by the military's Jewish experts. The policy basically stated that Jews entering and residing in Japan, China, and Manchukuo should be treated the same as other foreigners. No effort should be made to attract Jews to these areas, except for businessmen or technicians who could be useful to Japan.

The Japanese had a history of discouraging immigration. Declaring that Jews would be treated the same as other foreigners may have appeared fair, but it was hardly welcoming. The exceptions for businessmen or technicians represented, however, an opportunity for refugees who qualified. These categories were never clearly defined, but the underlying idea was that a skilled mechanical engineer or rich capitalist would be more attractive than an industrious merchant or talented musician.

Although this policy was ambiguous, the ministry's repeated message to its diplomats was not; the ministry instructed diplomats to discourage refugees from going to Japan, although transit remained possible. Most diplomats obediently followed these instructions and strictly enforced such visa requirements as a verified destination and adequate funds for the journey. Sugihara was exceptional. Many Japanese diplomats issued visas that saved Jews, but only a few like Sugihara saved Jews by issuing visas. The distinction is subtle but vital, for Sugihara gave visas to those whom no one else would have, such as Susan and Nate Bluman.

Ultimately, Japan, a member of the Axis and a traditionally xenophobic nation, became involved in helping Jews out of a sense of isolation. This assertion may sound contradictory, but the isolation was political, not geographical. Japan was increasingly estranged from the United States in the 1930s, and the alienation bred profound misunderstanding of American interests in Europe and Asia.

The Japanese military's single-minded effort to develop the puppet state of Manchukuo economically and militarily prevented it from perceiving the depth of American and international disdain for its efforts. The United States opposed the existence of Manchukuo, whether a haven for Jews or not. The Japanese government's policy towards Jews assumed that the United States was interested in European Jews, about whom the Japanese knew precious little of value. They knew even less about the American Jewish community and its clout, or lack of it, with President Franklin Roosevelt.

In 1938, Japanese diplomats were confronted by Jewish refugees in large numbers. Seemingly without warning, the Japanese consuls in Europe found themselves in the thick of the action. Just as the Jews were no longer a group of people to be evaluated from a safe distance, the Foreign Ministry was no longer an inaccessible bureaucracy, but individual diplomats.

The documents tell the story. By following the chronology, it is possible to capture a sense of the times—the bewilderment of Japanese officials coupled with the uncertainty of Austrian and German Jews amidst the steady escalation of Nazi persecution. Certain diplomats stand out, for their voices were strong and their opinions influenced the headquarters stand.

Most Japanese diplomats, like their counterparts from other countries, were bystanders aware of the persecution of Jews. As bystanders, they were "neither perpetrators nor victims," but they had an opportunity to alter events by opposing the perpetrators; in doing so, they would become rescuers.[7] Very few selected this route; instead they trod the path of least resistance. They chose not to assume the authority to issue thousands of visas to Jews. Instead, they deferred to Tokyo.

The course of events in the European war overwhelmed the cautious bureaucrats in Tokyo. The refugee flow determined the official response, which was reflexively anti-immigration. The majority of refugees ended up in Shanghai, because it was the only door open to them; no one had invited them—neither the colonialist powers nor China nor Japan. On their way to Shanghai, many passed through Manchukuo, governed by the Kwantung Army. Once in Shanghai, the refugees gravitated to the most affordable area, occupied by the Japanese navy. Others traveled directly to Japan from Vladivostok and ended up in Shanghai after exhausting all other options for a destination.

In China, the military shaped the policy that local consuls followed. The "Jewish experts" stationed there expended tremendous energy writing reports, meeting Jewish community leaders, and trying to influence more powerful officers. The Foreign Ministry, did have a distinct role, although it was hampered by the military's general dominance in the cabinet and in China. Regardless of specific policy directives, immigration issues belonged to the domain of the third section of the Foreign Ministry's America Bureau, handling administrative matters that did not have major foreign policy implications. While the navy and army's Jewish experts were dreaming up Jewish refugee settlements that would supposedly alter the downward course of United States–Japan relations, the Foreign Ministry's department was routinely treating visa requests made directly to Tokyo by refugees and answering questions from consuls abroad.

Unlike diplomats assigned to large consulates such as the one in Shanghai, Sugihara Chiune had no one but himself immediately at hand to obey or seek for advice. He was the sole Japanese diplomat posted to Lithuania. His superior was the envoy to Latvia at the legation in Riga, an eight-hour trip by train from Kaunas. Moreover, the consulate had no prior records to which Sugihara could refer. Its history was short: Sugihara had opened it in November 1939 and would close it in September 1940.

Sugihara had been sent to Lithuania to monitor Soviet troop movements; the Japanese were anxious to learn where the Soviets were massing troops in Europe. He was expected to use his fluent Russian. He had joined the Foreign Ministry in 1919 after dropping out of Waseda University, where he had been paying his own way. The ministry was appealing because it would pay him while training him. Sent to Harbin to study Russian, Sugihara performed so brilliantly that he ended up teaching it. Yet despite his recognized intelligence and obvious linguistic gift, he had entered the ministry as a noncareer officer and remained so. When Sugihara reached Lithuania, he was thirty-nine years old and a vice consul with little prospect of major advancement.

Sugihara's decision to grant thousands of transit visas caught the ministry by surprise. His action also affected the Japanese embassy in Moscow and consulate in Vladivostok, when it became apparent that the documents of many refugees en route to Japan were not in order. The Moscow office generally turned away refugees, while the consul in Vladivostok hesitated to reject them. When the consul in Vladivostok knowingly permitted refugees with questionable visas to board ships bound for Japan, he demonstrated the courage to make a decision that would not be popular in Tokyo.

In Japan, the refugees were uninvited guests who overstayed their welcome. Orthodox Jews strolling the streets became a familiar sight for Kobe residents, who treated the refugees hospitably, but the strange Europeans made the local authorities nervous and suspicious. The anti-Semitic, restrictive immigration policies of Western countries prevented the refugees from leaving Japan. In the autumn months before Pearl Harbor, more than a thousand refugees with no emigration prospects were transferred to Shanghai, where they awaited the end of the war. The marooned refugees highlighted how ill informed the Japanese government was regarding other countries' immigration regulations and how deluded any hopes had been that the refugees could influence the United States. The Foreign Ministry in Tokyo failed to recognize the extent of the problem until the refugees were on the Japanese doorstep, and the military had never coordinated its settlement plans with the ministry.

In the end, most Japanese diplomats became rescuers by accident. The ambiguous policy of the 1938 Five Ministers Conference allowed room for interpretation. The third section of the America Bureau continued to process visa inquiries just as it always had, realizing too late that Japan was one of only a very few countries that would issue any kind of visa to a European Jew in the late 1930s and early 1940s. Such a situation allowed many Jews to obtain transit visas for Japan, despite the government's stated desire to avoid having to deal with Jews altogether. When docile diplomats in China deferred to local Japanese military authorities who were intrigued by notions of international Jewish power and capital, impoverished European Jews with no emigration possibilities elsewhere flocked to Shanghai.

Yet it is remarkable that more than 21,000 European Jews survived the war in China under Japanese jurisdiction. In the late 1930s and early 1940s, the world was far more anti-Semitic than it is today. One need only to recall the doomed 1939 voyage of the *St. Louis* carrying 917 German Jews who were rejected by Cuba, all of Latin America, the United States, and Canada—only to return to Europe, where many of the passengers perished. On many occasions, Jews arrived at the port of Tsuruga with false, incomplete, or missing documents, but the local authorities rarely sent the boats back to the Soviet Union, where the Jews faced deportation to Siberia.

Japanese policy saved Jews not out of humanitarianism but rather as a haphazard response to external conditions. It is, however, crucial to place Japanese actions in proper historical perspective. Saving Jews on a national level in the late 1930s and early 1940s did not necessarily garner widespread public approval. Picture Canadian beaches in the 1930s marked with signs "No Jews or Dogs Allowed." Imagine the dismay when Jews arrived in Canada from a Shanghai displaced-persons camp in the late 1940s only to confront greater anti-Semitism than they had experienced in wartime Shanghai, occupied by the ally of their enemy.[8] Criticizing Great Britain and the United States, Zorach Warhaftig, a recipient of a Sugihara visa and subsequent Minister of Religion in Israel, comments, "Against such a background, Japan's decision to grant thousands of refugees, driven from pillar to post, a foothold within its safe borders, must be applauded."[9]

The story of refugees escaping Europe to the Far East is little known and therefore easily disregarded or distorted. American and Japanese historians have not pursued it. In the annals of the Pacific War it has been overshadowed by a concentration on military history, analyzing the morass of the China war and strategic disasters in the South Pacific. In accounts of the Atlantic War it is rarely mentioned. At first glance, the journey of Jews to Asia may appear insignificant in view of the enormity of the European Jewish tragedy. But these refugees represent 24,000 gratefully saved rather than surely lost.

NOTES

1. Susan Bluman, interview by author, November 1994, Vancouver, tape recording.

2. Telegram from Acting Consul Sugihara Chiune to Foreign Minister Matsuoka Yōsuke, #22785 coded, #50, 28 July 1940, "Minzoku mondai kankei zakken: Yudayajin mondai," File I 4.6.0. 1–2, folder 10, Diplomatic Records Office, Ministry of Foreign Affairs of Japan, Tokyo [hereafter JPF (Jewish Problem File)].

3. Acting Consul General Sugihara, list of Japanese transit visas issued in 1940 by the consulate in Kaunas, "Gaikokujin ni taisuru zaigai kōkan hakkyū ryoken sashō hōkoku ikken, Ōshū no bu," File J 2.3.0. J/X 2–6, Diplomatic Records Office.

4. The figure for those who passed through Japan is based on two documents: (1) Between July 1, 1940, and May 31, 1941, 4,413 refugees arrived in Japan, and 3,092 departed. American Jewish Joint Distribution Committee [hereafter AJJDC], "STATEMENT: June 1st, 1941," 1 June 1941, AR #33/44, #725: Japan, General, Emigration, 1941 July-December, AJJDC Archives, New York. (2) Between July 1, 1940, and May 31, 1941, 4,664 refugees arrived in Japan. Hebrew Immigrant Aid Society (HIAS), "Jewish Transients in Japan," by Moise Moiseff, 25 July 1941, Record Group 245.4, series xvb/xvc, HIAS Reports, YIVO Institute for Jewish Research, New York. (Mr. Moiseff was a member of the Board of Directors of the Jewish Community of Kobe. I have not included those who traveled via Japan before 1940, since it was a "handful" between 1933 and 1939.)

5. The numbers vary widely, ranging from 17,000 to 30,000, depending upon

the secondary source. I have relied on three original documents. (1) AR #33/44, #461: China, General, 1941 January-July, AJJDC Archives, (2) AR 33/44, #725: Japan, General, Emigration, 1941 July-December, AJJDC Archives, (3) AR 33/44, #462: China, General, 1941 August-December, AJJDC Archives.

6. Johanna Meskill coined the phrase "the hollow alliance." Johanna Menzel Meskill, *Hitler & Japan: The Hollow Alliance* (New York: Atherton Press, 1966).

7. Ervin Staub, *The Roots of Evil: The Origins of Genocide and Other Group Violence* (Cambridge: Cambridge University Press, 1989), 20–21.

8. Sara Cohen, interview by author, Toronto, Canada, 25 December 1993, notes.

9. Zorach Warhaftig, *Refugee and Survivor: Rescue Efforts during the Holocaust* (Jerusalem: Yad Vashem, 1988), 235–36.

2

Before Japan Had a Jewish Problem: The War in China and Japanese Anti-Semitism

ON A WINTER DAY in February 1935, the Japanese consul general at Harbin met the leaders of the local Jewish community. After exchanging pleasantries, the Jews made their point. "We have lived here for thirty years," they said, and began to describe the wave of anti-Semitism accompanying Japanese rule. Indeed, the Harbin Jewish community was established, prosperous, and law-abiding. The Japanese were the brash interlopers, who had unilaterally created Manchukuo in 1932 from the region of Manchuria.

Consul General Morishima seemed uncomfortable. The Japanese army, dominating the cosmopolitan city of Harbin, was permitting anti-Semitic activities by White Russians, who had fled the Bolsheviks in the wake of the 1917 Revolution. Although touted as a utopian state, Manchukuo was not proving such for non-Japanese residents. According to his notes of this meeting, Morishima professed sympathy toward the Jews and acknowledged the gap between rhetoric and the reality of Manchukuo.[1]

Manchukuo had been flawed from its inauspicious beginning. Yet the Japanese government remained equally ambitious about and defensive over it. Japan believed that the existing Jewish communities could be used to aid the nascent state's economic development and the campaign to justify its existence. Thus emerged an intense interest in the potential of Jews living in China to influence Jews in the United States. This policy was riddled with ignorance, mistaken premises, and false hopes.

INTERNATIONAL ISOLATION

"I was seduced by that great expanse called Manchuria," recalled a Japanese settler. Manchuria possessed a tranquil beauty. "Cottonbud willows seem to dance in the shimmering waves of heat," mused another resident. From one's train window, "the red sorghum fields stretched on for an eternity and the evening sun set far, far away."[2] The lure of distance and freedom of space were always factors in Japanese descriptions of Manchuria.

For Japan, Manchuria was a great frontier, just as it had been for China. For centuries China's rulers had perceived the largely unsettled area as having strategic importance. In the 1500s the Ming regime feared the combined threats of invasion and Manchu separatism; it governed the frontier of South Manchuria through both civil and military rule. When the Manchus vanquished the Ming in 1644, they preserved their homeland by keeping North Manchuria as a hunting preserve, administering the entire region through a military government and restricting Chinese immigration. As late as the nineteenth century, Manchuria remained thinly settled wilderness.

The Russians too were taken with the huge stretch of Manchuria. In the mid-nineteenth century they negotiated the cession of the coastal provinces and in doing so became a Pacific power. But with their defeat in the Russo-Japanese War in 1905 they lost the southern tip of Manchuria, as well as the portion of Russian railroads passing through it. Russia's loss was Japan's gain.

Japan continued to consolidate its power. While Europe was preoccupied with World War I, Japan secured greater economic rights in Manchuria, issuing its Twenty-One Demands to China in 1915. By 1928, its actions had become even bolder. A faction in the Kwantung Army, the Japanese force in Manchuria, orchestrated the assassination of the Chinese warlord there. In September 1931, a group of army officers planted a bomb on the tracks of the South Manchurian Railway; when it exploded, they attacked the Chinese barracks to avenge the crime. The Mukden Incident, as the event was known, resulted in the Japanese seizure of Manchuria. In February 1932, Japan formally claimed Manchuria—renamed Manchukuo—as its own.

For Japan, Manchuria was a magnificent prize turned political morass—a "cradle of conflict," according to historian Owen Lattimore.[3] Within a year of the founding of Manchukuo, the League of Nations, with the Lytton Report, condemned Japan's actions. As a result, Japan left the League. Its withdrawal was seminal: Japan thereby isolated itself internationally. In need of friends, Japan and Germany drew closer together, and anti-Semitic ideas began to be disseminated more widely in the Japanese press.[4]

What was compelling enough about Manchuria to risk international reproach? Its sheer size appealed to Japanese officials, hungry for more space than that available in the crowded archipelago. As large as the northeastern United States, Manchuria offered an outlet for Japan's surplus population, along with fertile land to farm. Japan itself was smaller than the state of Texas and ranked among the world's most populous nations, with a density of more than 2,900 per square mile of arable land in 1930. Moreover, Manchuria was rich in natural resources and appealed to the armed forces as an abundant source of minerals and ore for the empire's military buildup.[5] The region also possessed strategic value as a buffer state between the formidable Soviet Union and other areas of China that Japan desired.

Eight hundred thousand Japanese colonists moved there in search of better lives, among them "bureaucrats, soldiers, farmers, shopkeepers, industrialists," and others. Like the American Wild West, Manchukuo attracted its share of misfits, dreamers, and adventurers, including young renegade soldiers involved in the February 26 Incident of 1936, a failed coup d'état that revealed how dangerous the army could be to the government.[6] Japan sent not only people but also capital: during its existence Manchukuo received more capital from Japan than India had from the United Kingdom during 200 years of imperial rule.[7]

Japan justified its involvement in Manchukuo in the "Asiatic Monroe Doctrine" of 1933, by which Japan claimed to promote peace in East Asia via the development of Manchukuo; three years later, this doctrine was supplanted by the concepts of "co-prosperity" and "co-existence."[8] Japan's misadventure in Manchukuo and China was a war of words as well as weaponry. Manchukuo was described as a region of *gozoku kyōwa* (harmony of five races). *Minzoku byōdō* (racial equality) was another tenet expressing Japan's effort to unify Asians against the white race, whose prejudice was well known. One needed only to look at the United States. In 1924 the U.S. Congress passed a law prohibiting all Japanese and Chinese immigration; Japan smarted from shame and humiliation. This added to the smoldering resentment over its snub at the Paris Peace Conference in 1919, when its call for a racial equality clause in the Covenant of the League of Nations had been rejected; some in the Japanese media had angrily called Woodrow Wilson a "hypocrite."

Given Japan's indignation over American treatment of its nationals and its proclaimed insistence on racial equality, it could not very well discriminate against Jews living in Japanese-occupied territory—at least not openly. Although Japan persecuted other Asians, Jews were Caucasians who were treated differently. Japan also feared the response of the international media, which it believed was controlled by Jews.

Manchukuo may have been beautiful, but it was a complex environment in which to conduct diplomacy. When Consul General Morishima met with the Harbin Jewish leaders, he tried to respond to their concerns in a way that recognized the validity of their comments but also the aspirations of the state he represented. The local White Russian newspaper *Nash Put* was slandering the Jews with the "poison of barbaric anti-Semitism," he agreed, and the repercussions would extend to Japan, for "curses and slander harm a country that proclaims racial equality as a principle."[9]

INTERACTION WITH HARBIN JEWS

Morishima needed to be responsive and careful, because Harbin was no rural backwater. The hub of Manchuria, the city boasted wide avenues and imposing architecture. The bustling metropolis was "like a foreign country" for many awed Japanese, who were thrilled by its beauty and liveliness. The churches were onion-domed, the villas turreted, and the markets and cabarets reminiscent of czarist days. In its heyday in the 1920s, Harbin introduced the striptease, the Charleston, and Dixieland jazz to China, by way of Paris via the trans-Siberian railway.[10]

For 13,000 Russian Jews, Harbin was home. Approximately 500 arrived in 1903 to help build the Chinese Eastern Railroad. By 1908, the number had increased to 8,000, with Jewish soldiers discharged at the end of the Russo-Japanese War electing to remain in Harbin, where they had been stationed. Other Jews followed, fleeing pogroms. The Jewish population peaked at 13,000 in 1920 in the wake of the Russian Revolution. Many Russian Jews chose to become stateless rather than obtain Soviet citizenship.

Harbin appealed to the Jews because the Russian government, and later the Soviets, permitted greater political latitude in distant Manchuria, for the Chinese Eastern Railroad. The railroad administration set policy in the railway zone, which was 1,000 miles long and fifteen miles wide. Since the authorities were more concerned with developing the area quickly than in enacting restrictive legislation, Jews migrating to Harbin and in lesser numbers to other cities in Manchuria, such as Manchouli, Hailar, and Tsitsihar, discovered a haven of economic opportunity and political tolerance in this strip. Far from such virulently anti-Semitic regions as the Ukraine, where pogroms had claimed more than 60,000 lives, they could lead refreshingly free, productive existences. When the Kwantung Army occupied Manchuria in 1931, the Harbin Jewish community was vibrant and close knit. Its facilities and services included several synagogues, religious schools, a Jewish hospital, two Jewish banks, two Jewish journals, and a Zionist organization.

By 1935, however, Harbin's stable Jewish population had declined dramatically, to 5,000. With the Japanese occupation international trade had decreased, driving many Jews to the large, thriving ports of Shanghai and Tientsin. But a greater problem was the charged political environment. When the Japanese occupied Manchuria, they began pressuring the Soviets to cede control of the Chinese Eastern Railroad. By employing gangs of fascist and anti-Semitic White Russians as spies and rabble-rousers to stir up trouble for the Soviets, the Japanese were able to acquire the Chinese Eastern Railroad rights in 1935. The gangs also fomented trouble for the Jews while on the Japanese payroll. White Russians working with the *kempeitai* (secret police) used their power to make unwarranted arrests. The violence escalated to heinous crimes. Simon Kaspé, a young Jewish pianist, was kidnapped for ransom and brutally murdered by Russian gang members in December 1933; Jews were frightened and outraged. The criminals had ties to the Japanese police in Harbin, who tried to excuse the crime and actively subverted the trial.

Alarm over the botched investigation reached Shanghai, where N. E. B. Ezra, the feisty publisher of Shanghai's Zionist newspaper, *Israel's Messenger*, actively corresponded with Japanese officials. In November 1934, Ezra portrayed the situation for Jews in Harbin as "desperate": he appealed, "American papers are now saying that Jewish plight in Harbin is due to Japanese influence. What an advertisement and a slur on your good government!"

Always one to foster positive relations between Japan and the Jewish community in China, Ezra was miffed that Shigemitsu Mamoru, the Vice Minister for Foreign Affairs, had not responded to his letters. "I am not writing to Shigemitsu any more. I wrote him enough and duly expect him to act and move in the matter. It is hard to bear this burden because it is a pressure from a friend and not an enemy of our people. Please do something and not let the conscience to lull."[11]

But Ezra soon set aside his vow to stop corresponding with Shigemitsu. He complained to him hotly of the editor of the anti-Semitic *Nash Put*—"Cannot some steps be taken to muzzle a crazy man who is seeking to create a massacre of innocent souls in Manchukuo?" Shigemitsu never responded, but Ezra did not stop writing Japanese officials about the worsening situation of Harbin Jews until his untimely death in 1936. Ezra repeatedly reminded the Japanese that their declarations of racial equality included the Jews residing in occupied territory, and that the world would take notice should Japanese actions fall short of their words. Ezra knew that diplomats would be sensitive to the reverberating effects of Japanese actions in Manchukuo and China.

But Japanese diplomats were not in charge in Manchukuo. The Kwantung Army was. Duplicitous proclamations of racial equality were common operating procedure. The scheme to obtain the Chinese Eastern Railroad from the Soviets even if it involved alienating a pacifist, nonthreatening group such as the Jews exemplified the nature of the China conflict in general. It was, as James Crowley writes, "a perilous mission inspired by imperial ideology not circumscribed by careful or credible strategic calculations."[12] In comparison to diplomats, soldiers were not sensitive as to how their words might be construed. There was no direct correspondence between words and actions: their statements were in the service of their actions.

That is not to say that diplomats did not have a presence. The Foreign Ministry concentrated on China. In 1934, there were seventy diplomats in the United States, while there were 232 in China. By 1941, the American figure had increased to eighty-two, while the China figure had virtually tripled, to 640.[13] Despite these impressive numbers, however, in Manchukuo the Kwantung Army maintained a tight grip on the government, as the appointment of the commanding general as ambassador shows.

In 1936, Kasai Tadakazu served as a junior diplomat in the Manchukuo Affairs Bureau, the Manchukuo equivalent of the Japan's Ministry of Foreign Affairs. He had not chosen the Manchukuo ministry; the Kwantung Army had. After graduating from the famed Harbin Gakuin academy, where he had studied Russian, Kasai was assigned to the border station of Manchouli. Along with his job came a new citizenship; suddenly Kasai, a country boy from the same quiet prefecture as Sugihara Chiune, received dual citizenship from Japan and Manchukuo. Kasai did not meet many Kwantung Army officials while working in Manchouli, but he was conscious of the army's power. He noticed that his Chinese and Manchurian colleagues were not allowed to do important tasks. "Unlike what one learned in school regarding equality, the reality was different. There was discrimination."[14]

Kasai's experience matches the later recollection of Shigemitsu Mamoru. When the Manchukuo Affairs Bureau was formed in May 1932, it was placed under the jurisdiction of the War Office, not the Foreign Ministry, leading Shigemitsu to reflect in 1958 that "for all practical purposes Manchukuo came under the administration of the Army."[15]

The Kwantung Army acted inconsistently. While employing the slogans of an ideological war, it permitted persecution of non-Japanese. Also, while observing the Jewish population drain from Manchukuo to China, it considered the value of exploiting the Jews for Japanese gain. Little more than a year after Manchukuo's establishment, the Kwantung police chief issued a report entitled "Regarding Jews in Northern Manchuria," one that combined data with a section of suggestions. Jews in Manchukuo appeared to feel negatively toward the Japanese, the police chief found, but their opinions should not be publicized. Rather, the Jews should declare their sympathy for Manchukuo and be encouraged to solicit foreign capital. In addition, he argued, the Jewish press should report favorably on relations with Japan. Japan could not very well act contrary to its claim of an open door and racial equality. While the Jews were Japan's enemies, the report concluded, Japan could use them.[16]

This approach was typical of Japan's own version of anti-Semitism in the 1930s: the overriding theme was that of the Jew as enemy, but using the Jews was a compelling argument. The traditional stereotype, imported from Europe, of the "greedy Jew" took on the softer, more appealing patina of the "wealthy Jew." The Jew with money or influence was someone the Japanese would welcome and court, for his gifts could be put to good use. There was a precedent for Jewish assistance to Japan—Jacob Schiff, whose aid during the Russo-Japanese War was instrumental and legendary. As president of Kuhn, Loeb, and Co., Schiff had helped Japan raise almost $200 million on American markets, which Japan used to purchase much needed weapons and ammunition. For his efforts, Schiff became the first foreigner awarded the Order of the Rising Sun by the emperor. Driven by his hatred of czarist Russia and its history of persecuting Jews, Schiff became a symbol in Japanese eyes of the rich American Jew.

Using the Jews was never as easy as it may have appeared on paper. Despite the recommendations to control the Jewish community and present a positive image abroad, bad news did spread. In February 1935, Rabbi Stephen Wise, the prominent leader of the American Jewish Congress, visited the Japanese ambassador in Washington to request an explanation of the Japanese authorities' encouragement of anti-Semitic activities by White Russians in Manchukuo.[17] Still the unsettling actions continued. In the summer, Japanese police raided one of the Harbin synagogues in search of " 'arms and or banned literature.' " N. E. B. Ezra breathlessly described the unwarranted attack on the Jewish community: "The entire compound of the Synagogue was encircled with police and every nook and corner of the House of God was searched lasting over an hour, and of course, nothing of discriminative nature was found, after which the police left the Synagogue, warning all the local papers not to publish a single word about the incident under the penalty of imprisonment!"[18]

It should come as no surprise that the warning not to breathe a word of the search was clumsy and useless. *Israel's Messenger* and the *Shanghai Times* carried articles, and the news was disseminated abroad. Yet the searches continued, one occurring during Yom Kippur, a solemn High Holiday, in autumn 1935. In Great Britain, the Joint Foreign Committee, composed of the Board of Deputies of British Jews and the Anglo-Jewish Association of Britain, expressed its dismay over incendiary slander in *Nash Put* and the shocking invasion of Harbin's synagogue and influential Jews' homes. Over the course of many months, Fujii Keinosuke, acting ambassador to the United Kingdom, exchanged telegrams with Consul General Satō Shoshiro in Harbin on how to respond to these concerns.[19]

At first, Satō excused the search as an effort to protect the emperor of Manchukuo on a tour of Harbin; the police had acted on a tip about the synagogue. There were no special measures directed particularly at Jews. The authorities were only trying to maintain public safety. The attitude of *Nash Put*, however, was provocative, and Satō hoped to change it.[20]

Ambassador Fujii duly informed the Joint Foreign Committee. But when he wrote Satō several months later about more abuses of Harbin Jews, the consul general kept him waiting almost five months. He finally sent a detailed report addressing seven major crimes, ranging from unlawful arrests to kidnapping and murder, perpetrated against Jews from Manchukuo's establishment in March 1932 until April 1936. Placing the blame squarely on anti-Semitic White Russians, Fujii called the unfair treatment of Jews in Manchukuo "harmful and useless." Abraham Kaufman, the leader of the Harbin Jewish community, was quoted. Unlike Ezra, he was dispassionate in recounting the terror that he and others had experienced, but at the end he warned, "The circumstances of all harm to Jews are continually published in Shanghai's *Messenger* and in the *Beijing and Tientsin Times*, and Jews worldwide are stirred up."[21]

MISTAKEN PREMISES REGARDING JEWS AND THE UNITED STATES

Dr. Kaufman had already learned a hard lesson. Almost three years earlier, in an oration at Simon Kaspé's funeral, he had publicly expressed his outrage. While the thousands of mourners were stunned by the vicious murder, the Japanese police were horrified by Kaufman's outburst. Kaufman was advised that he risked imprisonment or deportation.[22] Still, Kaufman, a longtime resident of Harbin did not cease working to protect his community. He headed the Jewish Hospital and served as a skilled negotiator for the Jewish community. Kaufman was respected by all who met him, including the Japanese rulers of Manchukuo. When he warned that overseas Jews would be alarmed by the events in Harbin, he struck at the heart of Japanese fears. In particular, the Japanese were concerned about the reaction of American Jews to the problems in Manchukuo.

In February 1938 Consul General Shiozaki in San Francisco wrote Foreign Minister Hirota that "since the Anti-Comintern Pact, Jewish Americans have harbored ill feeling towards us." They were observing Japan's attitude towards the "Jewish problem." In addition, newspaper articles would "slander" the Japanese side by claiming that the Japanese government had embarked upon a program of Jewish persecution, and Jewish groups were systematically hindering Japanese development in the Far East.[23] Shiozaki correctly labeled this information false, particularly the notion that Jewish organizations would methodically hamper Japanese plans in the Far East. But he might have added that Japan should balance its concern over the negative press with some cold calculations regarding the power of American Jews.

Jews constituted a minority in the United States, "only 3.6 percent of an indifferent public," according to Michael Marrus.[24] A number of Jewish organizations, representing different missions and often in conflict with one another, could hardly offset the Jewish weakness in numbers enough to improve United States–Japan relations. Also, prominent Jews hesitated to use their influence, lest it might aggravate anti-Semitism in the United States.

Anti-Semitism in the United States was widespread. A July 1939 poll showed that 31.9 percent believed the Jews had too much power in business and that something should be done. In July 1942, 44 percent thought that Jews had too much power and influence.[25] These figures are ironic and sad, given the Holocaust's vicious, relentless progression by the summer of 1942. Even well into 1943, Sam Rosenman, a Jew and Roosevelt speechwriter and aide, feared that "if too much attention were paid to the plight of the European Jews, American anti-Semitism would increase," writes Doris Kearns Goodwin.[26]

Diplomats posted in the United States failed to inform Tokyo that the same restrictive immigration law of 1924 that prohibited Japanese immigrants also severely limited Jewish ones. The Immigration Act did not have separate categories for refugees and immigrants; the State Department would subsequently use this "lack of distinction" to hamper the refugee flow.[27] Since most of the refugees applying for Japanese transit visas in Europe from 1938 on hoped to go to the United States, this information would have been vital for Tokyo. Instead, the Foreign Ministry was surprised and distressed when more refugees ended up staying in Japan than departing, because they could not obtain immigrant visas for the United States. A similar situation occurred in Canada and Latin America.

The United States was not interested in welcoming either Asians or Jews to its shores, and its attention was firmly focused on Europe. By the summer of 1937 Hitler had preoccupied the United States, and only Pearl Harbor succeeded in distracting it. What attention was directed toward Asia was expressed as sympathy for China. Between the eruption of the Sino-Japanese War in July 1937 and the outbreak of war in Europe in September 1939, a number of pro-China American groups appeared on the political scene, and they advocated an end to American appeasement of Japan.

Dr. Maurice William of the American Bureau for Medical Aid to China even hoped to use American Jews to "help swing American support away from Japan and toward China." In 1939, he proposed a plan to settle German Jews in China, a scheme by which China would choose the refugee participants and American Jews would provide finances. Jewish publishers, movie moguls, radio station owners, financial industry captains—all "political and industrial figures of first importance"—would publicize their appreciation for China's largesse. As a result, American public opinion in general would be roused, leading to a stronger boycott of Japanese goods and pressure to end the sale of military weapons to Japan. William considered Henry Morgenthau, Jr., proof of his proposal's potential: "As a concrete demonstration of Jewish capacity for usefulness to China, one might point to the $25 million loan recently advanced by the American Government through the whole-hearted cooperation of Mr. Morgenthau, Secretary of the Treasury of the Government of the United States."[28]

William was pro-China, anti-Japan, and susceptible to common prejudices regarding Jews. He assumed that the implied reference to Secretary Morgenthau's religion would be understood, and he accepted the stereotypical view of the times that the American media and financial world were dominated by Jews.

Japanese officials mistakenly viewed Japanese relations with China and with the United States as distinct unless the United States chose to link them. But it became impossible for the United States to have amicable relations with both China and Japan once the East Asia conflict was depicted as a battle between right and wrong. By 1937, when Japanese bombs hit Chinese cities and killed large numbers of civilians, China was considered the victim and Japan the criminal. As John Dower notes, "Because air raids against civilian populations had become so commonplace by the end of World War Two, it is easy to forget how shocked the Western powers were when the Japanese began bombing Chinese cities in 1937, and how much Japan's actions at that time served to convince most Europeans and Americans that this was a race and nation still beyond the pale of civilization."[29] By 1937, the United States was already taking sides with its deep pockets: it provided direct aid to China's Nationalist government through a program in which it paid gold or dollars for silver.[30]

In step with their country, American Jews did support China. Among the most vocal was the prominent Rabbi Stephen Wise. In January 1937 he wrote, "China is still one of the world's few bulwarks of democratic potential or actual, as Japan is one of the most dangerous centers of Fascism. If we without protest permit China to be overwhelmed and Chinese unity to be smashed, ours will be a terrible sin!"[31] Months later, he supported a boycott of Japanese goods. "I am in favor of taking any action against Japan, short of war, or what may lead to war, that will make it impossible for Japan to continue its relentless and criminal war against China."[32]

Wise viewed Germany and Japan as fellow fascists. Jewish businessmen from Manchukuo and an unofficial Japanese emissary subsequently approached him in 1938 and 1939 about Japanese proposals to settle refugee Jews in China, but Rabbi Wise responded coldly until the summer of 1940, shortly before the Tripartite Pact was concluded. By then, Japanese interest in the Jews was fading, even as thousands of Jews were making their way to Japan.

Rabbi Wise's repeated rebuffs to Japanese overtures did not dampen their interest in him. In January 1939, Consul General Tsurumi in Harbin reported a conversation between Dr. Kaufman and Wise. The Jews in Manchukuo were living in a peaceful paradise, courtesy of the local authorities, Dr. Kaufman had said; Rabbi Wise had been pleased and had conveyed hearty congratulations to his brethren in Manchukuo. Rabbi Wise had great stature in the American Jewish community and in "American government circles," Tsurumi wrote to his superior. Indeed, he was said to receive a New Year's telephone call from President Roosevelt.[33]

This conversation sounds manufactured. It is difficult to imagine Rabbi Wise condoning the Japanese authorities in Manchukuo and cheering on fellow Jews there when he was adamantly opposed to Japanese rule. The reference to a paradise sounds more like a Japanese expression about Manchukuo than Dr. Kaufman's choice of words. The detail of the New Year's call was the kind of tidbit that appealed to the Japanese, because it represented a specific example of a link to Roosevelt, whom Japanese officials consistently misread.

Japanese officials believed erroneously that President Roosevelt was loyal to the Jews. Roosevelt had appointed more Jews to higher positions than any other president in history, with Jews holding almost 15 percent of his top appointments.[34] But this statistic did not mean that he adhered to the wishes of the American Jewish community at large or that he cared deeply about the European refugee problem. American Jews, in consistently supporting the president's four election bids and his political platforms, proved more loyal to Roosevelt than he was to them. Roosevelt refused to identify the refugee problem as primarily concerning Jews. After a White House conference concerning refugees in April 1938, an attendee noted, "While the President did not specifically say so, it was clear that he was anxious to avoid using the term *Jewish* refugees."[35] Several months later at the Evian Conference, initiated by Roosevelt to address the crisis, the designated term was "political refugees"; "Jew" was absent, by design.

To be sure, the president did have a full political agenda. In late 1938 and early 1939, Roosevelt felt the conflicting pulls of the tendency toward isolationism and of the tradition of granting asylum. The Depression, a defining and sobering experience for most Americans, was still devastating lives and dampening aspirations in 1939. Although the soup kitchens were closing, the economy was sputtering, with a 17 percent unemployment rate.[36] The plight of German Jews appeared distant, less pressing than domestic concerns and the claims of competing constituencies, despite the concerns of the American Jewish community and liberal groups. After the war began in Europe, it was still easier for the visionary, poll-savvy president to speculate about solutions to the postwar refugee problem than to convince himself, Congress, and the American people that serious resettlement schemes and alterations to immigration quotas should be initiated immediately.[37]

A 1939 Japanese report focused on minor details without considering the big picture. "President Roosevelt's 'brain trust' has many influential Jews and Secretary of State Hull's wife is also Jewish," wrote the authors, "and these two big names are always acting in the limelight."[38] The Intergovernmental Committee on Refugees, the result of the Evian Conference, was cited parenthetically as an indication of the activity of the brain trust and Secretary Hull.

In fact, three Jews, versus eleven non-Jews, had participated in the preparatory Advisory Committee meeting for the Evian Conference. Only two, Henry Morgenthau, Jr., and Bernard Baruch, may be characterized as Roosevelt advisors; Rabbi Wise, the third participant, was invited because he was the leader of the American Jewish Congress and the World Jewish Congress. Further, Secretary of State Hull did not demonstrate any particular affinity for Jews because of his wife; rather, the elderly statesman from Tennessee was a clever politician who knew how to play issues. When Eleanor Roosevelt urged that 5,000 German Jewish children be permitted into the United States whose parents had been transported to Auschwitz from Vichy France in 1942, she was automatically opposed by Breckinridge Long, an anti-Semitic State Department official who did more than anyone in the United States government to obstruct Jewish efforts to obtain American visas. Secretary of State Hull intervened, but only because humanitarianism would reap political gains. Hull's reaction to foreign refugees was common among leaders of nations and of the nation-states themselves. It lacked a moral imperative, illustrated the importance of appearances in politics, and betrayed a failure to understand the Nazi threat to Jews.

Meanwhile, Japanese officials were swept up by the pro-Nazi atmosphere in Japan. The Japanese press accepted Nazi portrayals of Roosevelt as a Jew and emphasized Roosevelt's links to allegedly greedy capitalist Jews. Yet, however strong the tendency to swallow Nazi propaganda, there were important differences. Germans viewed Jews as repugnant, "an Asiatic element polluting the racial purity of Europe"; the Japanese neither identified Jews as fellow Asians nor viewed their own Asian identity as inferior to the Nazis. Nor did they find everything about Jews repellent. "For the Japanese, Jews were an abstract symbol of avarice and aggression, but also of intellect, ingenuity, and material success," explains Ben-Ami Shillony.[39]

Between autumn 1938 and winter 1941 Japanese officials saw links between Jews in Manchukuo and Jews in the United States, who they assumed had ties to the president. Meanwhile, American Jews deferred to Roosevelt, and Roosevelt conducted the business at hand, which in his mind had little to do with the Jews. When the Finance Committee on Lithuanian Yeshivoth, associated with the American Jewish Joint Distribution Committee (known as the "Joint"), convened in October 1940 to consider how to rescue 200 yeshiva members in Lithuania, Rabbi Teitelbaum stated the "25–30 families—who are in extreme danger, should be brought to the U.S. immediately." Later however he agreed with several committee members that "no approach be made to Washington before election."[40] When the election was over, perhaps they could obtain American visas.

Little did the concerned rabbi know that the emigration opportunity for European Jews would be over by the second half of 1941, little more than six months away. The time constraint grew even tighter when the Soviets declared that by the end of January 1941 all refugees in Vilna (Vilnius), Lithuania, must either take Soviet citizenship or become stateless. Under that threat the yeshiva students and their families, still anxiously awaiting a favorable political climate in Washington, packed their bags and headed east to Japan. Many were unable to obtain American visas and ended up in Shanghai.

FOREIGN MINISTRY INVOLVEMENT WITH JEWS

Foreign Ministry officials appear to have been little more than messengers about happenings in their particular corners of the world, rather than insightful analysts of national and international trends. Despite the cosmopolitan orientation of the ministry, there was little grasp of the developing refugee problem. The failure to envision the many repercussions of the Jewish flight from Europe stems partly from the ministry's own troubles at home in Tokyo, where it was besieged by the military and was divided within between loyalties to the Anglo-American cause and to Nazi Germany. Add the inherent isolationism of Japanese immigration law, and the ministry's restraints become more understandable.

By the 1930s, the Foreign Ministry's position within the Japanese government was rapidly eroding. Buffeted by policies abroad and bullied by politics at home, it found itself seriously weakened. As early as 1924, when the U.S. Congress passed the restrictive immigration law, the ministry's policy of cooperation with the West brought it disgrace. Right-wing groups and the press in Japan berated civilian bureaucrats for the shameful situation. The ministry's continued efforts to arrest the deterioration of relations with the United States and England only brought it more reprobation and accusations of being "weak-kneed." By the 1930s, the army deliberately "took care to discredit the Foreign Office in the eyes of the public," asserts Kase Toshikazu, while other cabinet departments timidly deferred to the army and navy.[41] When a general and an admiral were appointed to the key posts of ambassadorships to Germany and the United States in early 1941, the damage was irreparable. In Manchukuo, the commander of the army had been concurrently the ambassador as early as December 1932.

Well before the ministry was confronted with Jewish refugees in 1938, it was forced to concede to the army's demand to develop closer relations with the Axis powers. In October 1937, a year before *Kristallnacht*, Joseph Grew, American ambassador to Japan, referred Secretary of State Hull to the Anti-Comintern Pact. "It will be recalled that the pact with Germany was engineered by the military and apparently without the knowledge or approval of the Foreign Office."[42] The treaty was tangible proof of the ministry's compromised position.

By 1941, the ministry had been effectively stifled by the dominance of the military. One young diplomat who returned to Japan after three years of study in the United States reflected later upon the ministry's broken voice and his own futile effort to help advance negotiations to avert war. "I saw the economic power of the United States and, compared with that power, personally I was convinced that there was no chance for Japan to win this war. But still in the climate then prevailing, if you had said that you would have been put into prison. . . . Nobody dared to oppose the military, the dinosaur which was about to go into this battle and eventually be defeated."[43]

Despite their broadened perspective gained from years of training abroad, Japanese diplomats could not put their skills to use to temper the government's course. No one could deny that they were superbly educated. Young foreign officer prospects were culled from the nation's finest universities, with those on the elite track often holding degrees in law from Tokyo Imperial University or Hitotsubashi University. Upon passing a rigorous entrance examination, they were subjected to even more education abroad. New recruits were primarily sent to the United States, the United Kingdom, France, Germany, or the Soviet Union to study language and history for three years. Those dispatched to the United States chose a college or university on the basis of the advice of superiors, selecting the best liberal arts institutions to learn English and cultivate friendships with Americans. Those sent to the Soviet Union had far less freedom, since they were shadowed by NKVD secret police agents (who suspected them of spying), but they still received a thorough education. One entering diplomat recalled a series of tutors who drilled him three hours a day in Russian, Russian history, Soviet history, the Soviet constitution, Marxist economics, and an unusual course on the international law of the Soviet Union.[44]

Men who entered the ministry as *ryūgakusei* (exchange students) while lower in rank than junior diplomats, enjoyed greater freedom abroad. They were paid less than junior diplomats and were not considered career officers, but they too studied overseas for three years. Katayama Junnosuke inadvertently became persona non grata with the Soviets because he spent so little time confined in the embassy. By the time he arrived in Moscow after learning Russian in Riga, Latvia, he was fluent and able to enjoy the city on his own. While the "regular diplomats" remained dutifully at their desks processing paperwork and studying problems, he spent his lunch breaks browsing in bookstores and his evenings at opera and dance halls, since his administrative job had set working hours. Six months into his delightful sojourn in Moscow, Katayama was repatriated.[45] Despite his abrupt departure, he probably learned more relevant information about life in the Soviet Union than his superiors, who were well educated but socially isolated.

While some exchange students ultimately enjoyed long careers in the Foreign Ministry, the ministry's expectations of them were not as high. The difference between career and noncareer officers was equivalent to "heaven and earth."[46] A former secretary remarked, "At the time, the Foreign Ministry was said to be the most liberal of government agencies, but of course the toilets and also the cafeterias were separate. It was awful."[47] Some noncareer officers did not feel as great an obligation to perform; they would never be candidates for major ambassadorial posts. In Europe, both young diplomats with promising careers and others who could not realistically hope for more than a consulship no matter what their capabilities came into contact with refugee Jews.

While a fine foreign education may have exposed diplomats to various political perspectives and alerted them to the danger of unquestioningly accepting the military's faith in Nazi Germany, education was not necessarily a substitute for independent thought, foresight, and immunity to prevailing political winds. The Foreign Ministry was not a discrete, united force opposing the ambitions of the military, particularly the army. "There were two major currents in the Foreign Office itself. The pro-German faction was very vocal, very assertive, and they were certain that Germany would conquer Europe. But the pro–United Kingdom and pro-Western faction did not like the domestic policy of Germany, and they were not sure that Germany would win eventually," recalled the diplomat who had feared that Japan could never win a war against the United States.[48] Although the pro-German faction was visible and active, it was considered a minority by many diplomats. It was, however, a minority that demonstrated an avid interest in Jews. Because it had allies in other cabinet departments, it appeared to be strong.

A diplomat's first post often influenced his political position—passionate support could be found where there was personal history. But until the mid-1930s, geographic differences did not matter much back at the ministry's headquarters in Tokyo. In 1934 the Europe and America Bureau was divided into the Europe-Asia and America bureaus, on the heels of the creation of a Research Division in 1933. In addition to the important, separate East Asia Bureau, the ministry also consisted of information, culture, treaty, and commerce bureaus, plus an administrative department. The Foreign Minister and Vice Minister consulted with the relevant bureau and section heads to formulate policy. The ministry's structure was revised just in time to be divided by international conflict and conflicting loyalties.

The Research Division proved prolific and political. In February 1936, it administered an institute named the *Kokusai Seikei Gakkai*, International Political and Economic Affairs Study Group. Ostensibly formed to provide the government with reliable information about the Jews, the organization published a journal called *Kokusai Himitsuryoku Kenkyū* (Research on International Secret Power), which appeared once or twice a year and was labeled "secret." The first four issues were devoted to the entire text of *Protocols of the Elders of Zion*, the notorious forgery that fascinated anti-Semites and justified their wildest fears of a Jewish conspiracy to dominate the world.[49] In May 1941, the journal was replaced by the monthly *Yudaya Kenkyū* (Jewish Studies). Miyazawa Masanori firmly terms the institute "a front organization for the Foreign Ministry."[50]

The Foreign Ministry also formed, in spring 1938, an interministry group called the Moslem and Jewish Problem Committee.[51] With more than thirty participants representing the Foreign Ministry, army, and navy, it was intended to "establish a basic policy towards the Moslem and Jewish problems in view of the international situation." Foreign ministry members included the heads of the East Asia Bureau, Europe-Asia Bureau, America Bureau, and the Research Division. Other members were the chiefs of the Army Affairs Bureau, the second division of the General Staff, the Naval Affairs Bureau, and the third division of the Naval General Staff.[52] In an attempt to unify national policy towards the Jews, the committee issued reports on the influx of Jewish refugees in China and Japan's strategy to deal with the problem. Although the membership list looks impressive, the committee's sources of information in China were none other than the military's Jewish experts Yasue Norihiro, an army colonel, and Inuzuka Koreshige, a navy captain.

Yasue himself was none other than the Japanese translator of *The Protocols of the Elders of Zion*. Writing under the pseudonym Hō Kōshi, he had produced the first complete version in 1924, having received the text from White Russian soldiers during the ill-fated Siberian Expedition in the early 1920s. Inuzuka had also participated in the Expedition and picked up anti-Semitic ideas. Both men had subsequently been dispatched abroad—Yasue to Palestine and Inuzuka to Paris—to study the Jews. Inuzuka had his own pen name, Utsunomiya Kiyo, and had authored anti-Semitic books and speeches. He was a fervent nationalist steeped in anti-Semitism; he believed that the Jews could be used for Japan's ends.

Inuzuka and Yasue were joined by Shanghai Consul Ishiguro Shirō when they first gathered in Shanghai in May 1939 on behalf of the Moslem and Jewish Problem Committee. They met regularly and produced lengthy, verbose papers. Much of their work involved straight reporting, such as data on the present refugee population. But they also boldly recommended their own pet plans, such as creating an exclusively Jewish settlement in Shanghai that would be controlled by the Japanese behind the scenes, and methods to solicit capital from British and American Jewish financial groups.

Even before Captain Inuzuka became a member of the committee, he had had the audacity to reprimand the Foreign Ministry for not doing enough concerning the Jews. In January 1939, he sent a twenty-eight-page report to the Moslem and Jewish Problem Committee of his "personal opinions" after a survey trip of the Jewish communities in Dairen, Tsingtao, and Shanghai. He was grateful for the army's cooperation in investigating the Jewish situation in Shanghai. As for the Foreign Ministry, "I got the feeling that the Foreign Ministry was not synthesizing the existing information well." "I would like," he added, "to request that your leadership be a little more active."[53]

In July, Inuzuka joined his colleagues Yasue and Ishiguro to request that the Foreign Ministry consider other countries' Jewish settlements and the issues of creating such settlements for German and Italian

Jewish refugees.[54] The suggestion revealed the committee's dogged effort to leave no stone unturned, but it also betrayed the members' ignorance. The only existing Jewish settlement at the time was Birobidjian in the Soviet Union, and it was universally recognized as a failure. Many countries were considering settlements during summer 1939, but very few were establishing them. Most countries had already tightened their immigration regulations to prevent Jewish refugees from entering.

Despite Inuzuka's and Yasue's diligent work and prolific output, their reports do not appear to have been widely disseminated among the various cabinet departments or within the Foreign Ministry. They were stamped with a number of impressive seals signaling departmental distribution, but perhaps they were neither read nor believed. Consider the puzzlement of Consul Kuroki, writing from the Middle East, the heart of the Moslem and Jewish worlds, in March 1938. Kuroki hedged in response to an article in the *Palestine Post* that Japan was persecuting Jews: "We hope it is a news with very little confidence as no official information has yet been received from our Home Government."[55] Two weeks later, Kuroki clarified his earlier statement. "Refering [sic] our previous Communique with regard to the 'Rumour of anti-Jewish movement in Japan' an official denial has been received by the Japanese Legation, Cairo. It was nothing but a false news which might be made accidentally by a foreign news agency in Tokio."[56]

Subsequently, Kuroki told a Japanese shipping company's agents in Haifa that "Japan was among the few countries which had encouraged the immigration of Jews from Germany and that Jewish immigrants were actually being employed in Government service and by the Universities. Japan would likewise welcome Jewish immigrants from Austria who belong to the liberal professions, while the immigration of workers could not be encouraged since they would find it impossible to compete with Japanese workers, owing to the latter's low standard of living."[57] The progression from ambiguity to clarity, and from indecisiveness to support for the Jews is orderly and dramatic. Even if one were to discount the positive slant because the news was intended for consumption in Palestine, Kuroki's words have little in common with the contemporaneous activity of any Foreign Ministry research organ.

Elements of the Foreign Ministry were anti-Semitic, but that does not mean that there was actual persecution of Jews by Japan. Japan permitted the immigration of Jews at this point, but Kuroki exaggerated when he used the terms "encouraged" and "welcome."

IMMIGRATION LAW

In the 1930s, Japan was not prepared to welcome anyone other than those specifically invited to come. Its immigration law—general and brief—reflected the country's traditional isolation. From January 1918 until May 1939, the law concerning the entry of foreigners into Japan contained only five articles. No distinction was made between entry and transit because the foreign population was so negligible. There was truth to a Japanese diplomat's observation, "Ours was a hermit country."[58]

At first glance, the lack of bureaucratic red tape might make it appear easy for foreigners to have entered Japan. Prefectural governors, not the central government in Tokyo, controlled entry. There were conceivably as many opportunities to enter as there were coastal ports dotting the archipelago. But as Joseph Grew explained, the case was otherwise: "The nub of the whole system lies in this delegation of wide administrative powers to the local authorities." In practice, the governors delegated authority to the prefectural police, and there was no way to appeal their decisions. Grew added confidentially, "The Government is not burdened with accusations or discriminatory or overly-strict immigration laws, but in effect all aliens whom Japan does not want can be and are quietly excluded."[59] The genius of the general instructions lay in their vagueness: one could not argue with or appeal what was not legally specified.

When the foreign resident population reached approximately 30,000, new regulations consisting of twenty articles were promulgated in March 1939. Foreign residents were required to register with the local police after thirty days in Japan, instead of the former more generous period of ninety days, and those suspected of "immorality, communism, or espionage" could be expelled more easily than before.[60] For the first time, the distinction between entry and transit was defined: entry visas would be issued to those staying in Japan for fifteen or more days, and visas for "passing through" would be granted to those staying less than fifteen days.[61] The prefectural governors retained their discretionary power to permit or prohibit entry.

The new legislation signified both a continuation of the status quo and a response to increased international tensions. Although police meddling had long been a bother for foreign residents, requiring foreigners to register frequently their movements was an official attempt to prevent espionage by those opposed to Japanese policy in China. When the English press in Japan reacted negatively to the provisions for increased police surveillance, Foreign Minister Arita warned prefectural governors that "every care should be taken not to arouse unnecessary misunderstanding among foreigners in enforcement of the new law."[62]

The American State Department was not as concerned as Arita. The rules were no surprise, since "any foreigner living in Japan is continually subject to police interrogation, to police inspection, and to an amazing amount of community interest in his affairs." "Retaliation" was not advised, since the rules were not new, they were not unreasonable for a country at war as Japan was in China, and because other countries, such as the Soviet Union, had similar ones.[63]

The Home Ministry, which was responsible for the legislation, and the Foreign Ministry, which was consulted by the Home Ministry, were more concerned with foreigners living in Japan than with those arriving. When the Japanese ambassador to the United States, Horiuchi Kensuke, sent Secretary of State Hull an explanation of the ordinance, he mentioned the importance of protecting and controlling foreigners staying in Japan.[64]

In Washington, the State Department's legal advisor perused Horiuchi's statement and Grew's comments on the same day in June 1939. He found that he and Grew concurred: Grew had determined, "By and large the new ordinance is not very different from those in force in most European countries."[65]

Although the Japanese legislation may have seemed current and similar to that of European countries, Japan had a special position, which no one remarked upon, as a transit point on one of the few escape routes from Europe. A more appropriate comparison may have been between Japanese legislation and that of other geographically remote transit centers, from which it was difficult logistically to deport unsuitable entrants or visitors. Other such countries proved far more suspicious towards and nervous about refugees, although the numbers of arrivals were hardly threatening. In the first four months of 1939, the Latin American states, which were both transit and destination countries, had "finally closed up altogether," wrote Robert Pell, assistant to the director of the Intergovernmental Committee on Political Refugees.[66] Indeed, when German concentration camps filled with Jews arrested en masse from 1938 on, many countries had stiffened their immigration requirements. Brazil had made Jewish immigration unviable by requiring baptismal certificates, and Bolivia left no doubt by declaring anyone with Jewish blood ineligible.[67] By comparison, Japanese legislation appeared mild and lenient.

To be sure, immigration could be restricted without the aid of detailed laws. When the American consulate in Yokohama inquired whether Isaacs Levy, a Moroccan Jew born in Palestine with a Japanese transit visa issued in Casablanca, would be guaranteed admission into Japan, the Foreign Section of the Water Police at Yokohama was resolutely noncommittal, asserting only the prefectural authorities could decide how long a foreigner could stay in Japan. But since consuls were supposed to investigate each applicant before issuing a visa, "It is extremely rare that a person in possession of a Japanese consular visa is refused admittance," recorded American Vice Consul Goetzmann in his memorandum of the meeting.[68]

Consuls had the right to issue visas, and the local prefectural authorities had the right to negate them. Even if rejections rarely occurred, the validity of visas remained questionable until the moment the local police stamped the visa and waved the applicant on. Refusing entry could be justified on the grounds that the person had become undesirable between the time he received his visa and the moment his ship anchored in Japan. For those suspected of becoming public charges because they were destitute, rejection was always possible. Many Jewish refugees were impoverished by the time they reached Japan; however, the local Jewish community negotiated and vouched for them. As long as the police were not capricious, which they seldom were, it appeared that the refugees were safe.

The key then to entering Japan successfully, whether for a brief or lengthy stay, was to obtain a visa in the first place. Entry visas for foreigners during wartime became increasingly scarce. Japan had been officially at war with China since August 1937; it had engaged in an undeclared war with China since 1931, a tense situation euphemistically termed "The China Incident." The nation was not in a receptive mood. More important, few refugees ever envisioned themselves residing in Japan; it required a geographic and emotional leap of faith. "I would have been double crazy," said Samuil Manski, to consider a country on "the other side of the world."[69] But Samuil's mother thought otherwise: Japanese transit visas could help the family reach the United States, where Samuil's father awaited his wife and children.

Whenever anyone applied for a visa from a Japanese consul, the diplomat was expected to address any questions to the third section of the America Bureau at the ministry headquarters in Tokyo. Why would consular officers in Europe ask the America Bureau about transit visas for Europeans who may have been traveling to Palestine or Australia rather than to the American continent? The third section of the America Bureau pertained to passports for the entire world, while the first section covered the crucial North American region, and the second section was responsible for Latin America. Originally, the association with the Americas made sense, because the third section was concerned with Japanese emigration to the United States and South America, especially in the wake of the notorious 1924 American immigration law. By the early 1940s, however, the connection between the third section and the other sections had become incidental. Each section operated independently, and unlike the other sections, the third section had no political agenda. Issuing visas was not considered political, but routine.[70]

The third section of the America Bureau was not alert to the potential political dimensions of visa and refugee problems. Although fleeing Austrian and German Jews had begun to arrive in Japan by the dozens, they did not raise alarm, because they honored their transit visas and promptly embarked for their destinations within fifteen days of their arrival. But no one looked across the Sea of Japan and the Yellow Sea to nearby Shanghai, where approximately 3,000 Jewish refugees were expected to arrive from Italy in January and February 1939. Both German and Italian ships were sold out for Shanghai until the end of March, the same month that the new entry and transit provisions were proposed in Japan.[71] So regular and numerous were the runs of refugees from Italy to Shanghai in 1939 and 1940 that Laura Margolis, a social worker sent to Shanghai by the Joint, described the voyage from Italy to China aboard Lloyd Triestino steamships as "a sort of 'ferry service.'"[72]

The trip between Italy and China had been reduced to a hop, but Japan remained psychologically distant from Europe and the rest of Asia. The Foreign Ministry bureaucracy continued to function under the premise that Japan, the world's most crowded country, was a place to leave, not a haven to reach. It would take some time before the ministry caught up with the course of events.

THE FAR EASTERN JEWISH CONFERENCES

Although the Jews had not yet fully captured the attention of the Foreign Ministry, they captivated the military. Every December between 1937 and 1939, the army orchestrated the Far Eastern Jewish Conference, held for three days in Harbin to promote goodwill between Jews living in Japan and Japanese-occupied areas in China. Exercises in international propaganda, the conferences highlighted the military's interest in using the Jews to influence Japan's international relations. Although the conferences were invested with great expectations, they failed to impress those for whom they were most intended—power brokers and policy makers abroad.

The Kwantung Army organized the three annual meetings, with the hope of arresting the continuing deterioration in United States–Japan relations. By having Jews who lived in Japanese territory proclaim their gratitude for the tolerant treatment by the Japanese authorities, the military's planners hoped to appeal to Jewish and national public opinion in both the United States and Great Britain. The conferences were an instrument to improve Japan's battered image.[73]

In the wake of the first conference, Japanese diplomats abroad found nothing to report.[74] Although the conference seemed to have attracted little notice, Colonel Yasue became an enthusiastic supporter and key organizer of the second conference. Posted to Dairen in 1938, Yasue led the Dairen Special Branch, a department under the intelligence bureau of the Kwantung Army. The conference was a perfect venue for him to pursue his interest in Jews, serve his country, and gather intelligence covertly in keeping with his job. Yasue was indefatigable.

To address the absence of foreign journalists in Harbin on the eve of the conference, he arranged a media blitz targeting Jewish presses in the United States and Great Britain.[75] These organizations, as well as Jewish groups and "eminent Jews," would also receive a total of 1,500 pamphlets printed in English, Russian, and Yiddish.[76] Yasue was enthusiastic and optimistic, but it is not clear whether his strategy succeeded.

One of the problems was that bad press negated Yasue's effort. "There is a mistake occurring among Jews in Manchukuo," Consul General Tsurumi wrote. "They think that Japan is acting in concert with Germany in persecuting the Jews." Tsurumi elaborated, "There is news of all sorts of trouble in Shanghai. Refugees pouring in there report that their arrival was strongly forbidden, and they had the impression that the Japanese leadership was stopping them." Tsurumi and Yasue worried that "the positive effects of the Far Eastern Jewish Conference will be overturned."[77] An exercise in public relations could not counter the weight of actual experience. The military, however, retained sufficient interest to hold another conference the following year; the fourth conference was canceled in 1940, owing to the Tripartite Pact.

If the intended international results of the conferences were inconclusive, the direct benefit to the local Jewish community was not. The first conference involved the creation of a recognized, unified Jewish body in Manchukuo—the Far East Jewish National Council. In exchange for cooperation with and loyalty to Manchukuo, resident Jews were allowed to maintain their own religious and cultural institutions. The Council exemplified the long-standing attempt of Jews to reside peacefully as an accepted minority rather than as uneasy outsiders. In 1937, not many anticipated another effect: the Council would be organized and ready to assist other Jews by the time the first trainloads of refugees arrived at the border station of Manchouli in less than a year. European Jews were about to flee east in their attempt to reach the West.

NOTES

1. "Japan's Consul General Morishima Criticizes the Slander of Jews," contents of his meeting with Jewish leaders published in three newspapers on 24 February 1935, JPF, folder 3.

2. Haruko Taya Cook and Theodore F. Cook, *Japan at War: An Oral History* (New York: The New Press, 1992), 56–57; Shinpei Ishii, "A Return to Wartime Manchuria," *Chūō Koron*, September 1991.

3. Owen Lattimore, *Manchuria: Cradle of Conflict* (New York: Macmillan, 1932).

4. Maruyama Naoki, "1930 nendai ni okeru nihon no hanyudayashugi," *Kokusai daigaku chūtō kenkyūjo kiyō* (1987–1988): 420.

5. Toshikazu Kase, *Journey to the Missouri*, ed. David Nelson Rowe (New Haven, CT: Yale University Press, 1950), 24, 135.

6. Cook and Cook, *Japan at War*, 56; Shunsuke Katori, *Mō hitotsu no Shōwa* (Tokyo: Kodansha, 1994), 44.

7. James B. Crowley, Introduction to "Designs on North China 1933–1937," in *The China Quagmire: Japan's Expansion on the Asian Continent 1933–1941*, ed. James William Morley (New York: Columbia University Press, 1983), 6.

8. James B. Crowley, *Japan's Quest for Autonomy: National Security and Foreign Policy: 1930–1938* (Princeton, NJ: Princeton University Press, 1966), 188, 191, 300.

9. "Japan's Consul General Morishima Criticizes the Slander of Jews," contents of his meeting with Jewish leaders published in three newspapers on 24 February 1935, JPF, folder 3.

10. Takeo Itō, *Life along the South Manchurian Railway*, trans. Joshua A. Fogel (Armonk, NY: M. E. Sharpe, 1988), 53; Nakamura Ryūko, interview by author, 6 April 1995, Minokamo, Japan, tape recording; Shimura Giichi, interview by author, 19 April 1995, Tokyo, tape recording: Paul Theroux, *Riding the Iron Rooster: By Train though China* (London: Penguin Books, 1988), 316.

11. Letter from N. E. B. Ezra to Dr. Oyabe, 2 November 1934, JPF, folder 3.

12. Crowley, *Japan's Quest for Autonomy*, 378.

13. Katsumi Usui, "The Role of the Foreign Ministry," in *Pearl Harbor as History*, 131.

14. Kasai Tadakazu, interview by author, 7 April 1995, Gifu, Japan, tape recording.

15. Mamoru Shigemitsu, *Japan and Her Destiny: My Struggle for Peace*, ed. F. S. G. Piggott, trans. Oswald White (New York: E. P. Dutton, 1958), 80.

16. Kwantung Police Chief, "Kita Man ni okeru Yudayajin ni tsuite" (1 April 1933), quoted in Miyazawa Massanori, "Shōwa zenki in okeru nihon no tai Yudaya seisaku," *Waseda daigaku shakai kagaku kenkyūjo* (July 1994): 66–67.

17. *Israel's Messenger* (5 April 1935), quoted in Maruyama, "Nihon no hanyudayashugi," 424.

18. Letter from N. E. B. Ezra to Ambassador Ariyoshi, ambassador to China, 9 September 1935, JPF, folder 3.

19. Telegram from Fujii Keinosuke to Satō Shoshiro, #25, 7 November 1935, JPF, folder 3.

20. Top secret telegram from Satō to Fujii, #1, 3 December 1935, JPF, folder 3.

21. Top secret telegram from Satō to Yoshida, United Kingdom, #1, 19 September 1936, JPF, folder 3.

22. Rena Krasno, *Strangers Always: A Jewish Family in Wartime Shanghai* (Berkeley, CA: Pacific View Press, 1992), 117.

23. Coded telegram from Shiozaki to Hirota, #5712 coded, #42, 28 February 1938, JPF, folder 3.

24. Michael R. Marrus, *The Holocaust in History* (London: Penguin Books, 1987), 171.

25. Marrus, *The Holocaust in History*, 162.

26. Doris Kearns Goodwin, *No Ordinary Time: Franklin and Eleanor Roosevelt: The Home Front in World War II* (New York: Touchstone, 1994), 455.

27. Henry L. Feingold, *The Politics of Rescue: The Roosevelt Administration and the Holocaust, 1938–1945* (New Brunswick, NJ: Rutgers University Press, 1970), 18.

28. Records of United States Department of State Relating to the Internal Affairs of China, 1930–1939, "To Dr. Hu Shih, China's Ambassador to the United States, from Maurice William, 31 May 1939," File 893.55J, National Archives, Washington.

29. John W. Dower, *War without Mercy* (New York: Pantheon Books, 1986), 38.

30. John King Fairbank, *The United States & China* (Cambridge, MA: Harvard University Press, 1981), 326.

31. Rabbi Stephen Wise, American Jewish Congress, New York, to Professor William Kilpatrick, Columbia University, New York, 7 January 1937, TL, Stephen S. Wise Papers, American Jewish Historical Society, Brandeis University, Waltham, MA.

32. Rabbi Stephen Wise, American Jewish Congress, New York, to Mr. Benjamin Wolf, New York, 1 November 1937, TL, Stephen S. Wise Papers.

33. Top secret telegram from Tsurumi to Ueda, #35, 12 January 1939, JPF, Far Eastern Jewish Conference folder.

34. Feingold, *The Politics of Rescue*, 9; Goodwin, *No Ordinary Time*, 102.

35. "Confidential Memorandum on White House Conference on Refugees," by Samuel McGrea Cavert, 13 April 1938, AR 33/44, #193: Organizations: Relations with Governments: United States Government, State Department, 1930–1944, AJJDC Archives.

36. See Goodwin's description of the Depression and staggering statistics on its breadth and depth. Goodwin, *No Ordinary Time*, 42.

37. See Harold Ickes's discussion of Roosevelt's chat in November 1939 and of Roosevelt's inability to acknowledge that the refugee problem concerned Jews. Also, the president did not endorse a resettlement plan for Alaska that was raised in Congress in early 1940 at the very time he was urging the Intergovernmental Committee on Political Refugees (IGC or ICR) to be more ambitious in envisioning solutions. Henry L. Feingold, "Roosevelt and the Resettlement Question," in *Rescue Attempts during the Holocaust: Proceedings of the Second Yad Vashem International Historical Conference in Jerusalem, April 8–11, 1974*, by Yad Vashem (Jerusalem: Yad Vashem, 1977), 150–151.

38. Top secret report, "Amalgamated Bulletin on Survey of Jews in Shanghai," 7 July 1939, JPF, folder 13.

39. Ben-Ami Shillony, *The Jews and the Japanese: The Successful Outsiders* (Rutland, VT and Tokyo: Charles E. Tuttle Company, 1991); 171.

40. "Meeting of Finance Committee on Lithuanian Yeshivoth," 21 October 1940, File 738, Emigration: Rabbinical Groups, 1940–1941, AJJDC Archives.

41. Kase, *Journey to the Missouri*, 17.

42. Department of State, "The Ambassador in Japan (Grew) to the Secretary of State," 1 October 1937, No. 2613, 765.94/50, *Foreign Relations of the United States: Diplomatic Papers*, 1937 vol. 1 General, 607.

43. Ambassador Takeuchi Harumi, interview by author, 2 February 1995, Tokyo, tape recording.

44. Ambassador Tokura Eiji, interview by author, 10 February 1995, Tokyo, tape recording.

45. Ambassador Katayama Junnosuke, interview by author, 31 August 1995, Tokyo, tape recording.

46. Katori Shunsuke, *Mō hitotsu no Shōwa*, 99.

47. Ibid., 100.

48. Takeuchi, interview.

49. Shillony, *The Jews and the Japanese*, 170.

50. Note that Miyazawa's translator refers to the *Kokusai Seikei Gakkai* as International Society of Politics and Economics and to *Kokusai Himitsuryoku no Kenkyū* as Studies of International Secret Power. I have elected to follow Shillony's translation, but the difference is minor. Miyazawa, "Japanese Anti-Semitism in the Thirties," 24.

51. Shillony explains the Moslem element as Japan's interest in encouraging the Moslem communities in China to abandon their support of Chiang Kai-shek. *The Jews and the Japanese*, 176. A former military officer, Maruyama Naomitsu, mentions that Japan also hoped to use a Moslem leader in Tokyo to foment anti-Soviet activities in an area ranging from Turkey to Indonesia. Ōno Masami, "Haran No Jigyōka Kyū-Manshū De Bōryaku," *Aera* (August 1995): 60.

52. Telegram from Foreign Vice-Minister Horiuchi to Army Vice-Minister Umezu and Navy Vice-Minister Yamamoto, Tokyo, #1491, 2 April 1938, JPF, folder 3.

53. Secret report, "To the Moslem and Jewish Problem Committee on Personal Opinions regarding the Present Situation of Shanghai Jews and Measures," by Captain Inuzuka, 18 January 1939, JPF, folder 13.

54. Top secret report, "Regarding the Management of Shanghai's Jewish Refugees," by the Board of the Moslem and Jewish Problem Committee, 18 July 1939, JPF, folder 13.

55. "Communique from Japanese Consulate Alexandria," 16 March 1938, JPF, folder 3.

56. "Communique Japanese Consul Alexandria," 2 April 1938, JPF, folder 3.

57. "No Anti-Semitism in Tokyo: An Official denial," 16 April 1938, JPF, folder 3.

58. Takeuchi, interview.

59. Records of U.S. State Department: Japan, 1930–1939, "From Grew to Hornbeck, Department of State," 10 January 1936, National Archives.

60. Ibid., "New Japanese Immigration Regulations Announced," from C. R. Cameron, American Consul General, Tokyo, to the Secretary of State, 8 February 1939, National Archives.

61. Ibid., "Promulgation of New Japanese Immigration Regulations," from Thomas A. Hickok, American Consul, Tokyo, 3 March 1939, National Archives.

62. Ibid., "Transmission of Translation of Ordinance Relating to Alien's Entry, Sojourn, and Departure," from Joseph C. Grew to the Secretary of State, 6 May 1939, File 894.11/79, Despatch 3868, National Archives.

63. Ibid., "From Division of Far Eastern Affairs, Salisbury, to JPS," 22 April 1939, File 894.55, National Archives.

64. Ibid., "Revision of the Ordinance Concerning the Entry of Foreigners," from the Japanese Ambassador to the Secretary of State, 11 May 1939, File 894.111/78, National Archives.

65. The legal advisor of the State Department stamped both documents on June 9, 1939. Ibid., "Transmission of Translation of Ordinance Relating to Alien's Entry, Sojourn, and Departure," from Joseph C. Grew to the Secretary of State, 6 May 1939, File 894.11/79, Despatch 3868, National Archives.

66. Department of State, "The United Kingdom Ambassador (Kennedy) to the Secretary of State," 19 May 1939, No. 1628, 840.48 Refugees, *Foreign Relations of the United States: Diplomatic Papers*, 1939 vol. 3 General, The British Commonwealth and Europe, 112–13.

67. John George Stoessinger, *The Refugee and the World Community* (Minneapolis: University of Minnesota Press, 1956), 38.

68. Records of U.S. State Department: Japan, 1930–1939, "Assurance of Admission of Aliens into Japan," from W. Garland Richardson, American Vice Consul, Tokyo, to the Secretary of State, 30 August 1940, File 894.111/87, Despatch 55, National Archives.

69. Samuil Manski, interview by author, 6 October 1995, Newton, Massachusetts, tape recording.

70. Much of this discussion is the result of an interview and subsequent phone conversation with Takeuchi Harumi, 2 February 1995 and 21 June 1995, Tokyo.

71. Top secret telegram from Consul General Miura, Shanghai, to Arita, #187, 17 January 1939, JPF, folder 6. Telegram from Miura to Arita, #1718, #123, 19 January 1939, JPF, folder 6.

72. Laura Margolis, "Race against Time in Shanghai," *Survey Graphic* 33 (March 1944): 1. AR 33/44, #463: China, General, 1942–1944, AJJDC Archives.

73. Maruyama, "Nihon no hanyudayashugi," 428.

74. Maruyama, "Asia taiheiyō chiiki ni okeru Yudayajin shakai," *Pacific Basin Project* 7 (Japan: International University, 1986), 22.

75. Telegram, from Tsurumi to Arita, coded #37659, express and top secret #229, 24 December 1938, JPF, Far Eastern Jewish Conference folder.

76. Top secret "Report on the Second Far Eastern Jewish Conference, Part I" by Army Colonel Yasue Norihiro, 30 December 1938, JPF, Far Eastern Jewish Conference folder.

77. Telegram, from Tsurumi to Arita, coded #38131, top secret #240, 29 December 1938, JPF, Far Eastern Jewish Conference folder.

3

Japan's Jewish Problem in 1938: Rhetoric Confronts Reality

SOMETIMES, the unexpected occurs—or, as the Japanese proverb goes, "a bird suddenly appears from where one is standing." Consider a cornered bird a metaphor for a frantic Jew, and one shares the perspective of astonished Japanese diplomats in Europe in autumn 1938. Jews were just as perplexed by their circumstances. Seemingly overnight, they were transformed from proud citizens into unwanted refugees.

Japanese diplomats in Europe were unprepared for the questions that Jewish applicants for visas posed by their very presence. Every time a refugee requested a transit visa from a Japanese consul, representatives of the Foreign Ministry abroad and at home in Tokyo were forced to consider the impact of their decisions on the German-Japanese alliance and the effect on Japan of permitting foreigners entry or passage. Japanese diplomats soon realized that one request was a harbinger of many. As a result, by December 1938 Tokyo had articulated a policy towards Jews that would remain in place until Pearl Harbor.

THE UNEASY ALLIANCE WITH GERMANY

The Japanese government never intended that the Anti-Comintern Pact, concluded with Germany in September 1936, would ally Japan with Germany in terms of European diplomacy. The Pact was considered a means to promote Japan's policy of southern expansion, the development of Manchukuo, and the stabilization of North China. Unlike

Germany, Japan increasingly viewed the agreement as a strong signal to the Soviets to stay away from its interests in China.

Germany was interested in maintaining its position in China, with whom it had significant trade. She became frustrated by the Japanese military's involvement with German business interests and helplessly watched profits shrink as the Japanese presence in North China expanded. The Japanese military treated German enterprises the same as those of every other country; it interfered at will. Germany was also concerned that Japanese aggression made communism more appealing to the Chinese. Within two years of the Pact's signing, it was obvious that Germany had gained little in the Far East, except an increasingly domineering ally emboldened by its treaty with a major European power.

Japan also was frustrated with Germany. Captain Inuzuka was angry that Japan was conducting a "punitive battle" in China "against the spread of communism" while Germany was supplying China with weapons and aiding her by importing tungsten.[1] Japan did not have sufficient trade with either Germany or Italy, who joined the Anti-Comintern Pact in 1937, to make Germany's relationship with China seem less threatening.

Japan saw no reason for Germany to be interested in China, and this extended to Japanese treatment of Jews there. "Our Jewish policy is a completely different situation than that of Germany," wrote Inuzuka in 1937. Jewish residents of Japan and Manchukuo were either stateless or possessed other citizenship. Inuzuka cited the small number of Jews—no more than 20,000—in comparison to Germany, where 600,000 Jews, about 1 percent of the population, held German citizenship. "While we should be on guard and devise a counterplan for the pernicious maneuvering taking place in the world by one element of the Jewish race, there is no reason that we should keep completely in step with the anti-Comintern countries," he elaborated, with his customary combination of anti-Semitic concepts and nationalist pride.

Japan never viewed the Anti-Comintern Pact as concerning Jews and was surprised when others perceived a connection. In 1938, Shigemitsu Mamoru, then ambassador to the Soviet Union, sent a report to Foreign Minister Ugaki that suggested Japan's relationship with Germany had created the perception of a German-Japanese bond in the eyes of Jews. "Fortunately, Japan has had no Jewish problem"; but now the Jews considered Japan a fascist country, owing to its opposition to communism, namely the Soviet Union, and the Anti-Comintern Pact with Germany. "Of course, they [the Jews] do not have the extreme animosity towards us that they do towards the 'Nazis,' but we need to research and comprehend the relationship with the Jews." The report assumed that the Jews possessed international political influence and supported communism, and it suggested further reading, including a book by Henry Ford, a well-known anti-Semite.[2] However flawed this analysis may have been, it demonstrates one of the unintended consequences of Japan and Germany's relationship.

By 1940, Germany and Japan were enduring a "passive friendship," observes Ernst Presseisen. Kase Toshikazu has called the Axis partnership "a paper alliance," a corollary to Johanna Meskill's famous term, "the hollow alliance." Kase wastes few words on the state of Japan-German relations: "Throughout the war there was little if any collaboration between Japan and Germany; each went its own way regardless of the other."[3]

The Racial Dimension

Nowhere was this more apparent than in the Japanese failure to understand that Hitler's war was a racial crusade of barbaric proportions. Despite its susceptibility to imported anti-Semitism, Japan did not initially view the refugees as victims of racial hatred. For Japan, the refugees were foreigners first and Jews second. They were unexpected visitors to Asia, rather than an ethnic group in flight.

Some Japanese may have read anti-Semitic texts, but few had practiced anti-Semitism. As members of a largely homogeneous society with little social friction, Japanese did not view Judaism as a threat to its native Shinto or pervasive Buddhism. Christians in Japan were a minority, constituting less than 1 percent of the population, and had suffered from persecution themselves. They did not discriminate against Jews; some, such as Holiness Church congregants, displayed sympathy and charity. Since Japanese were unable to distinguish between Gentiles and Jews, anti-Semitism was never the result of perceived physical differences between the two. After all, both Jews and Gentiles were Caucasian.

Japan could not comprehend the degree of Nazi hatred for Jews, but it was not alone in this matter. Countries far more familiar with anti-Semitism were surprised by Nazi fanaticism. Even when there was proof of actual extermination, they failed to realize what was happening. Yehuda Bauer has sought to explain the West's resistance in recognizing genocide in the face of a wealth of information available in 1942. Bauer observes, "[K]nowing usually came in a number of stages: first, the information had to be disseminated, then, it had to be believed; then, it had to be internalized, that is, some connection had to be established between the new reality and a possible course of action; finally, there came action, if and when action came."[4] If the truth was too horrible for the West to digest, imagine how easy it was for Japan to dismiss Hitler's words in the 1930s before they were turned into reality.

Part of the problem was Japan's decision to ignore consciously and discard the aspects of Hitler's racial ideology that it found insulting and incompatible with its own political interests. Although parts of *Mein Kampf* had been translated into Japanese as early as 1925, a full translation did not appear until 1942. Even then, it was not available to the public, out of fear of the detrimental effect that Hitler's inferior racial classification of the Japanese would have on Japan-German relations.

Manabe Ryōichi's pride in his version of *Mein Kampf*, published after Pearl Harbor, never wavered. Even when the book was brought before a war crimes tribunal that subsequently found Manabe guilty of complicity in the death of three American soldiers in Hankow in 1944, Manabe rejoiced over the evaluation of his translation. "Even the Americans said my version was impartial—a historical record." Once an unassuming scholar of German literature and language at the esteemed Kyoto University, Manabe had joined the Foreign Ministry in 1938 as a noncareer officer after being recruited by a pro-German diplomat. Assigned to the second section of the Research Bureau in 1939, he was appalled by the poor translations of German made from English and began to translate *Mein Kampf* on his own. Manabe sought dispassionate accuracy, but when the text was complete, army censors advised him that the section of the "excellence of the German race" would prevent the book's publication. Manabe reluctantly complied and erased that section, as well as an assertion that Japan would still be mired in the Tokugawa period had Commodore Perry not arrived at her shores. According to Manabe, his translation subsequently hit the best-seller list, with sales soaring to 100,000.[5]

It is not clear how widely Manabe's translation was disseminated within the Foreign Ministry. What is clear is that *Mein Kampf* was not fully recognized as a manual of Hitler's platform. Although the expulsion of the Jews from Germany and Europe was a direct result of Hitler's intent to preserve the Aryan racial community, Japanese consular records did not emphasize the racial background of visa applicants. Rather, lists and charts of applicants for visas always referred to nationality, only sometimes to race. Japanese consuls were aware that the people standing before them requesting visas were Jews, but how much did they actually comprehend regarding the seriousness of Hitler's plans, the danger driving Jews to abandon their homes and start anew, and the impact on Japan, which was beyond the isolation of the Tokugawa period but still operating under immediate post-Tokugawa-period immigration regulations?

Jews had fled to Asia before. At the end of the fifteenth century, Jews driven from Spain in the wake of the Spanish inquisition escaped to the Middle East, West Asia, and East Asia. Jews suffering from persecution in Europe had crossed Eastern Europe, Russia, and Siberia to reach China and East Asia.[6] After World War I, the Joint and Hebrew Immigrant Aid Society (HIAS) assisted Jews "stranded in Yokohama, of all places," to emigrate elsewhere, notes Yehuda Bauer.[7] Although Asia remained beyond the realm of the imagination of both Japanese diplomats and many Jews as a destination or a stop, it was already part of the history of the Diaspora.

"It was a festive sight, all the colored streamers connecting the passengers on the ship with the people on the dock," recalls Ernest Heppner of his 1939 journey to Shanghai, "but for us there was no one to wish us 'Bon Voyage' on our journey from an easy comfortable life to an unknown existence."[8] Heppner and his mother were among those who realized that they must leave Europe quickly. From autumn 1938 until Italy's entry into the war in June 1940, many refugees like the Heppners traveled aboard luxurious liners in a leisurely voyage that often began in Genoa or Trieste and wound down through Port Said and Aden, up to Bombay, down to Colombo and Singapore, and up again to Manila and Hong Kong before terminating in Shanghai and Kobe. The sooner one left, the easier it was to exit Europe.

Between June 1940 and June 1941, when Germany attacked the Soviet Union, refugees journeyed east via the far less elegant and comfortable trans-Siberian railway. Some of the first German Jews to arrive in Japan came via Siberia, Harbin, Pusan, and Shimonoseki before stopping in Kobe and Yokohama; they all possessed entry visas for other countries and moved on. None had transit visas for Japan.

Visas Were Unnecessary for Germans

Ambassador Ōshima never said much about Jewish refugees. "A man among men" in terms of demeanor, Ōshima was a heavy drinker and lover of all things German. Young diplomats faltered before him when periodically questioned about their language and cultural studies in Germany; they knew how fluent his German was, and perhaps they sensed a disdain for career diplomats. A lieutenant general sent to the embassy in 1934 as a military attaché, Ōshima used his 1938 promotion to ambassador to circumvent the foreign ministry bureaucracy in Tokyo. Along with Ambassador Shiratori in Italy, Ōshima was determined to achieve a tripartite pact even if it meant conducting unauthorized negotiations and selecting how much of Tokyo's requests were communicated. Considered "more German than the Germans" by fellow Japanese, Ōshima seems to have overlooked the fundamental

Nazi attitudes towards Jews in his pursuit of a closer alliance.[9] To be sure, he did not see many German Jews at the embassy. They did not need transit visas for Japan, just as Japanese did not need transit visas for Germany.

As early as March 1935, however, the Foreign Ministry had anticipated that German refugees might try to go to Japan, and it notified its ambassadors to follow the League of Nations' recommendations regarding identification and passports. Foreign Minister Hirota advised diplomats to issue travel certificates instead of passports and visas for stateless German refugees. Refugees who were German citizens should be treated as regular German nationals in accordance with Japanese law. Hirota also specified that there should be no special treatment for any German refugee; the provisions for stateless refugees were based on the precedents of Russian and Armenian refugees.[10]

No mention was made that the German refugees, whether stateless or not, would most likely be Jewish. This basic policy sufficed in 1935, because there were hardly any German refugees in Japan. The ministry's timing was appropriate: between 1935 and 1938, Germany's Schutzstaffel (SS) encouraged the emigration of Jews from Germany. The policy also preceded the Nuremberg Laws adopted several months later, in September 1935.

German Jews may not have needed visas for Japan, but they did for Manchukuo. "I issued visas to all without any kind of permission," recalls Kasai Tadakazu of his posting in Manchouli in spring 1935. Trains arrived twice a week, on Mondays and Thursdays. Applicants were few—twenty or less at a time, and they were en route to Shanghai, where some would stay, or Kobe, where they would depart for such destinations as Hong Kong, Singapore, and the United States. When asked whether he realized that these people were escaping persecution, Kasai replied, "Not really. It was still early. There was no need to ask why they had left; it didn't matter." Not yet, perhaps, but in 1938 it would matter much more.

THE REFUGEE FLOW BEGINS

Between fall 1938 and mid-January 1939, approximately 1,700 to 1,800 refugees traveled to Shanghai by ship, and eighty-two reached the Far East by rail via Siberia.[11] Most of the ship passengers and all of the railway passengers were Austrian Jews. The ships carried "a full load of passengers ranging from third class to deck," predominantly Austrian Jewish families.[12] The trains transported small groups of weary, penniless men.

Those who came via Siberia could only dream of deck cabins on a well-equipped ship. At the end of October, the first group arrived in

Manchouli: six men from Vienna, ranging in age from eighteen to thirty-six. They had no contacts in Asia, no jobs arranged in advance, and "no more than just ¥80 between them"—far less than what each one needed to proceed further. Their passports were prominently marked with a red *J*, and they spoke of the persecution that had prompted them to flee, saying that Hitler was "robbing Jews of the key to their lives."[13]

Austrian Jewish men were particularly at risk. Eichmann had arrived in Vienna after the Anschluss to enforce emigration, and he succeeded in a few months, through "a process of Jewish humiliation, discrimination, and expropriation that had taken five years to develop in Germany," writes Yehuda Bauer. In addition to organized efforts to compel emigration, " 'spontaneous' " outbursts by Austrian Nazis sent unmistakable messages to innocent Jews. Beaten, tortured, and evicted from their lifelong homes, they knew that they had no choice but to flee.[14] Of sixty-four refugees who entered Manchouli between October 27 and December 1, 1938, only ten were women, and these were all wives or daughters accompanying men.[15]

Within eight months, 45,000 Jews left Austria, in comparison to 19,000 during the same period in Germany. To be sure, conditions were also critical in Germany. Mass Jewish arrests had occurred in Germany in May 1938, when most were sent to Dachau. One month later, 1,500 Jewish men were seized, among them 200 accused of being "anti-socials" (able bodied) and the remainder of having a criminal record, even if the crime consisted of a single parking ticket. Their releases were conditional upon immediate emigration.[16]

Warnings from Vienna and Reaction by Tokyo

One of the first and most important indications of the Jewish panic in the Reich came from the consul general to Vienna in late September 1938. Consul General Yamaji Akira wrote Prime Minister Konoe Fumimaro, the imperial prince who was concurrently foreign minister. Yamaji was direct and concise in a coded telegram little more than two pages long that threw the Foreign Ministry into debate and action.

Austrian Jews—all of whom had German citizenship—were emigrating in large numbers. Some were coming to the Japanese consulate general to request visas for temporary stays, but Yamaji was explaining that entering and staying in Japan was very difficult because of the China Incident. In addition, Japan and Germany did not require visas. Yet the applicants were appealing for some kind of certificate in order to obtain transit visas from other countries. "Out of necessity," Yamaji wrote, the consulate had issued a basic statement: "German citizens do not require visas to enter and transit Japan."

Recently, Yamaji continued, all countries had either prohibited Jewish entry or applied limits, resulting in a dramatic increase for requests of these certificates—more than fifty per day. As a result, Yamaji had stopped providing statements, and, he warned, the entry of Jews could become a major problem. Yamaji had four urgent questions:

1. Could he continue to issue explanations that visas were not necessary?
2. What would the standard be if some kind of limit were set, such as funds to be shown on arrival? Emigrants could take very little money with them.
3. Could he issue basic travel certificates for stateless refugees in the case of stateless Jews whose relatives abroad would guarantee funds upon arrival or expenses after entry?
4. How did the ministry intend to handle the entry of Jews to Japan from now on?

From May through September, Yamaji had issued approximately 400 of the explanatory certificates. Jewish Germans held legal German passports that were valid for one year and could be extended. However, if they spoke negatively of Germany after their departure, extension could be refused, and they could become stateless.[17]

This telegram marked the first of many from Yamaji in which he consistently perceived the significance of events in terms of their consequences, beginning with the pressure to emigrate in 1938 and ending with the news of transports of Macedonian and Turkish Jews to Poland in May 1943. His questions displayed an awareness of the various details that were relevant if a bureaucracy was to function, such as the difference between handling stateless Jews and German Jews. Also, he demonstrated his own personal threshold. When there were only eighty requests a month for a simple, legitimate certificate, he obliged, but when the number jumped to fifty a day, he stopped and sought instructions.

Yamaji observed events but neither criticized nor endorsed them. Vienna was his third post in a German country; he had worked in Hamburg and Berlin from 1927 until 1934. He was "very pro-German," recalled his daughter Shigemitsu Ayako. Her father was "a very bureaucratic sort," whose allegiance to his country was paramount. "What was Japan's policy was his policy."

Yamaji supported Japan's relationship with Germany at the same time as his three children entertained Jewish friends at the official residence, above the consulate general offices, where Jews lined up for certificates and visas. The household was lively and open, with an adoring German nanny to supervise the activity. In this warm ambiance, a

Jewish friend of Ayako's elder brother Hide could freely admit, "The only one who is nice to me at school is Hide." Ayako became "best friends" with two "half Jewish girls" from her private school; they have since remained in touch for more than fifty years.[18] It is a curious image: young children, considered Jewish by the Nazis, uninhibitedly playing with their Japanese classmates while fellow Jews nervously queued below for official letters to escape the Vienna that so enthralled the Yamaji family. For Yamaji, welcoming affluent Austrian Jewish children into his home was clearly different from aiding refugee Jews to go to his country.

Yamaji was an astute, faithful public servant. Continuing to issue certificates may have struck him as devious when he could easily confirm his actions with Tokyo before proceeding. Was he also unnecessarily cold towards innocent people who asked for nothing more than a statement of fact? It would be easy to be judgmental now, since 210,000 Jews, 90 percent of Germany and Austria's Jewish population, were murdered during the Final Solution.[19] Yet, at the time, however horrible the persecution may have been, it had not yet escalated to genocide.

Other diplomats struggled with the dilemma of assisting Jews or protecting their careers. When Raoul Wallenberg arrived in Budapest in July 1944, 500,000 Hungarian Jews had already died. Ivan Danielsson, the minister of the Swedish Legation, had been issuing provisional passports to desperate Jews certifying to family or business connections in Sweden. But he reached his threshold after providing 700 certificates, for he feared the damage to the credibility of his office and to the existing certificates, as well as the effect on his career.[20]

To be sure, there was less risk in terms of Yamaji's personal safety in assisting Jews in 1938, when emigration was encouraged, than for Danielsson in 1944, when the Nazis were determined to murder as many Jews, and as quickly, as possible. The Japanese certificates were proper and could have been easily explained had questions arisen from either the Germans in Berlin or the Foreign Ministry headquarters in Tokyo, whereas the Swedish papers were suspicious at best. But it was also more difficult in 1938 to know that a refusal at any level of the bureaucratic procedure to escape the Nazis could have dire consequences for the trapped individuals, as well as repercussions for the country involved.

Yamaji sent his telegram on a tumultuous day that brought the world closer to war. Britain and France concluded the infamous Munich agreement that handed Hitler the Sudetenland. The Council of the League of Nations voted to apply economic sanctions against Japan. Konoe assumed the portfolio of foreign minister, replacing foreign ministers Hirota and Ugaki, who had resigned over the proposed creation of the Kōain "Asia Development Board," that would give the army power over matters concerning China. Once the Kōain was formed, the Foreign Ministry lost its diplomatic role in China, reducing its contribution to "diplomatic trivia," Yale Maxon observes.[21] Prince Konoe served as foreign minister for a month before Arita Hachirō assumed the post.

Although Yamaji did not mention what was occurring in Munich, the course of events may have made him anxious about managing an expected rise in requests for certificates to Japan. Despite the tension in the cabinet over the future of Japanese foreign policy, the Foreign Ministry responded to Yamaji within a week and also cabled all consular offices abroad the same day. The instructions served as the basis for an emerging policy towards the Jews: Japan did not want "foreigners being expelled by Germany and Italy"; the country was involved in the China Incident and had no space to shelter refugees; note that "refugees" was the public term, but it actually signified Jewish refugees; although the Empire did not want them to enter Japan and its colonies, transit was permissible; apply the existing "regulation governing the entry of aliens into Japan" to prevent people from coming. In addition, stateless refugees should not be issued travel certificates, although transit ones were not a problem if the refugees had completed entry procedures for a destination country and possessed more than ¥250 in funds. No certificates stating "a visa is unnecessary" should be granted to those refugees from countries not requiring visas for Japan: dissuade them from making passage to our country. These instructions were within the jurisdiction of the immigration regulation and were not special measures directed towards Jews. Finally, none of this should be publicized.[22]

The cable sent to Yamaji and the one forwarded to all other consular offices were similar in content. Written on behalf of Konoe, they were stamped by the America Bureau chief and the chief of the America Bureau's third section. But the latter cable, #1447, made an additional point: refugees of other nationalities should no longer be issued visas. Although only Austrian and German Jews were leaving Europe at this point, this point foreshadowed the course of Japanese policy towards future refugees. The instructions whisper of the quiet exclusion of foreigners to which Joseph Grew had referred two years earlier. The admonition not to announce publicly the ministry's measures would become a pattern in which Japan would appear to be welcoming refugees or at least treating them tolerantly, while actually discouraging them behind the scenes.

The policy resulted directly from a meeting of the Moslem and Jewish Problem Committee held the day the telegrams were issued. Assembled in order to determine a response to Yamaji's inquiry, the meeting also discussed the July Evian Conference, in which thirty-two countries had participated. The Committee noted the Evian Conference's preference for the term "refugees" rather than Jews, and the reluctance of various countries to provide shelter.[23] When the cables to Yamaji and other diplomats were drafted, the reference to Japan's lack of space to accommodate refugees and use of the term "refugees" were acknowledgments that Japan was not acting differently from the international community.

Yamaji was not satisfied with this response. Many Austrian Jews never inquired at the consulate, because they could travel to Japan without visas, in which case there was no way to stop them. It was "more or less impossible" to prevent people from going to Japan on the basis of Japan's foreign immigration law, especially when other countries were officially prohibiting immigration and applying limits. It would be appropriate, Yamaji suggested, if the Japanese government declared that it was prohibiting immigration. This would not have a major negative effect on relations with German, Italy, or other countries.[24]

From Yamaji's perspective in Europe, deterring refugees with a vague law that did not expressly prohibit entry until their arrival in Japan must have seemed weak and ineffective in comparison to the overt restrictions imposed by surrounding countries. He saw no reason for Japan to disguise its intentions to discourage entry when the prohibitions were so tough elsewhere.

Since the Japanese measures were neither detailed nor public, confusion reigned. If Yamaji worried that his government's instructions were toothless, the American consulate general in Tokyo believed the Japanese measures were more comprehensive than was the case. Shortly after Germany and Japan concluded a cultural pact in November, Consul General C. R. Cameron notified Washington that Germany had agreed not to provide passports to German Jews intending to go to Japan unless Japan granted entry visas first.[25] The Foreign Ministry denied the allegation, but it was picked up by two English-language newspapers in Japan. Meanwhile, the *Times* in London had reported that countries in the Near East and Far East were not applying limits to Jewish emigrants—"for instance, densely populated Japan is not refusing friendly nation treatment." The article cited the large number of Austrian Jews sailing to Shanghai, with some having Kobe as their destination.[26]

Then, *Kristallnacht* occurred, or as Yamaji put it, "The people's indignation exploded." When Herschel Grynszpan, a young Polish Jew, shot and killed Ernst vom Rath, secretary at the German embassy in Paris, local newspapers categorized the crime "a premeditated anti-German plot as well as a strategy to agitate Europe." Early on November 10, Yamaji wrote, a "demonstration" occurred in which twenty temples were torched, Jewish stores were attacked, and Jewish homes were searched, uncovering weapons, communist propaganda, and contraband foreign exchange.[27]

Fluent in German, Yamaji read the German papers every morning at breakfast, often reciting articles aloud. Nothing ruffled him as he reported this account. But by relying on German newspapers, he communicated only the German point of view, which depicted the Jews as international conspirators, created a pretext for further harsh legal and political measures, and understated *Kristallnacht*'s fury. In fact, almost every temple had been burned, thousands of stores had been vandalized, and more than 6,500 Jews had been seized in Vienna alone. Yamaji did not leave the safety of the stucco consulate to see the streets strewn with the debris of ransacked stores, hear the crunch of shattered glass under the heels of his freshly polished shoes, smell the smoke rising from the scorched ruins of temples, or ask citizens—Jews and non-Jews alike—about why this "demonstration" had resulted in so much destruction.[28]

Ernest Heppner knew that he had no future in Germany after *Kristallnacht*. He was "trembling, shaking with fear" as he watched his synagogue burn from afar. Events turned even more frightening when his elder brother Heinz was seized that day, along with other Jewish men, and sent to Buchenwald. Heinz Heppner was freed only when he showed proof that he would leave Germany as soon as possible.[29]

Germany was actively encouraging emigration—even providing information about tickets for Japan, the fees of Japanese ships, payment methods, and sailing schedules.[30] The Japanese desire to deter Jews was overwhelmed by the Nazi zeal to expel them.

Tokyo was becoming anxious, with its attention focused on Asia. While Yamaji was reporting on *Kristallnacht*, the Foreign Ministry was reminding all its offices abroad to obey its recent instructions in cable #1447. Fifty-five Austrian Jews aboard the steamer *Denmark* had departed Manila for Japan on November 7. "You [all consuls] should have them head to Shanghai, Hong Kong, and other places other than Japan," advised the America Bureau chief.[31]

Austrian Jews had every right to transit Japan, owing to Germany and Japan's agreement to exempt visas. All that Japanese consuls could do was discourage Austrian Jews from going to Japan; they could not stop them. Tokyo's alarm over fifty-five people, who may have departed for the United States or another destination within days, demonstrates the low threshold that Japan had for permitting foreigners at this time. Yamaji was correct: Japan's reluctance to publicize its policy would result in people continuing to go there, despite the country's desire to avoid having to deal with refugees altogether.

The *Denmark* soon arrived in Shanghai, where Consul General Hidaka spied twelve passengers disembarking. None, he observed, appeared to be refugees, and a Manila newspaper had published a photo of a group in "ordinary clothes" who were Austrian Jews en route to Japan.[32] Hidaka did not state how he decided that the twelve were not Jews. Perhaps, he was correct that the refugees were still on board and bound for Yokohama, but the passengers' clothing would not have revealed their faith unless they were Orthodox Jews. Many refugees disembarked dressed in their finest attire, often because it was all they had with them.

Well rested and relieved to be far from Europe, they had enjoyed their voyages, often the first stress-free period they had experienced in years. For weeks, they had nothing more pressing to do than revel in the slow tempo of a cruise, take in the breathtaking sights, and dine to their heart's content on generous helpings of delectable cuisine. "Hors d'oeuvres, spaghetti with meat sauce, cherry compote and a double helping of ice cream every day and night," recalled the renowned interpreter Hans Eberstark of his childhood journey to Shanghai from Trieste as a poor refugee.[33]

Rather than checking out the passengers' wardrobes, someone should have checked their passports for the conspicuous red *J* and the telltale middle names of Israel and Sarah. In August, Germany had issued a decree that Jews must either have a first name approved by the Interior Ministry or adopt the middle name Sarah or Israel; compliance was mandatory as of January 1, 1939. By October 5, all German passports held by Jews required the scarlet *J*. German Jews who were abroad at the time had up to six months to have their passports stamped by German consuls.

Less than two months had elapsed between Yamaji's initial warning that Jews were leaving Austria and Hidaka's notice that a group of Jews would soon arrive in Japan. The repercussions of *Kristallnacht* were beginning to reverberate throughout the world. Suddenly, the "Jewish Problem," which had intrigued elements in the Foreign Ministry from a distance, was coming close to home.

North China and Manchukuo

For refugees traveling via Siberia, the first Japanese authorities with whom they came into contact were often North China Army or Kwantung Army officials. Military officials may have appeared more predisposed to refugees than the Foreign Ministry bureaucrats in Tokyo, because they were interested in exploiting those who could be useful, but they did not offer a warm welcome when refugees actually showed up. The military listened to Tokyo and tried to follow Tokyo's directives—which is unusual in the annals of the war in China, where the Japanese army flaunted its independence from Tokyo.

In Tientsin, the police department handled foreign immigration. Major Taki, in charge of foreign affairs for the North China Army staff, headed the office and took a clear stand regarding Jews. The army was, he stated, inclined to permit the entry of Jewish refugees whom it had investigated and found acceptable. Jews could not be rejected, in view of Japanese trade and the import of foreign capital for North China's development. In addition, it was technically difficult to determine exactly who was being banished from Germany and Italy.[34]

A small established Jewish community of 2,000 lived in Tientsin and was prepared to assist refugees.[35] But Major Taki's words were not supported by action. When twenty-eight refugees arrived in Manchouli at the end of November hoping to head to Tientsin, they received Manchukuo transit visas. But when the *kempeitai* (secret police) in Shanhaikwan, the entry point to North China, contacted the army in Tientsin, they were told the refugees were to be prohibited from entering. What should we do when these people arrive in Shanhaikwan? asked the vice consul in Shanhaikwan of Tokyo. He foresaw " 'trouble' " when the refugees stalled in Shanhaikwan, after being forced to wait in Mukden on the way.[36] The lines of authority between the Kwantung Army and the North China Army were blurred when it came to the refugees, and the consuls were restricted to a secondary role. They were left to ask distant Tokyo for advice about problems after they occurred.

At the same time, another thirty refugees arrived in Manchukuo, and police intelligence predicted the number of arrivals could soon reach 1,000. Colonel Yasue, head of the Special Branch in Dairen, went to Changchun to discuss the growing problem with the Kwantung Army, and then to Harbin, where he met with consular officials and the *kempeitai*. They agreed that all refugees from now on would travel via Dairen to Shanghai and bypass Tientsin.

Colonel Yasue's intervention became pivotal. Meanwhile, the Soviet consulate general in Harbin was spreading propaganda and agitating Harbin's Jewish community by claiming that Japan and Manchukuo had begun an anti-Semitic policy. The Japanese consulate in Harbin responded by assuring Dr. Kaufman that Japan was not excluding Jews. The military invited Dr. Kaufman to Changchun, where the *Kyōwakai* (Concordia Association), a multiracial group sponsored by the Japanese, attested that Manchukuo rejected communism but not other races, though it could not shelter many refugees, because it was in a state of war.[37]

As Japanese consuls everywhere struggled to apply cable #1447, the North China Army said one thing and did another. For its part, however, the Kwantung Army had settled on a policy towards the Jews as early as January 1938. Forwarded by chief of staff Tōjō Hideki to Manchukuo director general Hoshino Naoki, the four-page report spoke of pursuing a policy behind the scenes and treading carefully so that the "sensitive" Jews "do not mistake our attitude as ranging from ingratiating to calculating." Further, "they should not grow presumptuous from becoming accustomed to our kindness." The report acknowledged the need for foreign capital to develop the country. The Kwantung Army headquarters was technically in charge of all Jewish operations in Manchukuo, though it delegated implementation to the heads of the Special Branch in every Manchukuo city populated by Jews. Manchukuo would fight the spread of communism as well as pursue the spirit of *gozoku kyōwa* (racial harmony) and *hakkō ichiu* (eight corners under one roof).[38] The Kwantung Army did not see any contradiction between its relationship with Germany and Italy and its treatment of Jews. The issues were distinct, and its image of Jews fit neatly into its conception of the Manchukuo state. Nor was it concerned with policy emanating from Tokyo, but the lack of interest may be due to the report's theoretical and academic nature; it was written not in response to impoverished refugees but in anticipation of wealthy Jewish investors appearing with capital that they wished to contribute to the imperial cause.

Army commander Ueda Kenkichi, who was also Japan's ambassador to Manchukuo, sent Arita a copy of this report in mid-November 1938. He was ten months late in notifying Tokyo, an eternity in diplomacy, which relies on written instructions, notes, and memoranda. But suddenly he found it expedient when refugees came to Manchouli. He had received cable #1447, Ueda confirmed, and agreed to handle along its lines Manchukuo entry visas for Jews driven from Germany and Italy.[39]

Refusing entry while promoting the spirit of racial equality and harmony was not easy juggling. The acting consul in Manchouli, Mr. Matsuda, realized this quickly when nineteen Austrian Jews arrived, intending to proceed to Japan or Shanghai. If he were to stop entry or transit, when the refugees had not violated the immigration law but had insufficient funds, he wrote, the refugees would suffer. As long as the Soviets did not stop issuing transit visas, more refugees would be aboard the twice-weekly trains from now on. A suitable policy was necessary.[40]

The immigration officials were confused. Austrian Jews did not need some minimum amount of money, because they were not stateless. The officials were correct, however, to evaluate them as not violating Japan's immigration regulation. Stopping them from proceeding was unrealistic: by the time they reached Manchouli they had traveled more than six thousand miles on the trans-Siberian railway alone. If they were to be effectively discouraged from making the trip, it had to happen at the Japanese consulates in Europe. If news of their rejection spread, Manchukuo's slogans would seem false.

The Soviet Wrinkle

Just as Germany did not discuss the effect of Jewish emigration on Japan, the Soviet Union did not explain its policy for issuing transit visas. The Soviets seemed to enjoy vexing Japan; their activities did not stop at the Harbin consulate's dissemination of propaganda about the Japanese exclusion of Jews. Their willingness to provide visas to Jews heading for Japanese territory created a test of Japan's true intentions.

Acting Consul Matsuda was concerned about the Soviet consular offices in Germany. They were recommending Japan to people who requested visas in order to go to Shanghai. In addition, they had drastically decreased the fees for visas.[41] All train passengers from Europe to Asia stopped at the Soviet border station of Otopol, some eight kilometers from Manchouli, where they received a departure stamp and left for Manchouli. If Manchouli refused entry, the Soviet authorities would not reissue entry or transit visas. Unless people were prevented from making the trip when they were in Germany or Poland, the Manchukuo authorities could not easily obey Tokyo's instructions.[42]

The problem was exacerbated when the Soviets decided to retaliate against the Japanese for claiming the right to refuse entry after the Soviets had permitted transit (although there were no cases of refugees who had reentered Soviet territory). Almost all Japanese passengers in Europe who planned to return to Japan via Siberia were denied transit visas, while Jews continued to receive visas even when they did not have Japanese ones. Foreign Minister Arita was exasperated with the Soviets. "They recommend going to Japan knowing that this is a spiteful move towards Japan and Manchukuo. In spite of Birobidjian, the so-called paradise for Jews, when they force these Jews out of the Soviet Union, one cannot help but say that their behavior completely lacks sympathy for the Jews."[43]

Jews knew that the Soviets had little sympathy for them. They breathed a sigh of relief when they left Soviet territory, grateful not to have been diverted to Siberia. Trains sometimes stopped at Birobidjian station, but no one ever disembarked. Samuil Manski did not even step outside; he preferred to watch his skin stick to the door handle in the frigid compartment. Martin Krygier vividly recalled his journey: "People swarming into the dining cars on stations with plenty of money, asking to be sold bread, which they could not get locally and being thrown out; Jews in Birobidjian telling a friend of mine: 'Well you are free men and we are Communists.' "[44]

Jews did not want to be stranded at either Otopol or Manchouli stations, with both the Soviets and the Japanese toying with their fate. The Soviets were inflexible, and the Japanese had not sufficiently clarified the Jewish policy for Japan and China. By December 1938, a more feasible policy had become crucial. If not, at the very least more Japanese nationals would end up traveling a circuitous route home across Europe, the Atlantic, North America, and the Pacific, while Jewish refugees crowded Manchouli station, the gateway to the empire of racial harmony.

THE FIVE MINISTERS CONFERENCE: POLICY UNTIL PEARL HARBOR

On December 6, Arita met with his colleagues for a Five Ministers Conference. The result was Japan's official policy towards Jews, which would exist with minor adjustments until early 1942.

The Soviet issue was just one factor influencing the need for a policy. Another was the Ministry's constant fielding of questions from foreign journalists about alleged discrimination against Jews.[45] In addition, Nazi spies were posted to Japan after the Anti-Comintern Pact, and they promoted Germany's anti-Semitic platform.[46] Soviet officials, Western commentators, and German agents all represented competing interests that had to be confronted. But most important, European Jews had discovered Shanghai, and in the words of Joint staff Laura Margolis, there they "streamed," with "the great mass immigration in 1939."[47] Japan formulated its policy just in time for an overflow of arrivals in spring 1939.

In 1938, the Five Ministers Conference served as Japan's inner cabinet. The group of five consisted of the prime minister, foreign minister, finance minister, and the ministers of the army and navy. The Conference created policy on foreign relations, national defense, and finance; it represented an attempt to avoid the domination of the Supreme Command.[48]

But the military still played a major role. Army Minister Itagaki is said to have been behind the Jewish policy proposal, and Colonel Yasue and Captain Inuzuka claim to have been behind Itagaki. After negotiating to allow the Tientsin-bound refugees to go to Dairen and Shanghai, Yasue rushed to Tokyo where he met with Itagaki, who subsequently suggested the Jewish policy that was agreed upon.[49] Inuzuka had already conferred with Yasue.[50] Although the roles of Itagaki, Yasue, and Inuzuka are not clear, the Army generally prepared policy drafts for the Five Ministers Conference at this time, and field-grade officers in the General Staff planned foreign policy.[51]

What is clear is that when Prime Minister Konoe, Army Minister

Itagaki, Naval Minister Yonai, Finance Minister Ikeda, and Foreign Minister Arita met on December 6, 1938, they decided upon a policy that resembled the Foreign Ministry's directives to its diplomats up until this point. There was, however, an added element—inviting businessmen and technicians who could prove useful to Japan.

The "Summary of Jewish Measures" as forwarded to Japanese consulates abroad began with a preface that made several points. The introduction stated: "As a rule, even though we should avoid actively embracing Jews who are expelled by our allies," if Japan were to act like Germany in radically expelling Jews it would not be "in the spirit of the empire's long-standing advocacy of racial equality." In addition, Japan had a "need to invite foreign capital particularly for economic development" and "should avoid worsening relations with the United States."[52] Accordingly, three principles were outlined.

1. Jews living in Japan, Manchuria, and China are to be treated fairly and in the same manner as other foreign nationals. No special effort to expel them is to be made.

2. Jews entering Japan, Manchuria, and China are to be dealt with on the basis of existing immigration policies pertaining to other foreigners.

3. No special effort to attract Jews to Japan, Manchuria, or China is to be made. However, exceptions may be made for businessmen and technicians with utility value for Japan.[53]

The third point suggests military involvement, since Inuzuka and Yasue were the primary instigators of capitalizing on Jewish capitalists for the gain of the empire. But regardless of its source, it provided room for interpretation to diplomats evaluating visa applicants, and an opportunity for refugees to present themselves as suitable immigrants to Japanese territories even if they envisioned residing permanently somewhere else. A final handwritten addendum to the typed policy summary mentioned that diplomats should request instructions in advance regarding the entry of capitalists and technicians.[54]

The drafts of the entire text are revealing. A crossed-out portion refers to allowing people beneficial to Japan into Shanghai, where there was "a complicated secret relationship"; putting such people to use would be an "internal operation." These points suggest the hands of Inuzuka and Yasue. Inuzuka would subsequently be posted in Shanghai, where he attempted to court wealthy British Jewish residents, such as Sir Victor Sassoon and Sir Ely Kadoorie; Yasue's work was clandestine by nature as head of the Dairen Special Branch.

But there is an additional note in some versions. It explains that the document was not the decision of the Five Ministers Conference but a presentation from the Foreign Minister to be sent to overseas consulates if the responsible authorities, namely the army minister and the home minister, consented. Perhaps Itagaki originally represented the opinions of Yasue and Inuzuka, while the Foreign Ministry worked on suitable wording for general dissemination that was subject to the final approval of Itagaki (whose authority involved China, where the military reigned) and of Home Minister Baba (who did not participate in the Five Ministers Conference but was responsible for immigration legislation).

Regardless of the original source, the summary represented interministry cooperation and an attempt to unify the government's policy overseas in Europe and elsewhere, where consuls needed to make quick decisions; in Manchukuo and in parts of China, where the army and navy were in charge; and in Japan, where Home Ministry and Foreign Ministry bureaucrats faced inquiries from both bureaucrats and potential emigrants.

Would this summary prove practical in stemming the flow of refugees to the Far East? Or was it more effective as an attempt to satisfy different political demands: by the Foreign Ministry and cabinet departments that did not desire foreigners, and the other by certain elements in the military intrigued by the possibility of receptive Jewish tycoons at Manchouli station or the port of Shanghai? Diplomats would request much clarification of the policy over the next two years. Within days, they would realize just how difficult it was to control the flow of refugees, even with a new policy that was intended to be timely.

The Immediate Aftermath

As the wording of the decision of the Five Ministers Conference was being finely tuned, hundreds of refugees were steaming towards Shanghai. One month earlier, the Foreign Ministry had expressed alarm over the impending arrival of fifty-five Jews on a European ship; in December, reports would refer to ten times that figure on a single Lloyd-Triestino liner heading to Shanghai from Italy. The Manchukuo border authorities were quickly becoming disenchanted by the arrival of penniless Jews, and the rhetoric of racial equality was employed less frequently. Shanghai, the destination of so many who had no other, was beginning to react negatively to the prospect of even more arrivals.

On December 9, Consul Kuga in Colombo wrote that approximately 900 German Jews had boarded the *Conte Biancamano* in Genoa armed with tickets to Shanghai and nine marks from the German authorities, the equivalent of little more than $3.50. "If almost all have no destination and do not disembark in Singapore or Hong Kong, they will end up causing trouble in Shanghai," Kuga warned.[55] Acting Consul General Gotō in Shanghai was worried; Shanghai was a city rife with rumors. He had heard that the ship carried five hundred German and Austrian refugees, the majority of whom would disembark in Shanghai. "The problem of sheltering and aiding the Jews is becoming grave," Gotō told Tokyo. To make matters worse, the head of the White Russian community had learned from the Italian consul general that Italy had recently deported 3,000 Jews to be sent to Shanghai.[56]

When the *Conte Biancamano* docked in Shanghai, it deposited seven hundred Jews from both Germany and Austria, exactly the average of what the diplomats in Colombo and Shanghai had estimated.[57] Dr. Sam Didner, a young doctor from Graz, Austria, was among them. After building a successful medical practice outside Vienna, he had become increasingly concerned by the tense climate of Nazi intimidation. When a Nazi decree stripped him of his medical license in summer 1938, he knew it was time to leave. Of course, he worried about Shanghai. Would his stethoscope be replaced by a shovel as he took any job he could find?[58]

As the situation worsened in Austria and Germany, other Jews pushed aside their fears of going to Shanghai. By the end of the month, Ōshima would cable that approximately 6,000 people had either already purchased ship tickets for the Far East or expected to do so. Of these, 3,000 would travel on Italian ships, 2,000 on German ships, 500 on *Nippon Yūsen Kaisha* (Japan Mail) ships, and the remaining 500 via other lines. "For German Jews who have been refused entry all over the world, the Far East is the only place of refuge," declared Ōshima. He advised "the necessity of quickly applying appropriate restrictions in China and Manchukuo."[59]

Coincidentally, as the *Conte Biancamano* sailed to Shanghai, the chief of the third section of the America Bureau requested that the other sections chiefs in the Foreign Ministry immediately share any differing opinions regarding the Home Ministry's revision of the existing immigration regulation, which dated from 1918.[60] Deliberations over the change in the law had begun almost a year before, in January; the timing was not a direct response to the reports of thousands of Europeans heading to the Far East. But the new law, with a distinction between entry and transit, would provide more guidance to diplomats evaluating visa applicants, and broader grounds for refusing visas.

Meanwhile, Manchukuo was wrestling with the impact of Japan's Jewish policy on its own immigration procedures. The head of the Manchukuo Affairs Bureau wrote that Italian and German Jews were arriving via Siberia without visas, and that "almost all are impoverished and need public and private assistance, and we do not want them to live here." Manchukuo had decided to permit transit, but not entry.

Problems, however, would occur when Manchukuo issued transit visas for the majority intending to go to Japan and Tientsin, since Japan had decided to prevent entry. "There is nothing we can do but to take steps so that people whom we do not want to reside here—these kinds of Jews chased from Germany and Italy—do not come." Seeking "to avoid the impression that we are discriminating between them and other foreigners," the diplomat added that foreigners (other than Japanese and Chinese) without visas from Manchukuo diplomatic offices abroad would not be permitted to cross the border. The exceptions were those who could be of use, such as technicians, and those with entry visas for countries besides Japan and China. The Manchouli authorities and ministers to Germany and Italy were instructed to refuse visas on the basis of "the difficulties of foreigners' lives in our country and the improbability of entering other countries." Finally, he said, other countries' diplomatic offices in Manchukuo were to be notified about this policy, especially the Soviet Union.[61]

This telegram encapsulates Manchukuo attitudes at the time. The Manchukuo official clearly perceived Manchukuo interests as separate from Japanese ones, since the Japanese policy of refusing entry was problematic for Manchukuo. He was concerned with the appearance of fair treatment, rather than its substance, so that Manchukuo would seem to be upholding its tenets of racial equality and harmony while employing the difficult conditions of living in Manchukuo as an excuse. Also, he continued to demonstrate interest in those who could serve Manchukuo's cause.

Southward in Shanghai, leaders in the International Settlement had no illusions about the possible use of refugees. An autonomous area dating from the mid-1800s, the Settlement operated under extraterritoriality and possessed its own police and government. By the end of December 1938, the Shanghai Municipal Council, the Settlement's diverse governing body, was becoming alarmed by the growing refugee problem. Far from enriching Shanghai, the refugees were "taxing to a grave degree the resources both of the municipality and of private philanthropy." The Shanghai Municipal Council was dominated by the British in numbers and influence, and they were no more predisposed to Austrian and German Jews than anyone else.

Cornell S. Franklin, the Council's chairman, sought to maintain stability. "There is to be considered not only the provision of accommodation and subsistence, but the degree to which any further number of refugees could be absorbed without still further impairing the standard of living of the present community." The international consular body should help stop more refugees from coming, specifically by notifying "interested organisations and shipping companies concerned." Franklin did not hesitate to characterize the unwanted arrivals as "Jewish refugees." He warned, "it will be the Council's duty to protect the community of the International Settlement" by prohibiting landing there should the numbers increase.[62]

Upon receiving a copy of this letter, Gotō cabled Arita to advise the Japanese shipping company of the International Settlement's plans.[63] Both Franklin and Gotō were dismayed by Shanghai's burgeoning refugee population of 1,000 to 2,100 Jews (which was approximately one-tenth of what it would become by the end of 1940).[64] Shanghai was beginning to demonstrate its lack of tolerance for European Jews. The 320 expected to arrive on the last day of 1938 could not anticipate a warm welcome.

Arita took a longer view than his acting consul in Shanghai. He did not remind Gotō of his suggestion one month earlier that fifty-five refugees reported to be heading to Japan be diverted to Shanghai and other places. Rather, he referred to the international political repercussions of arousing strong feelings either way regarding the Jewish problem. He wanted neither to damage Japan's friendship with Germany nor incite "American Jewish merchants," who had considerable influence over Japanese commerce with the United States. It was, therefore, dangerous to respond directly to the Shanghai Municipal Council's suggestion. After recommending a "neutral attitude," he warned that Japan should not become entangled in the problem—as much as possible, the rejection of Jews should be represented as the Shanghai Municipal Council's responsibility.[65]

As 1938 came to a close, the Foreign Ministry attempted to maintain a balancing act between preserving amicable relations with its allies and avoiding alienating American interests it wished to cultivate. It did not yet realize that Germany was intent on expelling the Jews from Europe no matter where they went. But it was aware that the United States was watching closely and was highly critical. The United States had already placed a "moral embargo" on such crucial materiel as aircraft, armaments, and engine parts, and the U.S. Commerce Department had advised American exporters to obtain an "irrevocable letter of credit" before accepting orders from Japan.

As the refugee problem became too large to juggle gently, Japan tended towards increasing restrictions—just as the flow from Europe was about to reach its height in 1939. The decision of the Five Ministers Conference would be tested in the months to come.

NOTES

1. Secret report, "An Introduction of the Lecturer of 'Jewish Influence Influencing the United States,'" Navy military dissemination defence unit, September 1937, JPF, folder 3.

2. "The Problem of Jewish Expulsion," from Ambassador Shigemitsu to Foreign Minister Ugaki, top secret #259, 2 August 1938, JPF, folder 4.

3. Ernst L. Presseisen, *Germany and Japan* (The Hague: Martinus Nijhoff, 1958), 235; Toshikazu Kase, *Journey to the Missouri*, ed. David Nelson Rowe (New Haven, CT: Yale University Press, 1950), 168.

4. Michael Marrus, *The Holocaust in History* (London: Penguin Books, 1987), 158.

5. Manabe Ryōichi, interview by author, 25 May 1995, Tokyo, Japan, tape recording.

6. Maruyama Naoki, "Asia taiheiyō chiiki ni okeru Yudayajin shakai," *Pacific Basin Project* 7 (Yamato-machi, Niigata-ken, Japan: International University, 1986), 3.

7. Yehuda Bauer, *My Brother's Keeper: A History of the American Jewish Joint Distribution Committee 1929–1939* (Philadelphia: Jewish Publication Society of America, 1974), 16.

8. Ernest G. Heppner, *Shanghai Refuge: A Memoir of the World War II Jewish Ghetto* (Lincoln: University of Nebraska Press, 1993), 31.

9. Ambassador Tokura Eiji, interview by author, 10 February 1995, Tokyo, tape recording; Yale Maxon, *Control of Japanese Foreign Policy: A Study of Civil-Military Rivalry 1930–1945* (Westport, CT: Greenwood Press, 1973), 133.

10. "Regarding German Refugees," from the Foreign Vice Minister to the vice ministers of the Home Ministry and Colonization Office; top secret #1023, from the Bureau chief to the head of the Kanto area; and top secret #45 from the Foreign Minister to every diplomatic office abroad, #35, 22 March 1935, JPF, folder 4.

11. "The Jewish Refugee Problem," undated, JPF, folder 4. (This one-page, typewritten document is included with October 1938 material, but the contents make it seem likely that it was produced in January or February 1939.) Note that most sources date the refugee flow by ship as commencing at the end of 1938, but three original sources give August 1938. An AJJDC document mentions August 1938, and a HIAS document refers to "a very small number" of "unvoluntary [*sic*] emigrants" who arrived in Shanghai. A JPF document mentions the August 15 arrival of thirty-two people. August was early, since it was just that time that emigration began to be encouraged in earnest under Gestapo supervision. It took most people months to prepare for the move, dispose of their property, and complete the necessary paperwork. See "The Victims of Hitler at Shanghai," *L'Univers Israelite* 18 (20 January 1939), AR 33/44, #457: China, General, 1939 January-June, AJJDC Archives; "European Emigration to China," by E. Kann, HIAS XV-C-3, YIVO, New York; and "Jewish Top Secret Information #5," by Naval General Staff, 27 January 1939, JPF, folder 6. On the Gestapo, see Lucy S. Dawidowicz, *The War against the Jews, 1933–1945* (New York: Holt, Rinehart and Winston, 1985), 374.

12. Telegram from Moriya Kazuo to Arita, #312, 19 November 1938, JPF, folder 4.

13. "Regarding Jewish Refugees," from Acting Consul Matsuda, Manchouli, to Arita, secret #213, 1 November 1938, JPF, folder 4.

14. Bauer, *My Brother's Keeper*, 225.

15. "Regarding Jewish Refugees," from Acting Consul Mimura Tetsuo, Man-

chouli, to Ambassador Ueda Kenkichi, top secret #258, 10 December 1938, JPF, folder 5.

16. Dawidowicz, *The War against the Jews, 1933–1945*, 99.

17. Coded telegram from Yamaji to Konoe, #28839, #39, 30 September 1938, JPF, folder 4.

18. Shigemitsu Ayako (Yamaji), interview by author, 9 May 1995, Tokyo, tape recording.

19. Dawidowicz, *The War against the Jews, 1933–1945*, 403.

20. Kati Marton, *Wallenberg* (New York: Random House, 1982), 77.

21. Yale Maxon calls the Kōain the China Affairs Board, though other authors like James Morley and Shigemitsu Mamoru refer to it as the Asia Development Board. Maxon, *Control of Japanese Foreign Policy*, 135.

22. "Regarding #39," telegram from Konoe to Yamaji, coded #26010, #33, 7 October 1938, JPF, folder 4; "Regarding the Entry of Jewish Refugees," top secret telegram from Konoe to the listed offices, #1447, 7 October 1938, JPF, folder 4.

23. "Theme of the Meeting of the Board of the Moslem and Jewish Problem Committee," undated, JPF, folder 4. The report mistakenly refers to representatives of twenty-nine countries at Evian, rather than thirty-two. Although this document is not dated, the contents make it clear that it was produced on October 5, 1938. In addition, the telegrams to Yamaji and all other consular officers refer to the consultations among the various ministries that occurred at this meeting.

24. "Regarding #33 and My #49," coded telegram from Yamaji to Konoe, #30567, #50, 17 October 1938, JPF, folder 4.

25. Records of U.S. State Department: Japan, 1930–1939, "Possible Discriminatory Treatment of German National of Jewish Faith," 29 November 1938, File 894.111/75.

26. Telegram from Shigemitsu, London, to Arita, #32341, #213, 2 November 1938, JPF, folder 4.

27. Telegram from Yamaji to Arita, #33254, #57, 11 November 1938, JPF, folder 4.

28. Yamaji employs the word "demonstration" in katakana rather than using a Japanese equivalent.

29. Heppner, *Shanghai Refuge*, 22, 24–26.

30. Zorach Warhaftig, *Refugee and Survivor: Rescue Efforts during the Holocaust* (Jerusalem: Yad Vashem, 1988), 197.

31. "Regarding the Passage of Jewish Refugees," top secret telegram from Arita to every consular head abroad, #1563, 10 November 1938, JPF, folder 4.

32. "Regarding Your Cable #1804," coded telegram from Hidaka to Arita, #33692, #3429, 16 November 1938, JPF, folder 4.

33. Jeremy Bernstein, "In Many Tongues," *Atlantic Monthly* (October 1993): 97.

34. "Regarding Your Cable 3156 (Regarding the Entry of Jewish Refugees)," coded telegram from Tashiro to Arita, #32208, #1045, 1 November 1938, JPF, folder 4.

35. In 1937, 2,000 Jews, half of whom were Russian, lived in Tientsin. *An-*

notated Catalogue, "Archives of the American Joint Distribution Committee 1933–1944," AJJDC Archives, 172.

36. Telegram from Vice Consul Kosakabe to Arita, #34887, #85, 28 November 1938, JPF, folder 4. Mukden was called Hōten by the Japanese.

37. "Regarding Your Cable #1447 (Regarding the Entry of Jewish Refugees)," coded telegram from Consul General Tsurumi to Arita and to Manchukuo, top secret #214 and #35190, #214, 30 November 1938, JPF, folder 4.

38. "Summary of Policy towards the Jewish Race," by the Kwantung Army Headquarters, 21 January 1938, JPF, folder 4.

39. "Regarding Manchukuo's Handling of Jewish Refugees," from Ueda to Arita, top secret #1451, 18 November 1938, JPF, folder 4.

40. "Regarding #52 (#72 to the Ambassador to Manchukuo)," from Matsuda to Arita, #34835, coded #56, 28 November 1938, JPF, folder 4.

41. "Regarding Top Secret #213 (#193 to Ambassador to Manchukuo)," from Matsuda to Arita, #34735, #52, 26 November 1938, JPF, folder 4.

42. "Regarding Your #3482 (#1139 to Manchukuo)," from Matsuda to Arita, #35308, urgent #59, 1 December 1938, JPF, folder 5.

43. "Regarding Jewish Refugees," from Arita to Ueda, coded and very urgent #1152, 5 December 1938, JPF, folder 5.

44. Samuil Manski, interview by author, 6 October 1995, Newton, Massachusetts, tape recording; Martin Krygier, "The Making of a Cold Warrior," *Quadrant* (November 1986): 40.

45. "Regarding the Jewish Problem," from Arita to Ambassador Saitō, Washington, #364, 2 December 1938, JPF, folder 5.

46. David Goodman and Masanori Miyazawa, *Jews in the Japanese Mind* (New York: The Free Press, 1995), 111.

47. Laura Margolis, "Race against Time in Shanghai," *Survey Graphic* 33 (March 1944): 1.

48. Seiichi Imai, "Cabinet, Emperor and Senior Statesmen," *Pearl Harbor as History: Japan-American Relations 1931–1941,* ed. Dorothy Borg and Shumpei Okamoto (New York: Columbia University Press, 1973), 65, 70.

49. Yasue Hirō, *Dairen tokumu kikan to maboroshi no Yudaya kokka* (Tokyo: Yawata Press, 1989), 109.

50. Inuzuka Kyoko, *Yudaya mondai to nihon no kōsaku* (Tokyo: Nihon Kōgyō Shimbunsha, 1982), 77.

51. Maxon, *Control of Japanese Foreign Policy,* 134.

52. "Summary of Jewish Policy," in coded telegram from Arita to various embassies with directions to forward to others, #3544, 7 December 1938, JPF, folder 5.

53. Goodman and Miyazawa, *Jews in the Japanese Mind,* 111. (This is a translation of the actual text included in a number of documents in folder 5 of the JPF.)

54. Coded telegram from Arita to various embassies with directions to forward to others, #3544, 7 December 1938, JPF, folder 5.

55. Telegram from Kuga to Arita, #35979, #104, 9 December 1938, JPF, folder 5.

56. "Regarding Your #1963 (Re. the Passage of Jewish Refugees)," from Gotō to Arita, #36510, coded #3700, 14 December 1938, JPF, folder 5.

57. Telegram from Hidaka to Arita, #36822, coded #3718, 17 December 1938, JPF, folder 5.

58. James R. Ross, *Escape to Shanghai: A Jewish Community in China* (New York: The Free Press, 1994), 4, 8, 16.

59. "Regarding Your #3544 (Regarding Jewish Refugees)," from Ōshima to Arita, #37477, coded #790, 23 December 1938, JPF, folder 5.

60. "Proposed Revision of Foreign Immigration Law," from chief of the third section of the American Bureau to every division and section head in the Ministry, 9 December 1938, JPF, folder 5.

61. "Regarding Jews Chased from Germany and Italy," from the head of the Foreign Affairs Bureau to the counselor at the Japanese Embassy in Manchukuo, secret #1821, 9 December 1938, JPF, folder 5.

62. Letter from Cornell S. Franklin to Dr. A. J. Alves, 23 December 1938, JPF, folder 5.

63. Coded telegram from Gotō to Arita, #37785, #3805, 26 December 1938, JPF, folder 5.

64. Coded telegram from Gotō to Arita, #38170, #3851, 30 December 1938, JPF, folder 5.

65. Coded telegram from Arita to Gotō, #2068, 30 December 1938, JPF, folder 5.

4

Increasing Restrictions in 1939 and 1940

IN DECEMBER 1938, State Department advisor Stanley K. Hornbeck commented, "There are for practical purposes now two Japanese Governments, one in Japan and the other in China."[1] Hornbeck was commenting on the army and navy's general dominance in China, but his observation could have applied to Japan's policy towards the Jews. In Shanghai and Manchukuo, the two main regions in China where Jews transited and entered, the Japanese navy and army, respectively, ruled. The local consulates contributed opinions but functioned mostly as messengers to Tokyo. Only back in Japan did the government operate according to its traditional delegation of powers. But even in Japan, the jurisdiction of the Ministry of Foreign Affairs was circumscribed; it deferred to the Ministry of Home Affairs when petitioned directly by Jews seeking to visit Japan. The Home Ministry took a less cosmopolitan view towards admitting foreigners, no matter how eloquent their pleas and valid their appeals.

In early 1939, Japan was besieged by disturbing signals from both Germany and the United States. At the end of January, German emigration agencies administered by the Central Office for German Jewry were reorganized to emphasize emigration or "evacuation." Shortly after, Hitler erased any optimistic interpretations of "evacuation," swearing to pursue "the destruction of the Jewish race in Europe."[2] In February, the United States decreed a cessation of credits to investment-hungry Japan. In forcing Jews to leave Europe, Germany was encouraging them to go to Asia, one of the few outlets available.

For its part, in taking punitive actions the American government was sending Japan strong signals of disapproval that could not be easily swayed by such a peripheral political issue as other countries' Jews. But these larger trends were not analyzed for their impact on Japan and its Jewish policy.

On February 27, Foreign Minister Arita stood before the House of Peers and announced, "Jewish residents in Japan are to be treated in the same manner as other foreign residents. . . . Jews who arrive at Japanese ports must comply with the Immigration Law, in common with all foreigners, but they never will be denied entry simply because of their race," he added. The headlines of the local English newspapers summarized Arita's vow. "Will Treat Jews Equally, States Arita," proclaimed the *Japan Times*, "Jews Will Receive No Discrimination, Arita Reiterates," emphasized the *Japan Advertiser*, edited by a prominent Jew named Wilfred Fleisher.[3] Cables disseminating the foreign minister's comments were addressed to the Associated Press in New York and the United Press in San Francisco.

If one were not familiar with the nature of Japanese immigration law and the specific telegrams sent to consuls in Europe advising them to discourage Jewish refugees, it might have seemed that Arita's statement was an official welcome to European Jews; the Japanese government appeared to be taking the high road morally. The truth was different. Still, in comparison to the behavior of other countries' diplomats in Asia, the ambiguity of Japanese policy allowed flexibility. Nowhere was this more apparent than in Shanghai.

SHANGHAI

"Incredibly, Shanghai was free from the twin curses of passports and visas!" recalls Ernest Heppner of having completed customs in Shanghai without incident in early 1939.[4] His euphoria was short-lived. Shanghai assaulted the senses: it was alternatively beautiful and horrible, inviting and repelling, and inspiring and distressing. The magnificent view of the stately Bund, the waterfront business district, was followed by the sight of war-torn areas strewn with ruins and rubble. The aroma of fresh pastries, savory sausages, and brewed coffee in the open-air cafes at many restaurants opened by transplanted Europeans was diminished by the stench of raw waste wafting from the waterways. The strains of classical music emanating from the instruments of refugee musicians, among Europe's finest, were accompanied by the raucous arguments of people living in close quarters. Shanghai was a busy, hectic, crowded city of deep divisions between rich and poor and Chinese and foreigners. A metropolis of 4,000,000 Chinese and less than 100,000 foreigners, Shanghai was a melting pot.[5] Although it did not require visas, the city was not receptive to the world's homeless and stateless.

No one wanted to go there. "Shanghai was an unknown entity and seemed a terrifyingly strange place to emigrate to," recalled Evelyn Pike Rubin of her family's reluctance while still settled comfortably in Austria in 1938. Her family expected American immigration visas any day. "We are better off waiting here in civilized Breslau rather than in some godforsaken rathole," was how she described her father's sentiment.[6]

Although he felt that he had no choice, Ernest Heppner had numerous questions about the wisdom of forsaking Breslau for Shanghai. "[H]ow would one get there? how would one live there? were there other people besides Chinese living there? who had ever heard of anyone but criminals going to Shanghai?"[7]

They did not know that Shanghai—famed for its beauty and exuberant cultural life, including riotous nightclubs—had once been dubbed the "Paris of the East." The International Settlement and French Concessions were European-style quarters where longtime, wealthy foreign residents resided in splendor in elegant mansions. British residents of the International Settlement, including Sephardic Jews holding British citizenship, directed far-flung trading companies and socialized at the Shanghai Club. The Ohel Rachel and Beth Aharon synagogues, founded by wealthy Sephardic families, attracted devout worshippers.

Shanghai had more to offer than refugees may have initially thought. But the most recent arrivals began near the bottom of the economic ladder. They were preceded by White Russian emigrés, who had arrived after the Russian Revolution, and Russian Jews who had arrived after the Revolution or moved from Harbin and other Manchurian cities later. Small store-owners seeking customers and people willing to do menial labor found stiff competition. Refugees were not considered eligible for some of the jobs that Chinese held at the lowest pay. By 1939, the rents of even the most humble apartments in the foreign concessions had become unaffordable; the battle-wracked Japanese-occupied zone was the only choice.

No matter where refugees found shelter, they lived perilously close to war. The foreign concessions were free from the hostilities of the Sino-Japanese War, but they were surrounded by the Japanese-occupied area, which was subject to attack, and by guerrilla areas. Itō Takeo, a South Manchurian Railway official, described Shanghai in the late 1930s as "a strange place from which I was able to see in great detail" even when "stray bullets at times flew my way."[8] Shanghai struggled under oppressive wartime conditions, rampant inflation, and a burgeoning Chinese and foreign refugee population. Every morning, the streets were littered with the corpses of malnourished Chinese who had died during the night. This sight greeted foreign refugees and immediately dampened any enthusiasm for their new home.

Shanghai had become a haven by default. W. Michael Blumenthal expressed mixed emotions: "We were grateful to be alive but we wanted, above all, to get away—to get away to another place—to go somewhere where we could begin a new life and turn our backs on everything that had happened in Germany and in the course of our headlong flight."[9]

The Consular Body in Shanghai

Leaving Shanghai was more difficult than reaching it. Authorities in Shanghai understood this and sought to stop refugees from going there in the first place. In January 1939, the Committee for the Assistance of European Jewish Refugees in Shanghai (CAEJR) wrote the Shanghai Municipal Council about the difficulties of meeting the basic needs of an increasing number of refugees.[10] The Shanghai Municipal Council promptly passed the problem to the international diplomatic community.

Michael Speelman, a CAEJR staff member, notified G. Godfrey Phillips, Secretary of the Shanghai Municipal Council, that London would no longer send funds to maintain German refugees. "I have reason to believe," he wrote, "that London thinks that the influx of refugees into Shanghai can be stemmed if it is found that no financial support is coming from London or New York." He warned that the CAEJR only possessed sufficient funds to last one more week.[11]

In meetings that occurred between January and March as ships full of refugees headed to Shanghai, consuls from seventeen nations, including the Axis and Allied powers, deliberated action to stem the influx. Despite their diverse politics, the diplomats comprising this Consular Body shared one characteristic—an inability to perceive themselves as moral agents able to induce change. Their reaction was the timeless one of governments hesitant to become involved in what they perceive as other countries' affairs. "With rare exceptions," writes psychologist Ervin Staub, "they protest only when they see their self-interest endangered."[12]

At the first meeting, the consuls from Germany and Italy stated that it was impossible to stop the flow of refugees. The Japanese consul asserted that Japanese jurisdiction did not extend to the Shanghai Municipal Council, and the American consul suggested that legal resolution was key. The issue was urgent; a Shanghai *Sunday Times* headline clipped by the Japanese consulate read, "Jewish Refugees From Europe To Number Some 4,000 By End of March."[13] But no one dared propose solutions that would involve assuming authority.

Instead, Consul General Neyrone, the Senior Consul, circulated for approval a letter in early February that spoke of "the earnest attention of my colleagues" and offered the statement, "The Governments are being urged to do everything possible to discourage persons of little or no means from emigrating to Shanghai by means of publicity in the press and through the medium of posters in the various ports and railway stations and in shipping offices." These words were a feeble attempt to simulate action. Germany was actively advertising emigration procedures to Shanghai. Emigrants were rushing to railroad and shipping offices intent on booking passages or using tickets they had in hand already. There was nothing more sobering than a stay in Sachsenhausen or one of the other detention camps to convince Jews living in Austria and Germany that it was time to go no matter what, especially when their release was conditional upon proof of plans to emigrate.

No one confronted the issue that the problem was not the overcrowding of Shanghai but racial persecution in Europe. Neyrone even wondered, "How one would define a refugee? If it was a question of money," he added, "who was to say where the dividing line in a monetary sense between refugee and non-refugee was to be drawn?"[14] It was not a question of money, but money was inevitably mentioned early in every discussion.

The Japanese were rankled by their Axis partners. That summer, Consul Ishiguro would comment that Italian vessels transported many more refugees than Japanese mail steamers, because Germany cooperated more with Italy's efforts. If only Japan had been provided the same favorable conditions, he complained; the implication was that Japanese ships would have been able to generate more revenue if they had carried more passengers.[15]

The deliberate legal and extralegal persecution driving people from their countries was never confronted in Shanghai. But back in Berlin, a German Foreign Office official was not so discreet. Germany did not want the Jews: they could go anywhere. Only out of deference to the "inconvenience" caused to the German community in Shanghai, he explained, were shipping companies being notified of the problem.[16]

The *China Weekly Review* did not blame the consuls for their reluctant measures but rather chastised the foreign concessions for their selfish desire to stop refugees, adding that "neither the International Settlement nor the French Concession has spent a dollar—yet—on the care of Jewish refugees." The newspaper doubted whether the Consular Body could influence the flow of refugees but asserted that was not the point. "A more sensible and humanitarian suggestion would be for the Consular Body to advise the authorities of the Settlements to bestir themselves and help the unfortunate refugees to establish themselves here."[17] But no one possessed the imagination or vision of a Raoul Wallenberg, perhaps because none of the consuls viewed assisting Jews as their mission, especially at this stage of the crisis, when it was easier to ignore the signs of terror from afar than to recognize them. The Jewish problem was just one more item on the consular body's regular agenda.

In March, the same month that the Consular Body decided to follow the Senior Consul's proposal, Consul General Miura reviewed the population figures for refugees in the International Settlement and in the Japanese sector. Although there were only 300 refugees in the Japanese sector and five times that many in the International Settlement at this point, he was concerned, characterizing the United States, Great Britain, France, and the Soviet Union as taking "the attitude of bystanders."[18]

In fact, all seventeen nations represented in the Consular Body were bystanders, including Japan. But by the summer of 1939, Japan would reach a threshold of tolerance and take restrictive action in advance of other countries. Before that, various Japanese diplomats would follow the movements and actions of one of Shanghai's most esteemed residents with great concern.

Sir Victor Sassoon

The man who attracted such interest was Sir Victor Sassoon, a Jewish tycoon with British citizenship. The Sassoon family had originally hailed from Iraq until emigrating to India and subsequently to China. Among the most influential Jewish families in the Far East, the Sassoons accumulated great wealth from international trading and banking concerns. By the late 1930s, Sir Victor headed the empire and served as one of Shanghai's most generous philanthropists.

Captain Inuzuka and other Japanese officials were interested in cultivating Sassoon's friendship in order to obtain his capital. Sassoon embodied Japanese dreams of Jewish wealth. One needed look no further than the Bund to see evidence of his riches. Sassoon House, a magnificent hotel and office building crowned by the famed Cathay Hotel, was just one of his impressive properties. Sassoon lived in the penthouse and hosted extravagant parties there.

Sir Victor cut an elegant figure. Wearing a monocle, he needed a cane after his leg was hurt in a Royal Naval Air Service accident. With his elite British education and fine British accent, Sir Victor carried himself with confidence. Outspoken and protected by a mantle of wealth, Sir Victor disdained Japanese military involvement in China.

During a February 1939 trip to North America, Sassoon gave interviews to journalists in New York, Chicago, and Vancouver. His subject was always the same: Japan had a dire need for capital in order to achieve its plans of economic development in China; if the United States, Great Britain, and France stopped exporting to Japan, he said, the China Incident would be resolved quickly, leading to a Japanese withdrawal from China. "The Japanese people are seriously gasping economically and socially from the costs of the Incident," Sir Victor said in New York.[19]

The Naval General Staff responded angrily, but the criticism sounds suspiciously like Inuzuka. Sassoon was negative because he and the other heads of Jewish financial groups were afraid that the Japanese military would ruin the economy in areas where their businesses operated. "This must be the Jewish plan trump card towards us."[20] Reference to a "trump card" in terms of Jews' alleged ulterior motives towards Japan was a particular Inuzuka flourish. Inuzuka could not help but be dismayed by Sassoon's comments.

Continuing to Chicago, Sassoon resumed his theme. Even if Japan was victorious, development in China would not be possible without loans from the United States and Great Britain. "The Japanese should respect the right of powerful Caucasians," Sir Victor asserted.

Such a comment might have elicited a diatribe in a Naval General Staff report, but the diplomatic cables from Consul Masutani in Chicago and Consul Kondō in Vancouver summarized the gist of Sassoon's interviews without passing judgment.[21] The diplomats acted as timely messengers of news but not analysts.

Despite Sassoon's vocal opinions voiced abroad and his cold shoulder toward Japanese overtures at home in Shanghai, Japan's desire to tap into Sassoon's millions did not fade. As late as July 1940, the Asia Bureau produced a report on using Sassoon's businesses to establish a self-supporting economy. Rather than citing the consuls' faithful communication of Sassoon's comments, the paper emphasized the Naval General Staff analysis that Sassoon felt threatened because his businesses would be adversely affected by Japanese development in parts of China. Of particular interest was Sassoon's alleged $200 million in "idle capital"; and the report enumerated means to obtain it.[22] By this time, there was little hope of Sassoon cooperating with Japan, but the funds at stake were too huge to resist. The Commerce Bureau in the Foreign Ministry even delegated authority to various ministries for future purchasing of the necessary goods that Sassoon's wealth would make them able to buy in plenty.

Issued the day after the United States Congress approved a licensing system for American exports that would require permits for many items exported to Japan, the report seems in retrospect like a wild gamble. Although written by a Foreign Ministry department, it was the result of a Kōain meeting. It illustrates how little weight Japanese diplomats' information carried at this point and how prominent the military was in China. Even if Masutani and Kondō had added several sentences explaining public reaction to Sassoon's comments and evaluating how seriously to take them, it is doubtful whether anyone would have remembered, as the China Incident continued to flare and United States–Japan relations deteriorated. It was far more comfortable for the military to entertain a fantasy than to evaluate the contemporary situation objectively. By the end of the month in July 1940, the military would be forced to confront reality when the United States restricted export licenses for such items as aviation motor fuel and heavy melting scrap, materiel vital to the Japanese war effort.

A Threshold in Spring 1939

If Sir Victor Sassoon personified the image of Jewish wealth so enticing to the Japanese, the thousands of European refugees landing weekly in Shanghai were a source of compounding frustration. In March 1939, the police of the Shanghai Municipal Council estimated that the number of refugees would double to more than 8,000 by the end of June, since passages on German and Italian ships bound for Shanghai were completely booked. Of those who had already arrived, 957 lived in charitable shelters, 1,211 received financial relief, and 271 had been provided loans to start businesses.[23] Those reduced to staying in the shelters shared one large room, where sheets were used as dividers and the only furnishings supplied were steel bunk beds. Half the refugee population was impoverished. Sir Victor Sassoon and his European coreligionists represented a dichotomy.

The Jewish Problem Committee hoped to exploit both. Alert to the growing numbers of refugees, it decided to consider concrete measures in accordance with the policy set at the Five Ministers Conference in December 1938. These included investigating a settlement for the refugees, appealing to the financial groups of British Jews (surely a reference to Sassoon), obtaining other Jewish capital, and using the Jews in China to bring about a positive change in the opinions of the American public and American policy makers towards Japan.[24] Inuzuka, Yasue, and Ishiguro were interpreting liberally the Five Ministers Conference directives when they decided to research a refugee settlement.

To be sure, the problem of scarce shelter warranted attention. The Shanghai Municipal Council's estimate soon proved correct, for 1,700 refugees landed in April, and 1,800 were expected in May. But no settlement space was available. More and more settled by default in Hongkew, Wayside, Yangtzepoo, and Chapei, all located in the so-called Japanese defense sector. Poor refugees haphazardly seeking shelter in the Japanese area was not what the Jewish Problem Committee had in mind. The Committee's plans were more bureaucratic and optimistic; they were designed to meet Japanese requisites for investment rather than the basic needs of people in crisis.

Captain Inuzuka did not hesitate to criticize Germany and Italy for abrogating their promises to limit the refugee influx. But there was no reason for "the Empire's embrace of Jewish refugees" to mar the sentiments of the Anti-Comintern Pact, he reiterated.[25] German-Japanese friction continued as Germany fanatically pursued its policy of emigration and Japan sought to enact its own Jewish policy and preserve its autonomy.

Meanwhile, the diplomats posted to the consulate in Shanghai did not communicate well with their German counterparts. One former Japanese diplomat recalls that no one spoke German at the consulate, and no one at the German consulate spoke Japanese. When the Japanese invited their German colleagues to the consulate in a gesture of goodwill, they sent invitations in Japanese, which the Germans could not read. When no one from the German consulate showed up, the Japanese were appalled by their ally's apparent rudeness.[26]

The projections for the refugee population continued to rise. By the end of May, Acting Consul General Satō had notified Arita that the figure could reach 30,000 by the end of the year and 100,000 within several years. Satō mentioned a Jewish source for his figures. As difficult as it was to believe that the number could jump from 8,000 to 30,000 within the year, the first estimate was reasonable; little did Satō or his sources know, however, that the second projection was hopelessly unrealistic, because by late spring 1941 Jews would be unable to escape Europe.[27]

The spring of 1941 seemed like the distant future during the spring of 1939. By early June, Japanese patience with the new arrivals in Hongkew was beginning to wear thin. The Jewish Problem Committee suggested restricting landings in the Japanese sector, except for refugees already en route to Shanghai.[28] These recommendations preceded major action in August to stem the tide of refugees to Shanghai. Miura wrote Arita about the decisions of the Committee, but he did not comment on them.

What was the position of the Shanghai consulate as the number of refugees residing in the Japanese area rose from 300 in March to approximately 4,500 in June?[29] It deferred to the Naval Landing Party, which ruled the Japanese sector. "Very weak" is a description of the Japanese consulate in Shanghai often repeated by former diplomats. Shanghai was not a desirable post, because diplomats knew that the navy dominated all matters. Perhaps because they were so powerless, the various officials did not distinguish themselves in their reports to Tokyo. Even Ishiguro, a member of the Jewish Problem Committee, is difficult to discern, though the personalities of his colleagues Yasue and Inuzuka illuminate the documents.

Summer 1939

By summer, the Jewish Problem Committee was caught in a paradox. On the one hand, it was officially proposing a Jewish quarter in Shanghai in the hope of exploiting Jewish wealth, and it was stressing the importance of not alienating the Jews. On the other hand, it was recommending limits on entry into Hongkew. Simultaneously, the Committee had swallowed whole the myth of international Jewish influence, even while witnessing people reduced to finding shelter in a tense military zone. The concept of a settlement for refugees who could be productive for Japanese ends was like whistling in the wind. One has to credit the Committee members for imagination, inasmuch as their daily exposure to the lives of the refugees suggested not productive economic gain in a number of years but hard times for people who could barely survive day to day. The settlement idea was also out of touch with the international political situation.

The unabated influx of refugees to Shanghai and the German emphasis on emigration created a crisis situation that was not predisposed to orderly settlement. On the same day in early July that the Jewish Problem Committee issued yet another paper on the refugee situation and methods to obtain American capital, the *Times* of London reported the establishment of the Reich Jewish Association in Germany. "The aim of National Socialism remains that of removing every single Jew from the Reich and the purpose of the present decree is not to provide the Jews with a basis for further existence in Germany, but, on the contrary, to hasten their departure," commented the article.[30]

There was no time for the Japanese leisurely to produce long papers on the need to consult and research various measures. A meticulously drawn graph of foreign Jewish capital flowing into Japan and Manchukuo had little to do with reality. To be sure, Jewish relief agencies abroad were sending funds to Shanghai, but they were attempting specifically to assist the Jews, not the Japanese.[31]

Japanese attempts to influence American policy makers via the establishment of a settlement were seriously mistaken. Despite appearances, the American government viewed as cynical the settlement proposals of other countries. Ambassador Joseph Kennedy criticized Britain's offer to settle refugees in Guiana. "The general effect of this program will be to place them in a strong moral position of which they plan to make full use in the international press."[32] Kennedy was an isolationist and at best not predisposed to the Jews, but his views were shared by many Americans who viewed other nations' proposals as publicity campaigns rather than possible solutions to a grave problem. It was doubtful whether Japan would win kudos for helping Jews, especially when the United States notified Japan at the end of July that it would abrogate the Commercial Treaty of 1911. United States–Japan relations continued to deteriorate. The number of Jewish refugees in the Japanese sector continued to swell, reaching approximately 15,000 by August. According to the Joint, "almost the entire Jewish population in Shanghai" was residing in the Japanese area—a grave problem for the Japanese authorities.[33]

August Restrictions

Foreign Minister Arita believed there were only 5,000 refugees in the Japanese sector, but even this figure was high enough to require action. In early August, he instructed Ōshima to explain to the German Foreign Office that refugees should be stopped from going to Shanghai, because they would no longer be able to live or do business in the Japanese sector. Arita advised that negotiations be conducted quietly so that the issue could not be used as propaganda harmful to both Japanese-Jewish relations and Japanese-German-Italian relations.[34] Arita did not view Japan's relations with European Jews and with its ally Germany as mutually inconsistent. Since Germany was still promoting emigration at this point, Arita's balancing act was possible, if awkward and ill conceived.

Arita's cable provided a concise summary of the situation in Shanghai and made no mention of Ōshima's well-known pro-German sympathies. Like any other diplomat, Ōshima, in spite of his rank as a lieutenant general, was expected to follow the Foreign Minister's instructions. Arita also sent the same cable to the Japanese ambassador to the United States.

Diplomats took pains to convince Jews that the impending restrictions were not anti-Semitic. Officials tried to preempt criticism before the local newspapers began publicizing Japanese regulations on entering the defense sector. Miura presented a memorandum to Ellis Hayim, the CAEJR head, in the presence of naval squadron officers and Captain Inuzuka. "In spirit that all races are equal and sympathizing with plight of Jewish people Japanese authorities have thus far placed no restriction upon their coming into area controlled by Japanese forces." This statement employed the familiar rhetoric about racial equality. That was straightforward enough, but the syntax became confused when the statement continued in an attempt to urge understanding. "Humanitarian attitude of Japanese Authorities would be much appreciated," it read, "especially in view of fact that this area has not returned to normalcy as yet and havoc wrought by hostilities has caused a dearth of houses there."[35] To be sure, the translation was stiff, and the grammatical subject in Japanese sentences can be difficult to identify. The resulting impression, however, is that the Japanese were congratulating themselves for their behavior and requesting recognition from others—not the customary behavior of true humanitarians. The statement rang hollow.

On August 12, *China Press* confirmed Japanese fears with the headline, "Ban Placed on Jews by Nipponese."[36] Although the article was not an editorial but an interview with a navy spokesman, the headline said it all. No matter how delicately put, Jews had been targeted as undesirables in the Japanese sector.

The *Shanghai Times* reported the development less melodramatically in its story, "Jewish Refugees Must Register to Reside or Do Business in Hongkew." It read in part, "Taking action to curb the influx of Jewish emigrés into areas north of the Soochow Creek, the Japanese Naval Landing Party authorities announced yesterday that all Jewish emigrés residing in the Japanese Defence Sector or engaged in business there or intending to reside there or transfer their domicile to that area must register with the Jewish Immigrants Relief Committee by August 21." Those who did not register on time were prohibited from entering. Most important, all new arrivals would be prohibited from moving to the area. This was the most devastating point. The navy spokesman attempted to justify the action: references were made to CAEJR's wish that a "constructive step" be taken "to curb the influx" and the Consular Body's failure to do so, resulting in a "case of 'passing the buck.' "[37] The navy believed it had no choice but to take action.

Note the contrast between Miura's circumlocution and the navy spokesman's candor. Miura sounded more even cautious when he notified the German and Italian representatives, Acting Consul General Bracklo and Acting Consul General Farinacci. "I have the honour to suggest that I would be gratified if you could arrest the attention of your Government," Miura proffered, "so that they might take steps within their power to stop the emigration of Jewish refugees to Shanghai, because such steps would, in the light of the local situation, save various frictions and benefit the refugees already arrived."[38] To be sure, diplomatic discourse was and is often couched in understatement, but Miura's timid language did not match the bold action taken by the navy. Both the appearance of a navy spokesman at the press conference announcing the Japanese restrictions and his forthright style showed who was in charge. The local Japanese diplomats were left to temper the tone of regulations that were in fact too stringent to downplay.

Within several days, the repercussions of the Japanese action spread as the International Settlement and the French Concession "took parallel but independent action" to block the arrival of more European refugees. Five thousand Jews who were en route to Shanghai or had paid for their passage aboard fifteen different vessels were immediately affected by the domino effect of the other foreign concessions' following the Japanese lead. G. Godfrey Phillips suggested that the Shanghai Municipal Council would consider assisting 2,000 of those caught by the new developments in Shanghai if the Japanese would accommodate the other 3,000.[39] The doomed voyage of the *St. Louis* was too recent for refugees to ignore. Emigrés were left in limbo as tension climbed in Europe in the weeks before the German invasion of Poland.

The copycat behavior of the other concessions in immediately applying restrictions in August 1939 did not result from a discussion of the European crisis. Nor did it reflect a serious appreciation of the effect of cutting off refugees from one of the few remaining sanctuaries in the world, however disappointing Shanghai may have been to the nervous arrivals. The concessions were representative of their national affiliations. When it comes to nations, writes Henry Feingold, "They have no souls and no natural sense of morality, especially when it concerns a foreign minority which is clearly not their legal responsibility."[40]

The Autumn Outcome

At the end of September, Neyrone tested the rigidity of the Japanese regulations and the meaning of Miura's polite words when he requested that 350 refugees who were unable to board the *Conte Biancamano* in Genoa on August 16 be permitted to head to Shanghai. These individuals would have beaten the Japanese deadline had the war in Europe not interfered with their ability to leave Genoa on time. Neyrone reiterated, "The juridical figure of 'refugee' has not as yet been defined in a clear and precise manner."[41] Apparently, Neyrone did not recognize that Nansen passports for stateless persons, issued by the Nansen Office of the League of Nations, and a scarlet J stamp were strong indications that the bearers were refugees.

Miura, however, soon recognized Neyrone's meaning between the lines. After a visit with Dr. Neyrone, he wrote Foreign Minister Nomura that Neyrone's letter was based on a request from the Lloyd Triestino company, which was concerned about losing profits if it had to refund ticket fares.[42] In a perfunctory letter, Miura rejected Neyrone's appeal on behalf of the "Japanese Authorities."[43] There was no further word regarding the 350 stranded Jews.

The Japanese stand, however, softened by the end of October, when refugee residents of the Japanese sector were permitted to send for relatives in Europe. The Shanghai consulate would issue entry permits "in limited numbers" after applicants had applied through the CAEJR. The exception, Miura explained to Ellis Hayim, had been made from a "humanitarian standpoint." He cautioned, "I may add that the procedure is not to be published, but instead is being sent to you and the shipping companies concerned."[44] That same day, Ishiguro notified eleven shipping companies of this change.[45]

While implying that appreciation for Japanese generosity was merited, Miura's admonition about keeping the news quiet suggests that the authorities feared a rush of refugees. He soon discovered that his painstaking effort to justify and enforce the navy's regulations was being frustrated, not by the Shanghai Jewish community or European Jews but by his own colleagues in Europe. He wrote Foreign Minister Nomura that Jewish passengers arriving in Shanghai revealed that the Japanese consulates in Europe were still issuing certificates, despite the August 2 decree.[46] Since consuls did not explain the restrictions on entering Shanghai, discreet efforts to ease the limits were meaningless.

Meanwhile, the Shanghai Municipal Council had modified its stand. At the end of October, it decided that adults who possessed U.S. $400 and children who had U.S. $100 would be permitted into the International Settlement. The CAEJR would process applications for consideration by the Shanghai Municipal Council. This new category of eligible emigrés was in addition to immediate family members of financially competent residents of Shanghai, those with employee contracts, and those with plans for marriage with Shanghai residents.[47]

Yamaji, ever vigilant in Vienna, asked Nomura several days later whether the reported $400 clause to enter Shanghai was true. The Vienna office of the Lloyd Triestino line claimed that the Shanghai Municipal Council had contacted the head office.[48] Yamaji was besieged with increasing numbers of people requesting visas from the consulate in light of "the increasingly violent anti-Semitic policy of this government and the advancing war situation." Yamaji listed three ominous events: the plan to establish a Jewish area in the Lublin region of Poland, with many people already deported there; the simmering aftermath of the assassination of the German diplomat in Paris the year before, including the burdensome one billion DM fine placed on the German Jewish community; and Hitler's recent emphasis on anti-Semitic and anti-British propaganda.[49]

Yamaji was a master of understatement. Hitler's anti-Semitic policies had already forced half the German Jewish population to emigrate from Germany and left the remainder indigent. The "war situation" referred to Germany's successful invasion of Poland. The "Lublinland" region was a harsh place, where many died within months of being sent there. The anti-British propaganda resulted from Britain and France's declaration of war on Germany the month before. These were all catastrophic events.

Perhaps it was fear that drove the Jews to the Japanese consulate in Vienna, because they were not required to apply there. German Jews still did not need visas for Japan (although Polish Jews living in Germany had become stateless). The $400 provision applied only to the International Settlement. The French Concession was treating German Jews as enemy nationals, by prohibiting them from doing business there. It is possible that the Shanghai Municipal Council had not clarified that point, knowing full well that most of the refugees would end up in the Japanese area; or perhaps the Lloyd Triestino office had misunderstood that entry was limited to the International Settlement.

Meanwhile, there was no word from Ōshima in Berlin. Ōshima may have mentioned Germany's anti-Semitic policy as a postscript in longer cables devoted to Japanese-German negotiations, and these cables were classified differently. But one cannot help but sense that Ōshima was too silent regarding the Jews. No matter how insignificant the Jews may have seemed to him, they were not so for Hitler, as history would show all too well.

Early 1940

By early 1940, the situation in Shanghai had settled. Restrictions imposed by the various concessions had proved effective. The *Jewish Tribune: The Organ of Indian Jewry* noted in March that an average of forty refugees a month had successfully entered Shanghai in the past two months.[50] After a meeting at the Japanese consulate, a CAEJR official realized that "it is the naval landing party deciding which permit is to be granted and which is to be declined, and not the Consular authorities."[51]

The Japanese authorities became more lenient in the spring, in order to manipulate the Jewish vote so as to obtain more seats on the Shanghai Municipal Council. At the time, the Council was composed of five British, two Americans, two Japanese, and five Chinese citizens. The Japanese put forward five candidates and considered the Jewish vote the key to victory. Miura admitted to Arita that the Shanghai consulate had begun to issue permits "in much increased numbers as a scheme to acquire Jewish eligible voters."[52] Michael Speelman, now the CAEJR chair, was worried. "I do not blame immigrants who sell their vote to the Japanese for the promise that permits will be issued for all their relatives to come to Shanghai," he confided, "but there is no doubt about that this creates a tremendous amount of antisemitic feeling here."[53]

The election strategy was strange and forced. The headline of a local newspaper exclaimed, "British-American Bloc Votes Equal Japanese; Jewish Holding Balance," and the article explained, "The Japanese are asking both Nazis and Jews to vote for them."[54] In the end, the strategy failed: the Japanese did not win additional seats, but 1,000 permits were issued to Jews.[55]

By June, the consulate had dramatically decreased the number of permits issued, to an average of one a day, in the wake of the inevitable overflow of refugees from the International Settlement into the Japanese sector. In spite of the slim chances of obtaining permits, "appeals are continuing and becoming very troublesome," wrote Ishiguro. Arrangements were made to transfer the responsibility of granting permits from the consulate to the naval administration, with the consulate's function reduced to a "window" for distributing and receiving applications. No one was disguising who was in charge at this point, though it is not clear whether the consulate deferred voluntarily to the navy, or was being forced.[56] Even if the consulate had not enforced a strict policy of granting visas, it was too late for many in Europe. Italy had entered the war on June 10, and the sea route to safety in Shanghai had evaporated overnight.

MANCHUKUO

It was still possible to reach Shanghai via Siberia and Manchukuo, but refugees needed a Manchukuo transit visa and an entry permit from the Japanese consulate in Shanghai. Just as the foreign concessions in Shanghai had become anxious over the steady and seemingly unstoppable flow of refugees in early 1939, the Kwantung Army and the Manchukuo Affairs Bureau viewed wearily the far smaller number of refugees crossing the border. Some refugees desired to stay in Manchukuo, where they had relatives or job offers. From the beginning, the involvement of Dr. Kaufman, the head of the Harbin Jewish community, was crucial.

In January 1939, Ambassador Ueda proposed several measures that did not favor refugees. While acknowledging that the local Jewish community would cover all costs while the refugees were in Manchukuo, he approved of neither entry nor transit for Jews driven from Germany and Italy. He added, however, that the *Kyōwakai*, the organization that had reassured Dr. Kaufman about Japanese intentions a few months, earlier, should negotiate with the local Jewish community regarding admitting skilled people. It was as if persecuted people and skilled technicians were mutually exclusive categories.

Ueda was obsessed with not admitting those he did not want. In the same cable, he repeatedly suggested that the German and Italian embassies in Manchukuo assume responsibility for sending refugees back.[57] This idea was unrealistic. It betrayed Ueda's identity as a general rather than diplomat, his lack of understanding of worldwide refugee crises, and his ignorance of Hitler's unequivocal and public vows to rid Europe of the Jews.

While Manchukuo officials regularly cabled Tokyo regarding refugee matters and generally followed Tokyo's policy, they appeared to operate with greater autonomy. Ueda, after all, wore the cloak of commander of the Kwantung Army, which reigned supreme in Manchukuo and North China. He could propose sending refugees back to Germany and Italy without being told that the idea was ridiculous.

Consul General Katō in Mukden discovered how misguided Ueda's recommendations were. A week after Ueda's proposals, he wrote Arita that twenty-nine German Jews from Austria had arrived in Mukden, where the German consulate assumed a "very cool attitude." "It is not feasible for us to pay their expenses," a German diplomat had stated. "They have arbitrarily escaped from Germany to profit from their livelihoods," he added, "and we will not actively help them."[58]

While Ueda seemed to forget that Manchukuo was founded on utopian aspirations, Acting Consul Matsuda recalled them when confronted by three impoverished Austrian women en route to Shanghai. When they entered, a Manchukuo official discovered that the women, ages thirty-one, forty, and forty-four, needed assistance in order to survive. Technically, they violated Japanese immigration law, since they were indigent, and they could be forced to leave. The official, however, decided that such action was not in keeping with the "real intentions of Manchukuo" and took a "broadminded viewpoint and carefully considered steps." Dr. Kaufman and the local synagogue assumed responsibility, and the women were able to proceed to Harbin, although two had husbands waiting in Shanghai.[59]

Was the official's action "broadminded" or self-serving? After all, no one disputed that Dr. Kaufman's support could always be counted on. There was no need for Manchukuo authorities to worry about feeding and sheltering them, no matter how helpless three unaccompanied women may have appeared.

Kaufman was called to action again that spring when fifteen people tried to enter Manchukuo from Shanghai without advance permission from the Kwantung Army. They sat marooned in the port city of Dairen with another party of six. A motley crew who did not fit the Five Ministers Conference conception of technicians and capitalists, the group consisted of five doctors, one decorator, two dancers holding contracts of employment at Harbin's "Fantasy Cabaret, and their spouses and children."[60]

Dr. Kaufman first appealed to the Kwantung Army in Harbin. When that effort failed, he spoke with Colonel Yasue in Dairen and Foreign Ministry officials in Shanghai. But the military, asserting its authority, refused to reconsider.[61] Subsequently, Kaufman visited Japan and called on the heads of the East Asia Bureau and the Research Division to negotiate a solution. Notes of their meeting refer to an impassioned plea from Kaufman, who was "sick at heart" regarding these groups. Kaufman warned of the repercussions if the refugees were unceremoniously sent back to Shanghai. "If British and American newspapers are able to sniff this out, they will exaggerate it as discriminatory treatment." Kaufman had "no other choice but to depend on help from the Japanese side," since his other attempts at mediation had failed. "If you have them enter, please assist me that after that, only those who have a guarantee from the Manchukuo Jewish community and employment will be permitted," Kaufman requested.[62]

Kaufman's intervention succeeded. The ambassador to Manchukuo vowed, "From now on, we will act in unison with Japan's policy towards Jewish refugees and refuse entry." This time, however, an exception was made for the doctors, decorator, and dancers delayed in Dairen.[63] Dr. Kaufman had demonstrated the finesse of a sharp negotiator. While realizing that a final decision would be issued by the Manchukuo side, he recognized the value of appealing to the Japanese side. He cautioned against arousing the wrath of the foreign press while promising that such an incident would not occur again. Finally, he suggested a future limit: "From now on, in general, if you let in 100–150 people a year, we would be very happy."[64]

Despite Manchukuo's alleged embrace of various races, its tolerance level towards refugees was low. Before entry to Manchukuo had been prohibited in October 1938, twenty-five people had come from Shanghai and stayed in Manchukuo; after October, fourteen of fifty-three people entering from Siberia had stayed, for a meager total of thirty-nine.[65] Kaufman's proposal of 150 people a year allowed some latitude for a higher number of refugee arrivals, but it was also smaller than the number of requests.

The Manchukuo embassy in Berlin reported that thirty to forty people a day applied for visas. Entry visas were generally not available. Like Japanese embassies abroad, the Manchukuo embassy explained, they were "answering verbally and refusing euphemistically," in order not to anger applicants. Applicants heading to Harbin with employment contracts or close friends were subject to thorough investigations. Friends in Harbin were evaluated on the basis of ideology, length of residence, their business situation, whether they could be trusted, and relationships with other foreigners there. Ten-day transit visas were possible, but the embassy was refusing to issue them to people heading to China for such reasons as Shanghai's increased population, lack of family members and no job opportunities there.[66] Any reference to China signified Shanghai, since North China was closed to refugees.

Clearly, emigrés could not easily obtain transit or entry visas from the Manchukuo embassy.

Settlement Plans

Yet Manchukuo was the region considered by Japanese and Jews alike as a potential site for settlements. Maruyama Naoki traces the concept of a Jewish settlement in Manchuria as far back as the years following the Russo-Japanese War, when the Jewish community approached the Meiji Emperor.[67] In 1933, N. E. B. Ezra advanced the idea of a settlement for as many as 50,000; other Jews proposed such plans in 1939. Also, officials at the South Manchurian Railway pursued plans from the late 1930s until autumn 1940, when the conclusion of the Tripartite Alliance nullified such overtures.

N. E. B. Ezra, ever active, was a man ahead of his time. He wrote Vice Minister Shigemitsu in September 1933 about a settlement for 1,000 families or 50,000 people in all escaping Hitler's anti-Semitic policies.[68] In August 1934, Shigemitsu responded negatively at a meeting with Ezra. "It is not possible to say anything definite just yet," he hesitated. "The country has many problems to adjust, it is just in its embryo, and, to my mind, such a movement is too big for the present."[69] This reaction dampened any hopes raised by Sugimura Yotarō, Japan's delegate to the United Nations, who had encouraged Ezra the previous autumn.[70]

In early 1939, Lew Zikman, a wealthy Jewish sugar refinery owner based in Harbin, approached the Foreign Ministry with plans to settle 200 families, or approximately 600 people, in Harbin. His ratio was far more conservative than Ezra's generous figure. Zikman envisioned the group working productively in factories manufacturing shoes and gloves. Offering to donate his own land, he discussed raising the funds for the plant from American relief groups and the local Jewish community. Any loans would be defrayed over five years. Zikman appealed to the Japanese authorities as if he was aware of the Five Ministers Conference tenets: "The fact that there are over 4,000 refugees in Shanghai would make it possible for us to select the most desirable elements and specialists." He also suggested that the mechanical shops work as subcontractors for the South Manchurian Railway. Zikman was open and candid. "Once again, I wish to repeat that my principal aim is to assist our co-religionists who are in dire distress, which I trust you will understand as a natural motive and at the same time I wish to point out that my most ardent desire is to act in conformity with the interests and principles of this country."[71]

Perhaps, Zikman repeated himself one too many times. Acting Consul General Taniguchi in Harbin wrote to Ueda and characterized Zikman's proposal as a "private plan to kill two birds with one stone" by assisting 200 families and contributing to Manchukuo's development with the imports of commodities from American Jews. Concerned about the "quite 'delicate' repercussions" of Zikman's plan, the consulate refrained from giving an opinion and passed the matter to the military, which was divided. Those opposing the plan felt that it was designed to assist European Jewish refugees; "Manchukuo industrial development is nothing more than an incidental result." Further, there was no guarantee that American Jews would send the sums needed to settle 200 families.[72]

Zikman had professed confidence that American relief agencies would support his cause; if they refused, he declared, "all moral responsibility will rest on them."[73] Yet Zikman downplayed the issue of morality when he discussed his plan with Jewish leaders. He wrote Dr. Cyrus Adler of Dropsie College in Philadelphia that one's moral stand towards Manchukuo was irrelevant when Jewish survival was at stake. "I believe that the Jewish people, in striving to attain their life and existence, should be far sighted and should base their position on laws and rights but not on moral sympathies and feelings, which are changeable," he confided. Zikman recollected the advice of another Jewish leader, Mr. Warburg: " 'It is hard to find a sauce which will be good for meat, fish and for ice cream.' "[74] Zikman believed that Manchukuo would be good for the Jews, even though it was far from an ideal state.

American Jewish leaders did not have an opportunity to consider the plan in a leisurely way. By the end of April, Ueda had advanced several concerns about the proposal. He feared the settlement of 200 families could be the beginning of large-scale Jewish immigration but was doubtful about the level of foreign capital that would be provided. He worried that giving permission to families this time would be a Pandora's box, for subsequent refusals would have major repercussions. Asserting that "we cannot expect European and American Jews to supply the large sums needed for business," Ueda advised: "Euphemistically discourage in a way that does not sound harsh."[75]

In light of Ueda's reaction, Dr. Kaufman's conservative suggestion to permit a maximum of 150 people a year into Manchukuo appears realistic. Although Zikman's plan was far more modest than that of N. E. B. Ezra, it was still ambitious. But even if he had projected a smaller settlement, it is questionable whether it would have succeeded. The American Jewish community was suspicious of any plan for a settlement in China.

In June 1939, Jakob Berglas proposed that 100,000 refugees emigrate to Kunming, the capital of Yunnan province, which was controlled by China. Kunming boasted an "eternal spring, beautiful landscape, (and) rich mineral resources," claimed Berglas, a businessman with offices in England and Germany. In his hotel room at the Cathay Hotel overlooking the Bund, Berglas envisioned a planned economy.[76] Although Berglas said that he had the support of provincial authorities, Americans who received his proposal were less enthusiastic. Alex Frieder, president of the Jewish Refugee Committee in Manila, wrote Charles Liebman, president of Refugee Economic Corporation in New York, that he was concerned that the plan originated from an individual and not a recognized organization. He called the plan "unofficial and shrouded with suspicion."[77] Berglas later expanded the possibilities to other parts of China, Argentina, Australia, and Brazil, widening the net to include not only Jews but other emigrants as well.[78] The Chinese government dismissed Berglas's plan as "premature."[79] Nor did the plan ever develop elsewhere.

Japanese authorities should have been warned by the quick demise of earlier proposals, but the attraction of a Jewish settlement was irresistible for Manchukuo industrialists and the army's Jewish experts. In 1939 the idea of settlement became a pet project of Inuzuka, Yasue, and Ayukowa Yoshisuke, the president of the Manchukuo Heavy Industries Development Corporation.

Manchukuo was not only the answer to Japan's problem of overpopulation and the embodiment of its dreams, but also the key to its national defense. An ambitious program of industrial expansion began in summer 1936 but foundered in the autumn of the following year, owing to bureaucratic snafus and the raging war in China that had flared with the Marco Polo Bridge Incident in July 1937.[80]

Meanwhile, from 1937 to 1941, the Manchukuo Heavy Industries Development Corporation was the major route for investment in Manchukuo.[81] Ayukawa was determined to raise capital. He had first pursued American sources in 1937 but was discouraged by the Foreign Ministry's strenuous opposition.[82] He tried again in early 1939, through an envoy, Tamura Kōzō. For the next year and a half, discussions would occur between Tamura and American Jewish leaders. But the talks never progressed to negotiations, because both sides were operating from different premises.

Tamura was a longtime resident of the United States, where he represented boiler manufacturer Tōyō Seikan. In a Joint memorandum, Tamura was described as "a very rich Japanese industrialist with large U.S. business connections."[83] Working with Captain Inuzuka in Shanghai and Ayukawa Yoshisuke in Manchukuo, he shuttled between New York, Tokyo, and Shanghai. On behalf of Inuzuka and Ayukawa, he suggested that Japan establish a settlement for 30,000 Jewish refugees in Manchukuo or China in exchange for ¥200 million in financial support. Some of the funds would finance the settlement, and the remainder would assist Manchukuo development.

The Foreign Ministry became suspicious of this private intermediary without government credentials. Foreign Minister Nomura notified Ambassador Horiuchi in Washington that Tamura had met with several prominent Jews, including Rabbi Wise, in New York in April 1939. Another was Frank Garson, president of Long Island Machinery, who became Tamura's regular contact. Nomura asked Horiuchi to forward his cable to the consulates in New York and San Francisco and to investigate Tamura's character.[84] The ministry had been slow to learn that Tamura had spoken with Jewish leaders; Nomura's cable was dated November. Horiuchi, however, responded quickly to Nomura's request. Providing basic background on Tamura, he commented that the appearance of Tamura's negotiations with Americans can be "direct like a short dagger, and there are occasions when this is efficient." Although Horiuchi did not know much about Tamura's actual proposal to use Jewish financial groups to fund a settlement and provide capital investment, he did know that one must have the approval of the American government, which would be difficult.[85]

It is unfortunate that Tamura seems to have had little interaction with Japanese diplomats in the United States. Horiuchi's statement about the necessity of American governmental support was accurate. No settlement scheme could advance without the knowledge and backing of the American government, because no Jewish organization would act without the government's endorsement. In his history of the Joint, Herbert Agar writes, "No middle course is possible. Either a private group of citizens operating abroad in peacetime and in war obeys its government, or else it becomes a form of conspiracy."[86]

At any rate, little occurred between Tamura's initial effort in spring 1939 and December of that year, when Tamura traveled to Tokyo to talk with navy, army, and Foreign Ministry officials. Despite Inuzuka's enthusiasm in Shanghai and the navy's initial interest, naval officers in Tokyo were not especially excited. Army officials foresaw problems if the settlement were located in Shanghai. Above all, both army and navy officials pointed to the Five Ministers Conference, which they did not believe favored the presence of refugees in Japan, Manchukuo, or China. A settlement scheme, they asserted, was not in keeping with that policy.[87]

Meanwhile, Frank Garson had sent a telegram to Tamura. He needed more information before organizing a trip of American Jewish leaders to Japan. "What profession refugee desired/How many are wanted/Where will they be located/What assurance that they will be employed in order to remain permanently/If satisfactory reply and invite from the government or reliable organization/Quite certain can arrange delegation/leave at once from here/Garson."[88] The cable format did not permit emphasis of the most important point: any overture should originate from the government or a recognized organization.

On December 27, army, navy, and Foreign Ministry officials met in Shanghai to consider Tamura's plan. The army vehemently opposed a Shanghai settlement in its weapons depot area, calling the plan "unexpected and exceedingly bothersome." Officer Sakurai, chief of staff of an army troop in Shanghai, resented hearing about this "thunderbolt" from the Army Ministry in Tokyo rather than the local experts. Naval Squadron Vice Chief of Staff Nakamura concurred; he would "by no means permit the implementation of a policy here related to the Jewish problem simply because there are experts on the Jewish problem."[89]

Nine months remained before the Tripartite Pact effectively canceled the plans of Tamura, Inuzuka, and Ayukawa. Considering the intermittent course of discussions within the Japanese government and with Jewish organizations, nine months was a brief period to realize a settlement involving so many refugees and so much money. In September 1940, Tamura was still talking with Garson, but there was no indication of concrete results.[90]

As late as November, the dogged Tamura had a meeting with a Joint official, Dr. Bernhard Kahn. "He used the entire hour, but did not say much practically," recalled Kahn. When Tamura resisted specifics, Kahn asked him, "Why we should not wait with any definite steps until the war is over—if no immediate project can be taken into consideration?" Tamura answered with a lengthy explanation of the need for Japan to have more "living space," raw materials, and industrial and agricultural development. Tamura also believed that American Jews could help "overcome the present unfriendly attitude of the United States." Kahn characterized Tamura's desire to solicit Jewish financial and political support as the "real object of his visit." While assuring Tamura that American Jews would be "very grateful" for Japanese government assistance to Jews, Kahn made a distinction between gratitude and political action. "I did not think the Jews of America would act as Jews," Kahn explained. "Only in the religious field would they act as Jews first, in any other endeavor they are first Americans, then Jews."[91]

Tamura and Kahn came from different worlds. Tamura's words were those of an ardent nationalist willing to pursue any means to satisfy Japanese ends—maintaining, expanding, and enriching the bloc of Japan, China, and Manchukuo. Kahn was deeply dedicated to the Joint, which represented American Jews willing to pursue charitable projects but unwilling to take a political stand contrary to that of their own government. The American government had no desire to contribute to the development of Manchukuo and, in Tamura's words, "the struggle for life and death" of the Empire.[92] By this time, Japanese-American relations were rapidly worsening. The United States had recently prohibited all exports of iron and steel scrap, exacerbating the Japanese struggle to which Tamura had referred. Also, there was still international denial that the situation in Europe was so horrible for the Jews.

Was there a link between settlement schemes conceived by Japanese military authorities and Manchukuo officials, and visas issued by Japanese diplomats abroad? If there was, the written record is either not part of the Jewish Problem File, does not survive, or never existed. Any cables regarding the scheme come from Shanghai, Tokyo, or the United States. The connection to Europe was not apparent, and significant coordination would have been necessary. Presumably, there were already enough refugees in Shanghai to fill such a projected settlement; no more needed to be sponsored with visas. The Japanese threshold for tolerating foreigners never expanded appreciably. Only in Shanghai, where the Japanese shared control with the foreign concessions, did refugee numbers increase before the navy took preemptive action in August 1939—which was still early with respect to the attempt of Jews to exit Europe.

Could there have been verbal instructions? That is possible, especially for a plan pursued extra-governmentally. But establishing a Jewish settlement would have been too big to hide, and the Japanese would have wanted to reap the benefits of favorable reports from the international media. In addition, there are enough cables in the Jewish Problem File that instruct diplomats to employ only verbal directions, rather than written records, for any secret to slip once the documents were handled by less discreet people. As it is, the Jewish Problem File is silent on the link between settlements and visas.

In spring 1940, the same time as the ill-fated Inuzuka, Ayukawa, and Tamura proposal was being suggested and sunk, the research division of the South Manchurian Railway was investigating a settlement for Jews. The Railway, also known as the Mantetsu, was one of the principal power brokers in Manchukuo. Its breadth and penetration of Manchukuo were awesome. Ranging over the entire territory of Manchukuo, the Railway managed nineteen businesses and dozens of affiliated companies. A sampling of its concerns includes sugar, spinning, steamships, woolen goods, glass, engineering, coal, and hydroelectricity.[93] In addition, it possessed the most complete statistical data on China and was staffed by the most informed Japanese specialists in Asian affairs.[94] The Mantetsu research division had between 1,000 and 2,000 employees, out of a total of 140,000 Mantetsu staff.[95] Although the staff represented a small percentage of the entire organization, it was a high-profile think tank that produced a multitude of reports, including material on Jews. The research division maintained close links with Japanese intelligence agents. Colonel Yasue, head of the Dairen Special Branch, assigned some Mantetsu research staff to look into the Jewish problem.[96] One result was a May 1940 paper on a settlement for 30,000 to 70,000 refugees. The report projected "a satellite town of an established metropolis" on prairie land for the Shanghai refugee population of 20,000, which was expected to increase naturally over time. The settlement would function as a planned economy; 6 percent of commercial space and 7 percent of industrial space could be privately owned. Individuals might each privately own sixty square meters of land.[97]

The space allotment and business opportunities were neither abundant nor appealing. Nor did the Joint find Manchukuo an attractive settlement site. Dr. Kahn described Manchukuo as a "buffer state" between the Soviet Union and Japan. He added, "It is in no way pacified. It is Japanese controlled with Japanese state economy. There is hardly any possibility for tradespeople or artisans to establish themselves there, and there is no chance for agricultural settlement."[98] Kahn's opinion is understandable, though settlement proposals anywhere were sparse. By this time, various countries' plans in places ranging from Africa to Alaska and from Madagascar to Mindanao had been abandoned.

The Mantetsu research division was aware of other countries' efforts and also produced a separate report on a Dominican Republic resettlement project the same month that it proposed a settlement in China. But by May 1940, the projected figure of 100,000 refugees quoted in the Mantetsu report had shrunk to a mere 500. With Italy's entrance into the war the following month, no more settlers were able to travel to Latin America. The Dominican Republic settlement remained very small and hardly served as a model for projects elsewhere.[99]

In the end, the Mantetsu research stands as records of unfulfilled dreams. On the one hand, the reports were no more far-fetched than many settlement schemes that died after a flurry of initial international fanfare—although in this case the Japanese had difficulty arousing interest from the worldwide media, since they were isolated politically. On the other hand, they appear as curious overtures by the Japanese towards American and European Jews, groups whom the Japanese did not understand.

Were the settlement plans as strange as other Japanese efforts to influence other groups? In the 1930s, the Japanese attempted to influence black opinion in the United States by encouraging a group that had split from the Black Muslims to support the emperor, cultivating to that end a relationship with Robert O. Jordan—known as "Harlem's Hitler"—and establishing a media service called the Negro News Syndicate. Their results were, according to John Dower, "desultory and largely ineffective."[100] Also, back in Manchukuo, the Harbin Special Branch established a Cossack village around 1935. It had two purposes: to assist White Russians, who would in turn provide intelligence on the Soviets across the border. The village supplied foodstuffs and horses for the Kwantung Army. The plan was that when and if war between the Soviet Union and Japan erupted, the residents would serve as members of the cavalry and as intelligence agents.[101]

Japanese gestures towards minorities were too calculated to be termed an embrace of many races and too unrealistic to succeed. In the end, the desire to stop refugees from coming to Manchukuo was far more profound and fervent than the will to create a working settlement. In August 1940, Ambassador Umezu in Manchukuo wrote Foreign Minister Matsuoka. Called an "emperor in actuality" by a former diplomat, Umezu did not waver in making his point.[102] Umezu reiterated that Manchukuo consulates issued only ten-day transit visas for those with destination countries and Japanese visas. "But people have begun to try to stay in Manchukuo," Umezu complained, "when their ships for Japan are delayed and they cannot board ships during the time period that their Japanese transit visas are still valid." Umezu offered only one solution to Matsuoka: "I request that you take measures that this repatriation does not occur from now on."

What was the source of Umezu's concern? Three Jewish men had reentered Manchukuo from Antung, when they hoped to have been en route to the United States. It is revealing that three men could raise such consternation at a time that a settlement for 30,000 and more was proposed. In addition, it is unlikely that the hapless travelers, Messrs. Jacob, Krautkopt, and Holland, were attempting to remain in Manchukuo. When their Japanese transit visas became invalid, they simply had no choice.[103]

JAPAN

Back in Japan, the Home Ministry kept a close eye on Jewish refugees, just one facet of its tight grip on Japanese society and the national psyche. The ministry's penetration of the society was deep: it managed elections, the local and prefectural governments, public speeches and meetings, and the press.[104] The Foreign Ministry deferred to the decision of the Home Ministry when refugees or their relatives residing in Japan applied to it for entry or transit visas. The frequency and eloquence of Jewish appeals was answered by the most terse of responses—either an affirmative or a negative. There was neither diplomatic dodging nor hope for appeal.

Bureaucratic red tape marred even the simplest transactions. When

Heinrich Steinfeld, a resident of Japan for more than thirty years, requested an entry visa for his wife's sister in Germany in February 1939,
the Kanagawa prefectural police issued one on behalf of the Home Ministry. But the outbreak of the war in Europe spoiled his relative's plans
to leave Naples in October on a Japanese steamer. Suddenly her booking became void when preferential treatment was given to Japanese
departing belligerent countries in Europe to return home. When the
woman tried to obtain a new, valid visa, the embassy in Berlin refused
without permission from the Foreign Ministry. Mr. Steinfeld turned for
assistance to the Kanagawa police, who sent him to the Foreign Ministry.[105]

Mr. Steinfeld's letter requesting a second visa was sad and polite. As
a longtime resident of Japan (he owned two homes and paid his taxes)
he offered evidence that he could support his sister-in-law. Neither Mr.
Steinfeld nor his relative posed any threat to Japan, or a visa would
not have been issued originally. When the request for a second visa was
routed through Japan, the bureaucracy complicated matters. It is unfortunate that the Japanese embassy in Berlin did not handle the second visa; responding to the request was within its authority. Embassy
officials were evading responsibility when they mentioned new regulations requiring Tokyo's permission. But Ōshima and his staff displayed no interest in Mr. Steinfeld's sister-in-law.

Mr. Steinfeld's name reappeared seven months later, when he asked
the third section of the America Bureau to issue entry visas for his
brother and sister-in-law. He told a sad story of loyal Germans stripped
of their rights by the increasingly drastic decrees of the Nazis. Mr. and
Mrs. Gideon Steinfeld were Christians of "Jewish parentage." Gideon
was a veteran of World War I awarded the Iron Cross, First Class, and
he had served as chief justice in the regional court of Breslau until his
retirement. (Since he was fifty-nine years old, his retirement may not
have been voluntary but by decree on the basis of his religion.) Steinfeld's relatives wanted to stay in Japan until permits for England,
where their son lived, became valid. Mr. Steinfeld was flexible. "Should
a Permit for entry and stay in Japan be entirely out of question, I would
be thankful if at least permission would be granted to live either in
Shanghai or in Peking/Tientsin." The Steinfelds, a middle-aged couple,
were willing to travel far out of the way to reach England. Meanwhile
the Battle of Britain was raging as the Luftwaffe was bombing the
southern coast of England. The distance to safety was terrifying long.

Steinfeld seemed to understand the sources of power in the Japanese
government. "I am not aware whether in that case the decision rests
also with the Home Office or whether the Imperial Japanese Navy or
Army are then competent. Please be kind enough to instruct me," he
requested.[106] Three weeks later, the Home Ministry instructed the chief

of the America Bureau to notify him that "permission for entry to Japan is difficult."[107] That was the last time that Heinrich Steinfeld contacted the Foreign Ministry on behalf of another Steinfeld caught in Europe; in 1941 he departed Japan for the United States.[108]

Hans Heller hoped to bring his sons from England to Japan. He wrote the America Bureau for entry visas for the two boys, ages sixteen and thirteen, who were in London. Heller and his wife had permission from the governor of Hyōgo prefecture to stay in Japan for one year, and they planned to proceed to the United States. Heller worried about his sons. "I have found Japan to be such a hospitable country and I would be grateful for the rest of my life if you could see your way to grant my pledge."[109] When entry visas were granted several weeks later, Heller was delighted by "such a human and sympathetic attitude. . . . The real nature of the Japanese nation is very often misunderstood abroad," he wrote, "and it will be my task to let all my friends throughout the world know the kindness Japan is showing to people who were so unfortunate as to be forced to leave their home country." In gratitude, Heller enclosed ¥50 for the Imperial Japanese Army, which the Foreign Ministry promptly applied to a telegram charge concerning Heller's sons.[110] If the Foreign Ministry had sought favorable press, Hans Heller would have been happy to provide it. With visas, his sons were able to escape the devastating bombing of London and the British internment of German Jews. There is no evidence, however, that the issuance of visas was driven by ulterior motives, such as influencing Jewish sentiment toward Japan. The granting of visas continued to be a bureaucratic process even when a request came from someone who met the Japanese stereotype of the powerful Jew.

In July 1940, Joseph C. Goltz requested "temporary stay visas" for his cousins in London, who were German citizens. They had begun the United States immigration process and held affidavits enabling them to immigrate to the United States in the autumn. Goltz was an American citizen and a managing director of United Artists who had resided in Japan almost two years. On impressive stationery bearing the letterhead of Mary Pickford, Charlie Chaplin, Douglas Fairbanks, Samuel Goldwyn, and Alexander Korda, Mr. Goltz wrote of his "distinguished relations in America who we hope will be able to hear that Japan was possibly the only country throughout the world in these turbulent times that would be kind enough to grant an asylum for two worthy people."[111] Mr. Goltz's cousins wished to stay in Japan only two months. Mr. Goltz could have been perceived as an influential, affluent American Jew holding an important position in the world of film and possessing a network of connections. But it appears that his request was handled in the same routine manner as any other. Three months later, the Home Ministry instructed the America Bureau that "entry to Japan is not possible." Mr. Goltz received the news on the day the Tripartite Pact was announced.[112] To be sure, his timing was unfortunate. Still, the conclusion of the Tripartite Pact did not prevent Jews from coming to Japan. Over 1,000 refugees were en route when Mr. Goltz's case was rejected.

The time lag in answering Mr. Goltz's request raises the possibility that he was given special consideration, even though the decision was unfavorable. But he was not the only one who endured months of waiting in 1940. Hugo Stern waited for more than five months to hear whether his children would be permitted to leave Vienna to join him in Japan. Stern had left his teenagers in Vienna when he and his wife went to Shanghai, where his wife died in 1939. He had moved to Japan when asked to share his expertise in turret lathes with an engineering company. "I am living in constant anxiety and unrest over the separation from my children," Stern pleaded. ". . . [T]he now orphaned children are longing for reunion with me so much as I do."[113] Despite repeated inquiries by his employer, F. & K. Engineering, on behalf of Stern's children, Stern waited from March until August for a decision. Finally, the Home Ministry granted approval, and Foreign Minister Matsuoka cabled Yamaji to issue the entry visas.[114] Between the time that Stern had grieved the loss of his wife in Shanghai and he received the affirmative response from the Japanese authorities, Jews from Vienna had been deported to the "Lublinland reservation" in an impoverished region of German-occupied Poland.[115] Stern was lucky his children were still in Vienna in August.

If a pattern can be discerned, it is that people had a better chance to bring in relatives who were children, rather than adults. The duration of the projected stay in Japan was not as important as the identity of the applicants. People who applied to the government bureaucracy for visas had no guarantee of approval; all they could do was hope. Those who went through the Kobe Jewish community, even if they had no clout themselves, had a better chance, because the community knew the corridors of power and had earned the trust of the authorities.

The Kobe Jewish Community

In 1940, the local Jewish population in Japan numbered approximately 1,000, with most residents living in Kobe, Yokohama, and Tokyo. Kobe was the home to the largest Jewish community, with approximately fifteen Ashkenazi families and ten Sephardic families, longtime residents of Japan. The Ashkenazi families formed an organization simply and aptly named "The Jewish Community of Kobe," but also known by its cable address of "Jewcom" Kobe. The Jewcom was close-knit, active, and politically astute. It tirelessly rallied around the

European refugees, many of whom might not have been admitted without its help. When its president, A. G. Ponevejsky, characterized his organization as "the only officially recognized Jewish body in Japan," he was not exaggerating.[116]

At first, the Kobe Jewish Community merely assisted refugees passing through Japan with entry visas elsewhere. Until late 1940 and the beginning of 1941, most refugees came from Germany and proceeded onward; "They might indeed have been classed as tourists, rather than as refugees," commented Mr. Ponevejsky.[117] Subsequent arrivals originated largely from Poland and arrived destitute and with their papers not in order. The Kobe Jewish Community tended to all their needs—food, shelter, medical care, and visa assistance. Support began the moment ships full of refugees anchored in the harbor of Tsuruga, six hours from the international port of Kobe. Vice president Moise Moiseff explained, "A member of the Jewish community meets the refugees on the makeshift boats on which they arrive and arranges for their care in Kobe. This representative is so thoroughly recognized by the Japanese Government that even American Jews have found themselves unable to land until the Kobe Jewish representative has given his consent."[118]

More than 4,000 refugees arrived in Japan when so many others, such as the worthy relatives of Mr. Steinfeld and Mr. Goltz, could not and did not. They had reached Kobe through a remarkable combination of courage, faith, persistence, and luck. For many, one of the first strokes of luck occurred in Lithuania.

NOTES

1. Department of State, "Memorandum by the Adviser on Political Relations (Hornbeck)," 10 December 1938, Despatch 166, 893.041, *Foreign Relations of the United States: Diplomatic Papers*, 1938, vol. 3, The Far East, 416.

2. Henry L. Feingold, *The Politics of Rescue: The Roosevelt Administration and the Holocaust 1938–1945* (New Brunswick, NJ: Rutgers University Press, 1970), 57; Lucy S. Dawidowicz, *The War against the Jews, 1933–1945* (New York: Holt, Rinehart and Winston, 1985), 161.

3. Articles, 28 February 1939, JPF, folder 6; Ben-Ami Shillony, *The Jews and the Japanese* (Rutland, VT, and Tokyo: Charles E. Tuttle, 1991), 179.

4. Ernest G. Heppner, *Shanghai Refuge: A Memoir of the World War II Jewish Ghetto* (Lincoln: University of Nebraska Press, 1993), 40.

5. *Escape to the Rising Sun* (Belgium: Diane Perelsztejn, 1990), film.

6. Evelyn Pike Rubin, *Ghetto Shanghai* (New York: Shengold Publishers, 1993), 49.

7. Ernest Heppner, *Shanghai Refuge*, 28.

8. Takeo Itō, *Life along the South Manchurian Railway*, trans. Joshua A. Fogel (Armonk, NY: M. E. Sharpe, 1988), 170.

9. W. Michael Blumenthal, "Shanghai: The Persistence of Interest," *Points East* 10 (March 1996): 4.

10. "Regarding #3805," from Miura to Arita, coded #1718, #123, 19 January 1939, JPF, folder 6.

11. Letter from M. Speelman to G. Godfrey Phillips, 13 January 1939, JPF, folder 6.

12. Ervin Staub, *The Roots of Evil: The Origins of Genocide and Other Group Violence* (Cambridge: Cambridge University Press, 1989), 88.

13. Telegram, from Miura to Arita, coded #2660 and #2666, #217, Parts 1 and 2, 28 January 1939, JPF, folder 6; "Jewish Refugees From Europe To Number Some 4,000 by End of March," *Sunday Times* (Shanghai), 29 January 1939, JPF, folder 6.

14. Telegram, from Miura to Arita, #726, 3 March 1939, including "Circular 56-C-IV," JPF, folder 7.

15. Report from Ishiguro to East Asia Bureau First Section Kimura, 27 July 1939, JPF, folder 7.

16. Department of State, "Chargé in Germany (Geist) to Secretary of State," 3 March 1939, *Telegram J/8, 893.55, Foreign Relations of the United States: Diplomatic Papers*, 1939 vol. 3, General, The British Commonwealth and Europe, 94.

17. "Jewish Refugees Should Be Welcomed And Assisted Here!" *The China Weekly Review* (Shanghai), 4 February 1939, JPF, folder 6.

18. Telegram from Miura to Arita, #806, 9 March 1939, JPF, folder 7.

19. Naval General Staff Third Division, "Anti-Japanese Propaganda in the United States by the Head of the Jewish Financial Combine in China," Jewish Information Secret #9, 7 February 1939, JPF, folder 6.

20. Ibid.

21. Telegram from Masutani to Arita, coded #4548, #9, 16 February 1939, JPF, folder 6. Telegram from Kondō to Arita, coded #5031, #17, 21 February 1939, JPF, folder 6.

22. Asia Bureau First Section, Report, "Regarding Using Sassoon Businesses to Establish the Empire's Self-Supporting Economy," 3 July 1940, JPF, folder 10.

23. Report, "Central European Jews—Arrival in Shanghai," 15 March 1939, JPF, folder 7.

24. Report, "Matters Agreed upon by the Jewish Problem Committee," top secret, 20 March 1939, JPF, folder 7.

25. Report, "Temporary Proposals Towards Jewish Refugees," 26 May 1939, JPF, folder 7.

26. Manabe Ryōichi, interview.

27. Telegram from Satō to Arita, #1773, 27 May 1939, JPF, folder 7.

28. Telegram from Miura to Arita, #17529, #1599, 10 June 1939, JPF, folder 7.

29. Yasue, Inuzuka, and Ishiguro, top secret report, "Survey Related to Jews in Shanghai," 7 July 1939, 1246, JPF, folder 8.

30. "New Nazi Plan for Jews: Emigration to Be Facilitated," *The Times* (London), 7 July 1939, JPF, folder 8.

31. Top secret report, "Survey Related to Jews in Shanghai," 1275.

32. Department of State, "U.K. Ambassador Kennedy to Secretary of State," 11 July 1939, Telegram 1729, 840.48 Refugees, *Foreign Relations of the United States: Diplomatic Papers*, 1939, vol. 3, General, The British Commonwealth and Europe, 130.

33. "Memorandum of recent events with respect to immigration to Shanghai," 18 August 1939, Paris, AR 33/44, #458: China, General, 1939 July-December, AJJDC Archives, New York.

34. Top secret telegram, from Arita to Ōshima, #20267, #491, 4 August 1939, JPF, folder 8.

35. Translation, from Miura to Arita, #2334–1, 10 August 1939, JPF, folder 8.

36. "Ban Placed on Jews by Nipponese," *China Press* (Shanghai), 12 August 1939, JPF, folder 8.

37. "Jewish Refugees Must Register to Reside or Do Business in Hongkew," *Shanghai Times*, 12 August 1939, JPF, folder 8.

38. Letter from Miura to Bracklo, Germany, and Farinacci, Italy, 10 August 1939, JPF, folder 8.

39. "Settlement, Concession Announce Decision of Ban on Future Arrivals," *China Press*, 15 August 1939, JPF, folder 8.

40. Feingold, *The Politics of Rescue: The Roosevelt Administration and the Holocaust, 1938–1945* (New Brunswick, NJ: Rutgers University Press, 1970), 304.

41. Letter (English) from L. Neyrone to Miura Yoshiaki, 28 September 1939, JPF, folder 8.

42. Telegram from Miura to Nomura, #623, 12 October 1939, JPF, folder 8.

43. Letter (English) from Miura to Neyrone, 11 October 1939, JPF, folder 8.

44. Letter (English) from Miura to Ellis Hayim, CAEJR, 28 October 1939, JPF, folder 8.

45. Letter (English) from Ishiguro to eleven shipping companies, 28 October 1939, JPF, folder 8.

46. Telegram from Miura to Nomura, coded #40046, #3132, 14 November 1939, JPF, folder 8.

47. "Entry of European Refugees," *Municipal Gazette*, 22 October 1939, JPF, folder 8.

48. Telegram from Yamaji to Nomura, 26 October 1939, JPF, folder 8.

49. Telegram from Yamaji to Nomura, coded #38472, #113, 31 October 1939, JPF, folder 8.

50. "The Jews in China," *The Jewish Tribune: The Organ of Indian Jewry* (March 1940), JPF, folder 9.

51. "Regarding Immigration," by Mr. Kann to Messrs. Ellis Hayim, M. Speelman, and H. Kadoorie, 13 February 1940, Shanghai, AR 33/44, #459: China, General, 1940 January-June, AJJDC Archives.

52. Telegram from Miura to Arita, confidential, coded #54093, #847, 10 May 1940, JPF, folder 9.

53. Letter, by M. Speelman to M. C. Troper, AJJDC, 6 April 1940, Shanghai, AR 33/44, #459: China, General, 1940 January-June, AJJDC Archives.

54. Undated newspaper articles, Shanghai, AR 33/44, #459: China, General, 1940 January-June, AJJDC Archives.

55. James R. Ross, *Escape to Shanghai: A Jewish Community in China* (New York: Free Press, 1994), 107.

56. Telegram from Ishiguro to East Asia Bureau First Section Secretary Uchida, 25 June 1940, JPF, folder 9.

57. Top secret telegram from Ueda to Arita, #35, 14 January 1939, JPF, folder 6.

58. Secret telegram from Katō to Arita, #22, 20 January 1939, JPF, folder 6.

59. Top secret telegram from Matsuda to Arita, #34, 18 April 1939, JPF, folder 7.

60. Top secret "Regarding Permission for Fifteen Jewish Refugees to Enter Manchukuo," undated, JPF, folder 7.

61. Telegram from Acting Consul General Taniguchi, Harbin, to Arita, #15111, #86, 18 May 1939, JPF, folder 7.

62. "Regarding Kaufman's Visit with East Asia Office Bureau Chief and Research Division Chief," top secret, 11 May 1939, JPF, folder 7.

63. Top secret, "Regarding Permission for Fifteen Jewish Refugees to Enter Manchukuo," JPF, folder 7.

64. "Regarding Kaufman's Visit with East Asia Office Bureau Chief and Research Division Chief."

65. Ibid.

66. Secret telegram from Foreign Affairs Bureau Political Affairs Head to the Secretary of the Japanese Embassy in Manchukuo, #792, 19 May 1939, JPF, folder 7.

67. Maruyama Naoki, "Asia taiheiyō chiiki ni okeru Yudayajin shakai," *Pacific Basin Project* 7 (Yamato-machi, Niigata-ken, Japan: International University, 1986), 17.

68. Ibid., 18.

69. *Israel's Messenger* (17 September 1934), quoted in Naoki Maruyama, "The Shanghai Zionist Association and Japan," pp. 17–18, paper presented as part of the symposium "Jewish Diasporas in China: Comparative and Historical Perspectives," Harvard University John K. Fairbank Center for East Asian Research, Cambridge.

70. Maruyama, "Asia taiheiyō chiiki ni okeru Yudayajin shakai," 19.

71. "Lew Zikman Proposal" (English), JPF, folder 7.

72. Secret telegram from Taniguchi to Ueda, #204, 4 April 1939, JPF, folder 7.

73. "Lew Zikman Proposal."

74. Letter from Lew Zikman to Cyrus Adler, 22 February 1939, Harbin, AR 33/44, #723: Japan, General, Emigration, 1939–1941 (March), AJJDC Archives.

75. Telegram from Ueda to Taniguchi, 24 April 1939, JPF, folder 7.

76. Letter from Jakob Berglas to the Chairman of the AJJDC, 15 June 1939, Shanghai, AR 33/44, #458: China, General, 1939 July-December, AJJDC Archives.

77. Letter from Alex Frieder to Charles Liebman, 3 July 1939, Manila, AR 33/44, #458: China, General, 1939 July-December, AJJDC Archives.

78. Records of U.S. State Department: China, 1930–1939, "Berglas Seeks Funds to Set Up Colony of 100,000 European Emigrants in Yunnan,"*Osaka Mainichi*, 10 August 1939, File 893.55J, Despatch 152.

79. *Shanghai Times* (24 June 1949), quoted in Marcia R. Ristaino, "Response to Ernest G. Heppner's comments on my paper: New Information on Shanghai Jewish Refugees: The Evidence of the Shanghai Municipal Police Files, National Archives, Washington, D.C.," symposium "Jewish Diasporas in China," 7.

80. Mark R. Peattie, *Ishiwara Kanji and Japan's Confrontation with the West* (Princeton, NJ: Princeton University Press, 1975), 214, 216.

81. Yukio Chō, "An Inquiry into the Problem of Importing American Capital into Manchuria: A Note on Japan-American Relations, 1931–1941," trans. Edgar C. Harrell, in *Pearl Harbor as History: Japan-American Relations 1931–1941*, ed. Dorothy Borg and Shumpei Okamoto (New York: Columbia University Press, 1973), 392.

82. Maruyama, "Asia taiheiyō chiiki ni okeru Yudayajin shakai," 29.

83. Cover to Memorandum from B. Kahn, 20 November 1940, New York, AR 33/44, #723: Japan, General, Emigration, 1939–1941 (March), AJJDC Archives.

84. Top secret telegram from Nomura to Horiuchi, Washington, #31359, #482, 16 November 1939, JPF, folder 8.

85. Telegram from Horiuchi to Nomura, coded #41451, 24 November 1939, JPF, folder 8.

86. Herbert Agar, *The Saving Remnant* (New York: Viking Press, 1960), 65.

87. "Regarding the Problem of Sheltering Jewish Refugees," #4, 26 December 1939, JPF, folder 8.

88. Telegram (English) from Mr. Garson, New York, to Mr. Tamura, 20 December 1939, JPF, folder 8.

89. Telegram from Miura to Nomura, #198, 29 December 1939, JPF, folder 8.

90. Inuzuka Kyoko, *Yudaya mondai to nihon no kōsaku* (Tokyo: Nihon Kōgyō Shimbunsha, 1982), 482.

91. Memorandum from B. Kahn, 19 November 1940, New York, AR 33/44, #723: Japan, General, Emigration, 1939–1941 (March), AJJDC Archives.

92. Ibid.

93. Itō, *Life along the South Manchurian Railway*, 124–25.

94. Peattie, *Ishiwara Kanji and Japan's Confrontation with the West*, 109.

95. "Jiyū e nos tōsō," *Chūnichi Shimbun*, 9 April 1995, 30; Ito, *Life along the South Manchurian Railway*, 212.

96. Ōno Masami, "Haran no jigyōka kyū-Manshū de bōryaku," *Aera* (August 1995): 60.

97. Report, Mantetsu Special Survey Group, #4, May 1940, JPF, folder 10.

98. Letter from B. Kahn to Rabbi Stephen S. Wise, 7 June 1940, New York, AR 33/44, #723: Japan, General, Emigration, 1939–1941 (March), AJJDC Archives.

99. Henry L. Feingold, "Roosevelt and the Resettlement Question," in *Rescue Attempts during the Holocaust: Proceedings of the Second Yad Vashem International Historical Conference in Jerusalem, April 8–11, 1974*, by Yad Vashem (Jerusalem: Yad Vashem, 1977), 166.

100. John Dower, *War Without Mercy* (New York: Pantheon Books, 1986), 174–75.

101. Ōno Masami, "Haran no jigyōka kyū-Manshū de bōryaku," 59.

102. Takeuchi, interview.

103. Telegram from Umezu to Matsuoka, #979, 20 August 1940, JPF, folder 10.

104. Yale Candee Maxon, *Control of Japanese Foreign Policy: A Study of Civil-Military Rivalry, 1930–1945* (Westport, CT: Greenwood Press, 1973), 14.

105. Letter (English) from H. Steinfeld, Tokyo, to Department of Foreign Affairs, 27 November 1939, JPF, folder 8.

106. Letter (English), from Heinrich Steinfeld, Tokyo, to the third section of the America Bureau, 28 June 1940, JPF, folder 10.

107. Telegram from Home Ministry *Keihokyoku* to the chief of the America Bureau, #54, 19 July 1940, JPF, folder 10.

108. Letter from Henry M. Steinfeld (formerly H. Steinfeld, Tokyo) to the American Jewish Joint Distribution Committee, 12 February 1941, San Francisco, AR 33/44, #723: Japan, General, Emigration, 1939–1941 (March), AJJDC Archive.

109. Letter from Hans Heller, Kobe, to the third section of the America Bureau, 21 May 1940, JPF, folder 9.

110. Letter (English) from Hans Heller to Dainobu Kenzi, third section of the America Bureau, 7 June 1940; letter (English) from Dainobu to Heller, 12 June 1940, JPF, folder 10.

111. Letter (English) from Joseph C. Goltz to the Bureau for Emigration Applications, III Section, Ministry of Foreign Affairs, Attention Kenzie Dainobu, 2 July 1940, JPF, folder 10.

112. Telegram from Home Ministry *Keihokyoku* to chief of the America Bureau, #100, 26 September 1940, JPF, folder 10.

113. Letter (English) from Hugo Stern to Home Ministry and Gaiji-ka Department, 20 March 1940, JPF, folder 10.

114. Telegram from Home Ministry *Keihokyoku* to chief of the America Bureau, #62, 6 August 1940; telegram from Matsuoka to Yamaji, #26819, 9 August 1940, JPF, folder 10.

115. Martin Gilbert, *Atlas of the Holocaust* (New York: William Morrow, 1988), 40.

116. Letter from A. G. Ponevejsky, president of the Jewish Community of Kobe, to the Joint Distribution Committee, 18 February 1941, AR 33/44, #723: Japan, General, Emigration, 1939–1941 (March), AJJDC Archives.

117. Ibid.

118. HIAS, "Jewish Transients in Japan," by Moise Moiseff, 25 July 1941, Record Group 245.4, series xvb-xvc, HIAS Reports, YIVO.

Diplomat Sugihara Chiune at the time of his posting to Kaunas from 1939 to 1940. Courtesy of Taishō Shuppan and Sugihara Yukiko

Klaudia, Chiune's first wife, in kimono. Klaudia and Chiune met and married in Harbin. Courtesy of Takechi Yūji

Chiune and Klaudia visit the Sugihara homestead in Japan. Many would remark on how foreign Chiune seemed, and Klaudia clearly stood out. Courtesy of Takechi Yūji

Seemingly a lifetime apart and a world away, the Sugihara family in Lithuania: Yukiko's sister Setsuko, Chiune, Chiaki, Hiroki, and Yukiko. Yukiko would give birth to a third son, Haruki, in Kaunas. Courtesy of Taishō Shuppan and Sugihara Yukiko

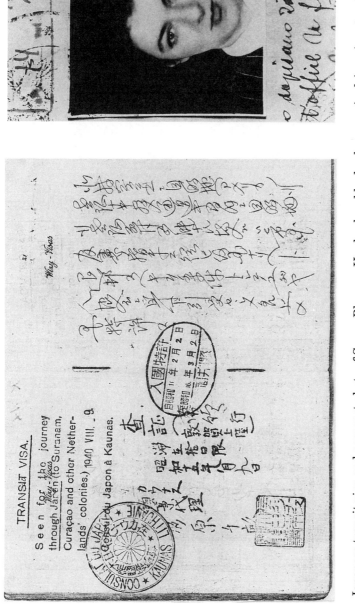

Japanese transit visa and passport photo of Susan Bluman. Her husband had only an expired American tourist visa, and Susan had no passport of her own. Despite these gaps, Sugihara issued the Blumans a visa. Courtesy of Susan Bluman

Refugee luggage in Kobe, Japan in 1941. In general, Germans managed to bring large trunks and bags, but Polish Jews often fled with very few belongings. Courtesy of the family of Kōno Tōru from the collection of Tokyo Metropolitan Museum of Photography

Father and son in Kobe. Occasionally, children arrived alone in Kobe—most accompanied their families, using a parent's visa, and enjoyed a carefree experience. Courtesy of the family of Tabuchi Kaneyoshi from the collection of Tokyo Metropolitan Museum of Photography

Refugee pondering the next stop. Parents had far more worries, as they wondered where and when their perilous flight would end. The photographer was taken with the furrows in this man's brow, which expressed not only a sense of "forlornness," but also a "tenacious strength." Courtesy of the family of Tabuchi Kaneyoshi from the collection of Tokyo Metropolitan Museum of Photography

Conferring in Kobe. Secular and Orthodox Jews, whether from cultural centers or isolated shtetls, were thrown together in their search for refuge. Making the daily rounds of embassies and relief organizations, they depended on each other for information. Courtesy of the family of Tabuchi Kaneyoshi

Resting in Kobe. Catching a nap outside was unthinkable for Jews trying to escape Europe in hiding. Masha Leon commented on the Japanese in Kobe: "Not that they were friends, but they let you live. Nobody threatened you. I had friends. You could walk down the street, and the weather was lovely." Courtesy of the family of Tabuchi Kaneyoshi

Celebrating in Kobe in spring 1941. Susan and Nate Bluman sit second and third from the right. Commemorating the Jews' flight from Egypt, this Passover seder held special significance. The matzo and fresh fruit were a treat for refugees all too familiar with privation. Courtesy of Susan Bluman

5

Sugihara Chiune: Extraordinary Diplomat

BETWEEN SEPTEMBER 1939 AND JUNE 1940, Lithuania was an island of independence in a turbulent Europe. Its neighbor Poland was split in two by the German-Soviet nonaggression pact of August 23, 1939. Susan and Nate Bluman were just two of 15,000 Polish Jews who spilled into Lithuania fleeing the Nazi advance from the west and the Soviet occupation from the east. They traveled by foot and sleigh, by night, and in the depth of winter to reach Lithuania—whose border was to be closed by mid-January 1940 and impossible to penetrate by March.

Any sense of safety was short-lived. "On June 15th, 1940, we went into the movies to see *Marie Antoinette* with Tyrone Power and Norma Shirer, and when we went in the Lithuanians were in power. When we came out of the theater, Russian tanks were rolling down the street and everybody was running madly trying to hoard food," remembers Masha Leon, who was nine at the time.[1] It was time to leave. Martin Krygier recalled, "We would not stay, come what might. But we already knew that in other parts of Russian-occupied Poland those who registered for departure abroad were the first to depart for Siberia. And yet, if we did not try—no matter how high the risk and how slight the chances—we would not go."[2]

In the midst of war, people depended on rumors for their information, and the rumor of deportation was undeniably true. "So strict was the regulation of residents of Soviet occupied Poland that none dared to apply to leave after seeing the example set by unnumbered thousands," wrote an American diplomat processing Polish visa requests in Kobe

in 1941. "In unnumbered thousands it is reported that they registered—to be removed in droves to northern Russia and Siberia."[3] The
refugees who dared to leave Europe possessed foresight and courage,
but they no longer had a home.

Where was one to go, when so few countries permitted immigration?
Polish Jews would gather at cafes and exchange information in Vilna,
the historic capital that had been part of Poland before the outbreak of
the war until reverting to Lithuania, which called it Vilnius. They anxiously awaited news. When the Soviets officially occupied the country
in June, they learned that all foreign consulates were to close in August. One day, someone mentioned that the Japanese consulate in Kaunas, now called Kovno, was issuing transit visas to Japan. Although
most refugees knew nothing about Japan and had never considered
going there, it was far from the war in Europe and that much closer to
safety. Suddenly, the idea of Japan, unfamiliar and exotic, became appealing.

THE JAPANESE CONSULATE

Kaunas had been the capital of Lithuania until that distinction re-
verted to Vilna in September 1939. Vilna was lovely and familiar—the
"Jerusalem of Lithuania," in the words of Napoleon—owing to its great
Jewish cultural heritage.[4] But Polish Jews were not there to visit the
yeshivas. No matter how far-fetched and possibly futile the news of
Japanese transit visas may have appeared, giving up a seat in a Vilna
cafe for the three-hour trip to Kaunas was worthwhile.

The consulate was one of three Japanese diplomatic offices in the
Baltic states; there was another consulate in Tallinn, Estonia, and a
legation in Riga, Latvia. The Kaunas consulate had been officially established in August 1939, and the designated diplomat, Sugihara
Chiune, and his family had moved there in November. Sugihara's home
and office were located in an unassuming building on a quiet residential
street. The simple setting gave no indication of the drama that would
occur within.

The Japanese consulate was an anomaly. The need for a consulate
appeared puzzling, since the legation to Latvia had also covered Lithuanian affairs since its establishment in 1937.[5] Why would another
office be necessary just two years later? No Japanese nationals resided
in Kaunas, where they might need diplomatic assistance. The only Japanese family in Kaunas was the Sugihara family.

Sugihara had been sent to Kaunas to observe German and Soviet
military activity in the area. As "new eyes in Lithuania," he would later
write, "My consulates' main task was to rapidly and accurately determine the time of the German attack." The Foreign Ministry selected

him because his fluent Russian would help him do so. Japan did not trust its ally Germany, and it feared the Soviet Union, with whom it had skirmished with devastating results along the border of Manchukuo in 1938 and 1939. If Germany and the Soviet Union fought, Japan would experience repercussions in the Far East. If the Japanese military wanted to prepare strategy in advance, particularly for the south Pacific, it had to learn what was happening in Europe. Although Sugihara's direct superior was Minister Ōtaka in Latvia, he generally corresponded directly with the Foreign Ministry in Tokyo, and he believed that the army was the source of the creation of his consulate.[6]

Stationing officials in the Baltic region—"the traditional tinderbox of Europe"—was useful for gathering valuable information. It was not unusual for a consulate to operate as an "observation post," according to a diplomat attached to the legation in Riga in the late 1930s. "This sort of information about the military situation on both sides of the demarcation line was quite important business," he said. "All diplomatic agents were searching everywhere because both sides started to concentrate a lot of divisions." Riga itself was a hotbed of international intrigue, according to another diplomat, where the Soviets, British, Americans, and French also posted officials to watch for military developments.[7]

There was no need to justify this function. After all, one of the primary roles of a diplomat is to become familiar with the people and places where he is posted. To be sure, a fine line exists between assembling information and collecting intelligence. During war, it is thinner than usual, since there is secrecy in strategies, suspicion among friends and foes, and much at stake.

SUGIHARA CHIUNE

It must have been lonely to be the only Japanese official in Kaunas, but Sugihara Chiune was accustomed to living in unusual places. By the time he arrived in Kaunas, he was a cosmopolitan man who had been exposed to other cultures since childhood. He had visited Korea, lived in Manchukuo for sixteen years, and worked at the embassy in Helsinki before being sent to Kaunas.

Kaunas was a long way from Yaotsu, a small village nestled in the mountains of Aichi prefecture outside Nagoya in central Japan. Yaotsu seemed a long way from everywhere. Cool even in the humid summer with clouds hovering close and hills thick with fir trees, Yaotsu was quiet, isolated, and protected. Sugihara Chiune, the second of five boys and a girl, was born there in 1900. But he did not pass his childhood in this serene setting; his father Kosui, a tax collector, moved the family repeatedly. Chiune attended three elementary schools in three different prefectures. By the time he graduated from middle school in 1917, his father was no longer even in Japan.

Kosui had left his family in Japan and headed to Korea when it was annexed by Japan in 1910. Once there, he discarded his civil servant garb and became an innkeeper. But his Japanese-style inn in Seoul never proved profitable. "He was always poor," recalled Nakamura Ryūko, Chiune's only sister and the youngest child, born in Korea. Part of the problem may have been that Kosui lent travelers money and allowed guests to stay who could not pay. Kosui's wife Yatsuko was troubled by the lack of money and rumors that her husband had a mistress. She rushed to Korea and stayed with Kosui until her death from cancer in 1921.[8]

Meanwhile, Chiune, independent at a young age, had left for Tokyo and a series of part-time jobs to support himself. In 1918, he entered prestigious Waseda University, among Japan's finest schools. One year later, he noticed an advertisement in the newspaper calling for exchange students for the Foreign Ministry. Chiune liked the idea of being paid to study; he promptly passed the entry exam and joined the organization that would change his life.

Sugihara entered the Foreign Ministry as a *ryūgakusei* (exchange student). This status would limit his prospects, no matter how well he performed. He would not enter as a graduate of elite Tokyo University, the source of many of the ministry's most prominent diplomats. If he was serious about a career in the ministry, he was commencing under restrictive circumstances.

Sugihara was soon sent to Harbin to study Russian. Within a year, however, he had to interrupt his studies to complete compulsory military training. After a year and three months of duty in the army, Sugihara returned in spring 1922 to Harbin, where he resumed his studies. Until his term as an exchange student finished in February 1923, he audited classes at the Japanese school of Russian language that would become the famed Harbin Gakuin. Funded jointly by the Japanese government and the South Manchurian Railway, the school was under the jurisdiction of the Foreign Ministry and had been created to train Japanese specialists in Russian research. Sugihara met and exceeded the school's expectations.

The following month, Sugihara went to Manchouli to continue to study Russian. At the time, General Hashimoto, head of the Harbin Special Branch (and later associated with two coup d'état attempts in 1931), asked Sugihara and Shimura Giichi, a friend of Sugihara from Harbin, to use Russians and Jews in Manchouli to gather intelligence on the Soviets.[9] Shimura said that Sugihara was "very skilled at gathering intelligence"—the right man for the job.[10]

In 1925, Sugihara returned to Harbin to work as a clerk in the Harbin consulate. He had recently married a beautiful woman. She was not Japanese: she was a stateless White Russian, whose family had fled the Bolsheviks. Her name was Klaudia; Chiune called her Yuriko, meaning "lily child." Sugihara's family was not troubled by his choice of bride. "No one in the family minded," recalled Ryūko.[11]

In Harbin, Chiune never seemed to mix with his Japanese colleagues. He and Klaudia lived in the Russian neighborhood, separate from the Japanese area. Rather than socializing with other Japanese, Chiune preferred to return to his home, where Klaudia's mother and siblings also lived. His sister Ryūko would visit occasionally and delighted in the lively, warm atmosphere and in Klaudia's kindness. "Mama spoke badly of the Jews, but Klaudia was quiet because her mother was so loud," recalled Ryūko. "Klaudia had Jewish friends," asserted Ryūko, though she never met any at Klaudia and Chiune's home.[12] In an interview one year before he died, Sugihara recalled that he had not been familiar with Jews before Kaunas. "We didn't have much knowledge of what they were. We knew that they were generally unwelcome in Europe, but that's all," he said. "We didn't like them or dislike them."[13]

While posted at the Harbin consulate, Sugihara began teaching Russian twice a week at Harbin Gakuin. His Russian was excellent—the result of a linguistic gift, an agile mind, diligent study, and daily communication with native speakers. "No one was as fluent as Sugihara," later commented Shimura.[14] Sugihara continued to teach at Harbin Gakuin even after transferring from the Foreign Ministry to the Manchukuo Affairs Bureau in 1932.

As a diplomat with the Manchukuo Affairs Bureau, Sugihara managed the Russia Section, where he helped handle the purchase of the Chinese Eastern Railway from the Soviets in 1935. Recognized as a tough negotiator, Sugihara apparently procured the rights that the Japanese desired to extend the South Manchuria Railway, after a year and half of consultations.

In 1935, he divorced Klaudia, to the dismay of Ryūko, who adored her. Rumors abounded. Sugihara was a ladies' man; he loved Klaudia, but he was not faithful. Klaudia did not want children, but Chiune did. A White Russian wife was a liability for a Japanese expert on the Soviet Union. One of Sugihara's responsibilities included gathering intelligence on the Soviets; perhaps he was perceived as being too close to the Russian community in Harbin, exposing himself to the possibility of leaking privileged Japanese information. Or Klaudia may have made him ineligible for his dream posting at the embassy in Moscow.

A diplomat who attended Harbin Gakuin after Sugihara remembered meeting a friend of Klaudia who criticized Sugihara for abandoning her.[15] Whatever bitterness existed, however, must have subsided with the passage of time. According to friends and relatives of Sugihara, upon their divorce Chiune gave Klaudia a large lump-sum payment, the total of his retirement fund from the Manchukuo Affairs Bureau. She stayed in touch with Chiune and Ryūko for the rest of Chiune's life, even after she had remarried, emigrated to Australia, and started anew.

At any rate, Sugihara had returned to Japan in 1935, leaving the Manchukuo Affairs Bureau. Within several months of his divorce, he married a young woman named Yukiko; their son Hiroki was born five and a half months later. Sugihara rejoined the Foreign Ministry and was assigned to serve as an interpreter at the embassy in Moscow. The Soviets, however, refused to issue Sugihara a visa, never offering an explanation. Instead, Sugihara ended up in Helsinki in 1937, as an interpreter to the legation. In comparison to eclectic Harbin and imposing Moscow, Helsinki was *"inaka,"* or country, in the words of a former diplomat. Helsinki was not important. It was merely the prelude to Kaunas.

SUGIHARA'S ENCOUNTER WITH JEWS IN KAUNAS

In early 1940, Katayama Junnosuke traveled by train from Riga to Kaunas, acting as a diplomatic courier. His trip required seven or eight hours. Arriving at the consulate to pick up documents, Katayama chatted with Sugihara over drinks. Only a few months into his stay in Kaunas, Sugihara was reflective. He told Katayama that he had produced a book on the Soviet Union for the Foreign Ministry while in Manchukuo, a feat no one else had accomplished. Katayama, certain only that Sugihara was not content in Kaunas, waited for Sugihara to elaborate on the reasons for his disappointment, but he never did.[16]

Kaunas may have been a backwater in comparison to Moscow, but it was not a sleepy little town. Solly Ganor remembers, "For decades it had been a favored asylum for all sorts of political refugees. It was a bit like some small Eastern European version of Beirut or Casablanca, with its Nordic gentiles, its Poles and Russians, its Germans and Jews, in a place forever on the border of the next war."[17] Kaunas had a large and active Jewish population. Lithuanian Jews, including Solly's family, felt comfortable there.

Solly Ganor celebrated Hanukah with Yukiko and Chiune Sugihara in December 1939. Meeting Sugihara at his aunt's gourmet food shop, young Solly spontaneously invited the diplomat to his family's party, to thank him for some Hanukah *gelt* money. The eleven-year-old child and thirty-nine-year-old diplomat had charmed each other. A chance meeting became a fateful encounter. " 'It is the first time I've had the pleasure of visiting a Jewish home, and I hope it won't be the last,' " Ganor recalls Sugihara saying. In the spring, Solly visited the consulate, where Sugihara gave him stamps for his stamp collection and warned him to leave Lithuania.[18] Months later, Sugihara also gave him a visa stamp for his passport.

Most of the time in Kaunas, Sugihara was trying to gather intelligence. He cooperated with Polish intelligence officers; in exchange for the use of Japanese diplomatic pouches transported by Japanese couriers to relay information among the Polish intelligence network extending from Warsaw to London, they provided him with intelligence on Soviet and German troop movements. Professional spies fluent in German and Russian, they were far less conspicuous than a lone Japanese diplomat. Part of Sugihara's arrangement with the Poles apparently involved issuing transit visas for Polish refugees. At the time, no one—neither Sugihara nor his contacts—foresaw that the Poles would turn out to be Polish Jews, not Polish soldiers who had escaped German prison camps. Nor did anyone expect so many.[19]

The first reference in the record to a Jewish refugee occurs in January 1940, when the ministry advised Sugihara to issue an entrance visa to Alfred Katz. Julian D. Bermann, the manager of Metro Goldwyn Meyer in Japan and Katz's brother-in-law, promised to serve as his guarantor. Katz worked for Metro Goldwyn Meyer in Lodz. His connection to his guarantor was strong, and his guarantor was reliable. Moreover, Katz planned to stay in Japan only one month before proceeding to the United States to see his sister.[20]

Katz's case appeared simple, but he did not receive a visa until more than two months had passed. On March 21, Sugihara wrote the ministry. "If I were to refuse him a transit visa, he would not be able to leave the country," wrote Sugihara. "Since this is an unavoidable situation, I have issued the visa as an exception." Katz's Nansen passport may have been the problem: Diplomats were not supposed to issue entry visas to holders of these passports. Sugihara knew the rules, but he had begun to assume authority to issue visas without waiting for confirmation from Tokyo.[21]

That spring, Polish intelligence agents approached Sugihara to offer intelligence in exchange for assistance. Also, Ayukawa Yoshisuke visited Sugihara at the consulate in March.[22] There is no record of the conversation between Ayukawa and Sugihara, but they shared an interest in Manchukuo. Did they also have an interest in the benefits of assisting Jews? It is difficult to imagine that Ayukawa could have foreseen the significance of Lithuania as a temporary haven for Polish Jews searching for escape routes from Europe, especially since Sugihara's own Polish contacts did not predict that. Yet, it is possible that Ayukawa and Sugihara talked about the Jews in general, since Ayukawa was in the midst of his effort to raise capital for Manchukuo, and Sugihara had spent most of his career there.

There was not much activity for several months. Perhaps Sugihara was busy relaying bulletins to Tokyo about the Soviet troop buildups in the region, but these cables have not been unearthed. As for visas, he did not ask Tokyo for instructions again until the end of July. On July 28, he sent a cable to Foreign Minister Matsuoka in which he detailed the "terror activities" accompanying the Soviet occupation. These included seizing the registry lists of political parties and subsequently arresting 1,500 people in Vilna and 2,000 elsewhere. "The majority are former Polish soldiers and government officials, White Russian commissioned officers, members of the ruling party of the former administration of this country, national parties ranging from the leaders of the Socialists to 'Bundists,' as well as 'Zionist Jews,' " Sugihara explained. Sugihara described an atmosphere of danger, concluding with the information that Jews were requesting visas from the consulate to go via Japan to the United States—as many as "one hundred people every day."[23]

Sugihara forwarded his cable also to the embassies in Germany and the Soviet Union, which was consistent with the contents of his message. It was routine to convey information to Germany, since the former ambassador, General Ōshima, had wanted a consulate in Kaunas in order to determine whether Germany and the Soviet Union would engage in war.[24] The emphasis of the entire cable is on the thoroughness of the Soviet occupation in eliminating any groups it perceived as enemies, and it was in keeping with Sugihara's role of watching the Soviets. The Jews were just one among several groups singled out.

Like Sugihara, other diplomats from other countries noted the increasingly tense situation in Lithuania. In March, the American legation in Kaunas wrote to Washington regarding the continuous state of emergency and the establishment of conscript labor camps for refugees.[25] At about the time that Sugihara wrote to the Foreign Ministry, the Lithuanian minister to Rome notified the Lithuanian legation in Washington that "secret arrests" were occurring throughout the country and that people had been deported to the interior of the Soviet Union by the trainload.[26]

Sugihara's statement about hundreds of Jews congregating at the consulate is arresting. But it becomes more striking when one realizes that however much Sugihara's correspondence matched that of his colleagues from other countries in other ways, no one else mentioned refugees inquiring for visas. In addition, no other Japanese diplomat had ever written Tokyo about such a large number. The question is whether Tokyo picked up the significance of the crowd outside the once-quiet consulate.

Tokyo could not have known how Sugihara felt looking through his window at people fighting to climb over the consulate's wrought-iron gate. "It happened suddenly, but my husband seemed to understand what was occurring," commented Yukiko. Sugihara may have been aware that refugees might come, but the scene was still disturbing. "People were wearing winter clothes in the summer, though it was cool there. Their clothes looked dirty," Yukiko recalled. "My husband didn't sleep that first night."[27] Indeed, Sugihara would later recall that the refugees "all seemed very tired and exhausted. I did not know whether they had any place to sleep in Kovno in those days, maybe they just slept in the station or on the street."[28]

In Japan, bureaucrats were losing sleep over a different matter. The Foreign Ministry was in flux. On July 22, shortly before Sugihara wrote, the second Konoe cabinet had been formed, and Foreign Minister Arita had been replaced by Matsuoka Yōsuke. Matsuoka, a former president of the South Manchurian Railway, held two portfolios: those of foreign minister and colonial minister. Matsuoka possessed power and personality, and he outshone Prime Minister Konoe. "There was no room in the Japanese political world for two such outstanding men on the stage at the same time," Ambassador Shigemitsu Mamoru later commented.[29] Matsuoka advocated power politics and practiced brinkmanship. Despite ten years in the United States and affection for the country, Matsuoka immediately reappointed General Ōshima as ambassador to Germany and Admiral Nomura as ambassador to the United States. These selections would prove devastating to the course of United States–Japan negotiations to avert war, just as Matsuoka's conclusion of the Tripartite Pact would cancel any hopes that United States–Japan relations would improve.

If there were a foreign minister who might be interested in Jews, it would have been Matsuoka. As president of the South Manchurian Railway from August 1935 to July 1940, he could have had direct contact with Jews. He certainly had one link to Jews: during his tenure, he hired Abraham Kotsuji, a Japanese scholar of Hebrew, to work as a Jewish expert in the Railway administration.[30] Now, with his concurrent cabinet appointment, he had the power both to contemplate and enact a settlement scheme. But his actions in office are more telling than his resume. The Tripartite Pact looms larger in history than any interest Matsuoka may have displayed in the Jews.

There is no record of Matsuoka's response to Sugihara's information, but Sugihara cabled again on July 31. He notified Tokyo that expropriation of industries was occurring in Lithuania as the Soviets tightened their grip. A week later, he inquired whether he could issue visas to applicants with Czech passports; the ministry replied several days later, on August 12th, that Sugihara could issue visas as long as the passports were valid and destination country procedures were complete. On August 13, he issued four transit visas to Czech citizens.[31]

Sugihara mentioned the Jews again on August 9. He asked whether a party consisting of Mr. Bargman and "approximately fifteen other influential Warsaw-based Jewish industrialists" might receive permission to stay in Japan one month before departing for South America. They intended to negotiate an offer of capital and experience to Japanese enterprises during their stay. (Sugihara was only issuing tenday transit visas at the time.[32] Sugihara seems to have been a conscientious, conservative diplomat: transit visas could be issued for up to fifteen day stays in Japan—Sugihara was stringent in providing only ten days. In addition, he was asking permission for one month before providing it.) On August 14, the ministry advised Sugihara to confirm that the Bargman party had completed the procedures to enter their destination countries before issuing transit visas. If transit visas were appropriate, the length of stay would be determined upon the group's arrival.[33]

The ministry was applying the immigration law provision that delegated the decision on length of stay to the local level. In theory, the prefectural governors decided, but in practice the local police determined stays. The ministry's response was prompt and predictable in terms of immigration regulations, but there was no sign of applying the Five Ministers Conference concept of welcoming capitalists. On August 14, Sugihara issued transit visa #1756 to Berko Bargman.[34]

Did Sugihara know about the Five Ministers Conference statement of 1938? He should have, since he was stationed in Finland at the time, and the legation had received the "Summary of Jewish Measures" forwarded on December 7, 1938. Perhaps this was why he specifically inquired about Mr. Bargman. However, a number of former diplomats do not recall hearing about the policy set at the conference. To be sure, they were junior diplomats at the time, but the least senior officers in the consulates were generally assigned to decoding incoming cables; they saw everything. Although the cable on Jewish policy undoubtedly arrived from Tokyo, it may have been neither memorable nor widely disseminated. Even if it was, the point is moot if the America Bureau failed to apply it by recognizing people who fit the statement's description of "desirable."

Regardless of Sugihara's level of knowledge, he had begun compiling a list of issued transit visas even before hundreds of Jews descended on the consulate. By July 29, the date that the ministry first received Sugihara's cable about Jews crowding in for visas, Sugihara had already issued sixty-eight; he had begun on July 9. There may have been more whose names went unrecorded. By August 14, the date that Sugihara was told to check the Bargman party's destination procedures, he had granted 1,711 visas.[35]

On August 16, the ministry cabled Sugihara that Lithuanians were arriving in Japan with visas from Sugihara but little else: limited funds and no destinations. "We cannot permit them to land here," telegram #22 read, "and we are troubled as to how to deal with this." Sugihara should not issue visas unless the refugees possessed entry visas elsewhere, travel funds, and sufficient money for the duration of their stay in Japan.[36] The ministry would remind Sugihara of these instructions several times.

Was Matsuoka aware that a small number of refugees would mushroom into hundreds in early 1941? Most refugees were unable to leave Lithuania immediately after obtaining a Japanese transit visa. They still had to acquire Soviet exit visas, and fear often stopped them. The few that made the two to three–week trip from Lithuania to Japan in summer 1940 presaged many more to follow. It is unlikely that Matsuoka knew and recognized this trend. Although correspondence with Sugihara and other diplomats posted abroad was conducted in the name of Matsuoka, it was routed through the relevant department. In this case, the third section of the America Bureau took charge.

Matsuoka was also extraordinarily busy. On August 23, he executed a purge of the Foreign Ministry, dismissing Anglo-Saxon advocates in favor of Axis supporters. He replaced four ambassadors, nineteen ministers, five embassy counselors, and most division heads.[37] Matsuoka sought, according to James Morley, to implement his "grand design," in which the Tripartite Pact would serve as a "lever in negotiations with the United States, not only regarding issues between the two nations, but also to persuade the United States to help terminate the Sino-Japanese conflict, to cooperate with Japan in mediating the European war." Japan also desired to strengthen the Axis for its own southern advance, and to prevent American intervention.[38]

What this meant for a diplomat still holding a post abroad was that his communications became secondary to the action taking place within the ministry in Tokyo. Shigemitsu Mamoru, then ambassador to the United Kingdom, wondered why his reports seemed to have no impact. He learned only later that his most important cables had not been circulated; cables from envoys in Axis countries had received preferential treatment.[39]

Kase Toshikazu, secretary to Matsuoka, believes that "Matsuoka probably did not see cables on the Jewish problem." Kase does not recall reading any himself. "Basically, it wasn't considered an important problem at the time. There were many other pressing concerns."[40] Indeed, the arrival of some foreigners with incomplete paperwork was a temporary nuisance, while the Tripartite Pact was momentous.

Still, Sugihara persisted. He asked the ministry essentially the same question on August 24 as he had regarding the Bargman group. This time he wrote about Leon Polak, a Polish Jewish industrialist, who was awaiting an entry visa for the United States. Mr. Polak's wife and children had already obtained theirs, but Mr. Polak's attempt to obtain a visa had been complicated by the withdrawal of the American legation on August 17. Sugihara added that Mr. Polak possessed sufficient capital abroad.[41] The ministry's response was automatic: Polak would be eligible for a transit visa only after receiving permission to emigrate to the United States.[42] This was the fourth time that Sugihara had been told to ascertain that refugees would be able to enter their destination countries.

It is curious that Sugihara asked about a single individual when by this point he was buried in a pile of passports. A man named Lewi Polak had already received a transit visa on August 21, before Sugihara ever asked Tokyo. Was this the same man? In any case, Sugihara had already issued 2,135 visas by August 24. Perhaps Sugihara was attempting to present a positive portrait of the future visitors to Japan in order to receive permission that he could later use to justify his actions ex post facto. Or did he know that it was more effective to present an individual case than to appeal on behalf of Jewish refugees in general?

If so, he abandoned the tactic in another message. "There are no Central and South American representatives nearby," he wrote. "These people are requesting our visas as the only transit country." Moreover, the visas were necessary for departure procedures of the Soviet Union to go in the direction of the United States. In light of this situation, Sugihara was issuing visas only to those with a "reliable introduction" who agreed to possess permission to land in their destination country by the time they boarded ships in Vladivostok, ship reservations to Japan and beyond, and the necessary funds that could be transferred from abroad to Japan. "Immediately I would like you to take measures to prevent people who have not completed procedures from embarking in Vladivostok."[43] People with visas from Sugihara were already arriving in Vladivostok to discover that the Japanese ship captains would not permit some to board since documents were missing.[44] Sugihara appeared to be following ministry orders, although he was also liberally interpreting them. Sugihara was giving refugees transit visas and the time to come up with entry visas and money.

By this point, Sugihara was pressured by a deadline, for he was supposed to have closed the consulate by August 25.[45] As Sugihara had noted, many other countries had already withdrawn their diplomats in advance of the Soviet occupation. Sugihara was working on borrowed time.

The shipping companies could not stop people with transit visas from boarding not only because the Soviet authorites had ordered such, but also because doing so "would damage faith in our visas." The message ended, "Please follow telegram #22."[46] The ministry stood by Sugihara's visas while warning him to obey his instructions, when Lithuanians began arriving in Japan without money or destinations. Since the Soviets were recognizing Japanese transit visas, the Foreign Ministry could not revoke them. If Japan treated its own visas as suspicious, the faith of others in the Foreign Ministry, its representatives, and their guarantees would suffer. By extension, the reputation of Japan and the Emperor would be tarnished.

By this time, it was too late to advise Sugihara, for he officially closed the consulate on September 4 and left for Berlin with his family. The list of visas he sent to the Foreign Ministry ends on August 26 at number 2,139. It was too late also because Sugihara had stopped listening; his wife Yukiko asserts that though he had already sent his diplomatic seal and papers to Berlin, he continued to write permits anyway from his hotel room in Kaunas and even his train window at the station, as he prepared to depart from Kaunas forever.[47] Sugihara had pushed to its limit the Soviet deadline to evacuate the consulate. If he had indeed continued to issue papers outside the legal confines of his consulate, he had exceeded his authority as a foreign diplomat in Lithuania.

It is difficult to estimate how many people received visas or hastily written permits from Sugihara. Mrs. Sugihara believes her husband stopped recording the number of visas and lost count.[48] Sugihara's own unpublished account recorded in Russian mentions visas for 3,500 Polish refugees.[49] Moses Beckelman, who supervised the Joint relief program in Lithuania, also estimated that 3,500 visas had been issued in Lithuania.[50] These numbers are not actually the same, because a family could use one visa, meaning that the latter figure could translate into visas for far more than 3,500 people. Hirsh Kupinsky, his parents, and sister all traveled to Japan on visa #873. Technically, only children under the age of sixteen could be included on an adult's visa, and each member of a couple was supposed to have his or her own visa. But Susan Bluman, with her photo affixed to her husband's passport, is proof that Sugihara did not strictly enforce these details. In addition, Sugihara mentioned Poles, but he also provided visas to Lithuanians, Germans, and other nationalities, including Americans like Moses Beckelman, who received #1890.[51]

There are several other gaps. How many refugees were Jewish? Prior to sending his actual list, Sugihara wrote Tokyo from Prague in early February 1941 that he had issued visas to 2,132 Lithuanians and Poles. This figure represents a slight deviation from his list of 2,139 people, who were primarily Polish and Lithuanian. But Sugihara continued, "Among them, I estimate approximately fifteen hundred Jews."[52]

How many visas were actually used? Most Lithuanians discovered that the Soviets would not permit them to leave, since they were considered Soviet subjects. Solly Ganor met this fate and ended up in

Dachau, where he survived the Death March in 1945. Others never applied for Soviet exit visas, out of fear. Some waited in Lithuania too long and were caught when the war spread east. As for those that made it to Japan, any refugees who had bona fide destinations would not be included in any subsequent reports by the Foreign Ministry on refugees stranded in Japan.

Finally, there is the question of forgeries. One of the Polish intelligence officers with whom Sugihara worked refers to two copies of Sugihara's rubber visa stamp, asserting that one was used to issue backdated visas in Vilna after Sugihara's departure from Kaunas.[53] A former refugee recalls "underground stampmaking shops" that produced phony visas for hundreds of refugees in Vilna by copying the Japanese characters. "Most of the visas were produced in Kaunas and Vilna after Sugihara left Lithuania."[54] Joseph Shimkin, a Joint worker in Vilna, also forged transit visas after Sugihara's departure. "We made a rubber stamp and, since he [Sugihara] didn't care whether or not people had passports, we actually stamped whole lists of people on a single piece of paper. And it worked."[55]

Refugees were driven to manufacture and obtain forgeries by the fear of expulsion into remote parts of the Soviet Union, even Siberia, which had begun as early as spring 1940. The arrests that Sugihara described in July were frightening and foreshadowed major deportations that continued until immediately before the Germans invaded the Soviet Union. Even those fortunate enough to possess Soviet transit visas and American immigration visas found themselves at risk. "There is danger that Russian transit visas will be withdrawn in the case of certificate holders and refugees with United States visas if they do not emigrate within a very short time (September 15th)," Dr. Kahn warned the World Jewish Congress on September 10, several days after Sugihara left Lithuania.[56] The refugees did not have much time. Approximately 200,000 Jews from the Baltic states and Rumania ran out of time, and they were exiled deep inside the Soviet Union.[57]

THE CURAÇAO CONNECTION

Phony visas were not the only fiction connected with Sugihara. In order to issue transit visas, Sugihara needed to know that the refugees had a destination, as the ministry had repeatedly reminded him. But for many Polish Jews, a destination was a dream—that is, until the small island of Curaçao in the Dutch West Indies appeared as a solution.

A visa was not necessary for Curaçao; only the permission of the governor was required upon arrival at its port. When Jan Zwartendijk, the Dutch consul in Kaunas, agreed to issue Curaçao papers omitting the caveat of the governor's approval, an ingenious strategy was set in motion. The Curaçao visas qualified as entry visas, and Sugihara could issue transit visas without breaking his government's rules. Soon, Sugihara had his clerk stamp passports with "TRANSIT VISA. Seen for the journey through Japan (to Suranam, Curaçao, and other Netherlands' colonies). Consul du Japon à Kaunas."

Three Dutch nationals, Nathan Gutwirth and siblings Rachel and Levi Sternheim, were among the first refugees to inquire about Curaçao. Consul Zwartendijk investigated and secured approval from L. P. J. De Decker, the Dutch ambassador in Riga. Zorach Warhaftig then asked the Dutch consul whether Polish refugees could use Curaçao and Surinam as destinations, and Zwartendijk agreed. Anywhere from 1,200 to 1,400 Curaçao visas are believed to have been issued. Gutwirth, a Telz yeshiva student, also obtained more Curaçao visas for other refugees, by going through the Dutch consul in Kobe after his arrival in Japan.[58]

Sugihara seems to have been involved in this plan from the start. One of Sugihara's Polish intelligence contacts asserts, "He was one of the first to come up with an official project to send Polish refugees via Japan to one of the small states off the South American coast [Curaçao]."[59]

Meanwhile, Laurence Steinhardt, the United States ambassador in Moscow, reported that the Joint representative in Kaunas had persuaded the Dutch consul to assure the Japanese consulate that "entrance visas to the Dutch possessions in the Americas were not required." Steinhardt believed approximately 2,000 Japanese transit visas with such destinations had been issued.[60] Joseph Shimkin also credited the Joint as the origin of this strategy.[61]

In the end, the identity of whoever discovered Curaçao in Kaunas is less important than its significance as a convenient fiction. The Curaçao visas underscored the weakness of Germany's and Japan's alliance and also the determination of Sugihara to aid the refugees. The Tripartite Pact had required Japan to cancel recognition of nations that surrendered to the Reich, but Japan continued to recognize the Netherlands until the Pacific War, despite its capitulation in May 1940. Sugihara could recognize the visas as legally valid even if they were dubious.

However implausible, it was possible that Curaçao would accept the refugees. Would Curaçao prove any different than Shanghai as a curious, distant haven for European Jews? Or was it a lovely mirage that disappeared when it came into view? The saga continued into 1941.

SOVIET EXIT VISAS

Once refugees had obtained Curaçao stamps as entry visas and Japanese transit visas, they became eligible for Soviet exit visas. Like the case of Curaçao, it appears that persuading the Soviets to agree to issue exit visas was a joint project. Mrs. Sugihara recalls that her husband asked a diplomat from the Soviet consulate in Kaunas to issue the visas, and Sugihara's own account offers confirmation.[62] According to Sugihara, the Soviet consul "thought a minute and just looked at me and said, 'OK, go ahead.' That was it. I knew they could get through."[63] Zorach Warhaftig also spoke with the Soviet deputy prime minister of Lithuania, Pius Glovacki. Mr. Glovacki received permission from Moscow; refugees began to receive visas.[64]

Personal intervention may have been the crucial factor, but there were other motivations. "The attitude of the Soviet authorities in permitting Polish Jews in Lithuania to leave that area is a surprise action," commented an American diplomat. "There may be several causes, ranging from the difficulty in assimilating these persons into the new Sovietized Lithuania scheme to more practical considerations."[65] Upon occupying eastern Poland in 1939 and the Baltic states and part of Rumania in mid-1940, the Soviet Union found itself with approximately 2,000,000 more Jews. Not all would be deported.

Finally, there was the matter of money. The revenue from exit visas could be converted into dollars, providing an unexpected source of foreign exchange for the Soviet Union. The trip to Vladivostok cost approximately $200, which was often defrayed by the Joint. Refugees who had the courage to place themselves and their passports before the NKVD, which issued visas on behalf of the Department of Interior, were most likely on their way to Japan.

TOKYO CAUGHT UNPREPARED

Tokyo had no idea how many visas Sugihara had issued in Kaunas, because Sugihara did not forward his list until February 1941, when he wrote from Prague explaining that he still had not finished organizing the papers from the Kaunas consulate and was in the midst of closing the Prague consulate general and opening one in Königsberg.[66] Little did Tokyo know that approximately 2,180 Polish Jews were en route from Lithuania, and that 1,000 had no options elsewhere.[67] They would begin to arrive en masse in autumn 1940 and continue until spring 1941.

The Foreign Ministry was slow to realize that visitors with visas from Sugihara were unlike the other refugees who were passing through Japan. Between July and September 1940, more than 1,000 German Jews arrived in Japan, but most had visas for the United States or Latin American countries. "These people were for the most part still well-clothed and in possession of funds; it was as the victims of Hitler that they aroused the most sympathy," commented the president of Jewcom.[68] They were the lucky ones, even the twelve-year-old boy and thirteen-year-old girl who arrived alone in August and September, with their occupations defined as "student."[69]

The Foreign Ministry did not respond immediately to this number, perhaps because the Jewish community in Japan was caring for the refugees' needs, and the refugees did move on. Yet, the Joint relief effort in Japan was already financially strapped. "ALMOST UNABLE COPE WITH ARRIVING REFUGEES," cabled Ernst Baerwald, the representative in Yokohama, in August. He was worried about "UNPAID PASSAGES" and "EXPIRED AND INCOMPLETE VISAS."[70] Still, the Joint coped.

The first specific reference to a recipient of a Sugihara visa appears in mid-September. Moses Kapman, a Lithuanian Jew, had received a visa in mid-July from Sugihara and traveled to Japan with his wife and son in August: His landing, however, was prohibited, since he possessed "just a little money" ($2.00 and $1.50) and did not have entry visas for Canada. He tried to enter a second time and was let in "at any rate."[71] It was easier to allow the Kapman family in than to refuse them.

One visa on which a small family traveled was not a red flag, because the list was dominated by Moscow, not Kaunas. Five others had received transit visas in Moscow without fully meeting requirements. But the name of Moses Kaplan—a Lithuanian Jew—appears on Sugihara's list as having received a visa on July 15, approximately the date listed in the ministry's report. "Kapman" must have been a typographical error.

Other locations appeared to cause problems and distract the ministry from what had occurred in Kaunas. At the end of September, the ministry sent a cable to Ambassador Tōgō in Moscow. "Refugees heading in the direction of the States with transit visas from Stockholm and Oslo have had little spending money," the ministry warned.[72] Ten people had been prevented from landing in Japan. As long as the government did not know about the refugees' financial straits, it was not alarmed. But when discrepancies were discovered at the port of arrival, concerns were raised, even over so few people. The flow of refugees was just about to increase and change. No longer would there be two handfuls of people whose disembarkation could be rejected, but dozens and then hundreds.

On October 5 Ernst Baerwald cabled the New York office that "MANY POLISH EMIGRANTS ALREADY ARRIVED (STOP) GREATER INFLUX FROM VILNA TO BE EXPECTED NEXT WEEKS."[73] By the end of the month, 300 Lithuanian-Polish refugees had arrived in Tsuruga. Fortunately, the Jewish Community of Kobe reported, "Our community has come to an understanding with the Tzuruga [sic] and local Police Authorities as to letting the groups pass without any difficulties under the personal guarantee of our Community." The Jewish community was grateful for the "exceptionally humane attitude of the Japanese Authorities who in every way facilitate the work of our Committee."[74] Some of these refugees may have had visas from Sugihara, but they also had emigration possibilities.

Meanwhile, Tokyo was reacting, although the problem of people with Curaçao visas had not yet developed. At the end of September, the chief of the America Bureau wrote the Home Ministry. "There are inconveniences resulting from the handling by our offices abroad," he admitted. Although only stateless refugees had been required to possess a set amount of money, the Bureau now recommended ¥25, approximately $6, a day, "regardless of whether those coming are stateless or not." The Home Ministry approved, and in early October the Foreign Ministry notified Japanese consulates in Europe, the Soviet Union, and China that visa applicants needed enough money to pay their passage to their final destination and ¥25 a day for the stay in Japan. This message was also sent to various shipping companies.[75]

Ernst Baerwald tried to reassure the America Bureau that all emigrants would be cared for by the Kobe Jewish Community and the Relief Aid Committee in Yokohama, with "no fear that they may become a public burden." The past four months had "clearly shown that no trouble had occurred with the Japanese Authorities and that many transports passed through Japan without any inconveniences."[76]

Refugees with Curaçao visas were on their way. Tokyo was unaware of them until a tip arrived from Consul Toyohara in Manchouli in early November: in a chart showing the destinations of Jews who had transited Manchukuo in October, forty-three were listed as heading to the West Indies. This was the first time that any reference to Curaçao, however indirect, had occurred.[77]

By late October at least twenty-six Jews who were heading to Curaçao reached Japan. None was refused entry.[78] Kaunas was still difficult to trace, because the origin of their visas was not listed. When previous addresses included Vilna, the city was listed as either Vilno or Vilnius. It would have been easy to miss the source of the visas as the Japanese consulate in Kaunas, because so many Polish cities were listed as prior addresses that the two Lithuanian cities of Kaunas and Vilna (and its variations) seemed insignificant.

Sugihara's belated attempt to notify the Foreign Ministry of his activities in Kaunas was an oversight. It was standard procedure for diplomats to send bimonthly breakdowns of issued visas; Sugihara sent the list only after the ministry requested it in early February 1941.[79] But even if he had sent his list promptly, the ministry may not have known that the visa recipients were Jews. Diplomats always listed the nationality of visa applicants, but only occasionally the religion. To be sure, as noted, German Jews were easily identifiable by their middle names of "Sarah" and "Israel" and the prominent *J* marking their passports. Polish Jews, however, were not easily recognized unless one was familiar with Jewish names. A bureaucrat processing paperwork in the America Bureau in Tokyo may not have studied the lists closely. There had not been any major problems until that point; why look for one now? After all, other diplomats in Europe were issuing visas. Sugihara Chiune was exceptional, but he was not alone.

PERSPECTIVE: OTHER JAPANESE DIPLOMATS

Between January 1940 and mid-March 1941, Japanese consulates in Europe issued transit visas to 5,580 people, although as of April 15, 1941, more than 2,500 recipients still had not arrived in Japan.[80] The Kaunas consulate was the source of more than 2,000 visas, and the remaining ones were most likely from other key locations in Europe. For example, in mid-February 1941, the ministry produced a chart on Jewish refugees who were in Japan as of February 8. Transit visas had been issued by the following consulates:

Berlin: 95 German and 1 Pole = 96

Moscow: 1 German and 1 Other = 2

Vienna: 5 Germans and 1 Other = 6

Hamburg: 9 Germans and 3 Others= 12

Stockholm: 11 Germans and 6 Others = 17

Prague: 2 Others

Sofia, Bulgaria: 3 Others

Riga, Latvia: 3 Germans and 2 Poles = 5

Kaunas: 14 Germans, 400 Poles, 11 Lithuanians, and 6 Others = 431

Others: 14 Germans, 4 Poles, 1 Lithuanian, 17 Others = 36[81]

Some refugees possessed ship reservations and destinations, and would be moving on. Others would be staying. One might make an educated guess regarding which consulates issued transit visas after strictly applying Japanese immigration regulations and which did not.

The cable traffic adds another dimension. Japanese diplomats in Sweden also issued visas. Before Sugihara's flurry of activity in summer 1940, Acting Minister Hirata wrote the Foreign Ministry in the spring that approximately twenty people waiting for immigrant visas for North America had proof of bank deposits, proof of approval from exchange offices, and sufficient funds for their stay in Japan. He was issuing entry visas. "In case these type of requests increase in the future," he added, "it is appropriate to issue visas to those who have been waiting a long time and who have sufficient funds."[82]

Arita provided the standard reply. Japanese transit visas could not be issued unless entry visas were in hand. If the applicant had an entry visa for another country, a Japanese transit visa should be granted, but not an entry one.[83] Although Hirata was concerned with a relatively small number of applicants, his decision to grant entry visas suggests that he was sensitive to the applicants' personal circumstances and oblivious of the decisions of the Five Ministers Conference.

The Stockholm legation continued to be open to refugees' appeals as late as March 1941. In February and March, approximately eight-four Jews received transit visas, out of a total of 190.[84] In this case, below the designation "German," a *J* was included. Acting Minister Kanda did not hide the visas; presumably, the applicants met the transit visa requirements. But by this time, the Moscow embassy was supposed to be the only Japanese diplomatic office issuing visas.

Stockholm was a site of intrigue. Like Kaunas, Polish intelligence operatives cooperated with Japanese officials. In this case, however, the Japanese contact was a military attaché—Onodera Makoto. The Jews who received transit visas were German nationals, not Poles. Was the atmosphere in Stockholm more conducive to helping Jews than that of diplomatic offices elsewhere? Sweden was neutral, but it harbored 3,000 European Jews between 1933 and 1943.

Studies of World War II rescue efforts have shown that the less directly a country was subjected to Nazi rule, the more possible rescue behavior became. This was the case in Denmark, where the king and his people subverted the Nazi administration to rescue the majority of Jews by secretly sailing them to Sweden in autumn 1943. Could that also have been the case for a Japanese office operating in Sweden? Since the early 1900s, the Japanese legation in Sweden had been responsible for Denmark and Norway. The Japanese legation was operating in an environment where rescue was a viable option. To be sure, Bulgaria was also neutral until March 1941 and would subsequently protect its Jews from deportation in 1943, but the Japanese legation in Sofia did not issue many visas. One reason may be that restrictive measures against Bulgarian Jews were not taken until February 1941; Bulgarian Jews may not have sensed danger until late in the period when flight and rescue were still possible.

Meanwhile, the Japanese embassy in Moscow was not as friendly as the legation in Stockholm. Tōgō, a leading diplomat, told Arita in May 1940 that he was "discouraging" both German and Polish Jews from going to Japan. Tōgō did not think that Japanese-Soviet relations would benefit from providing Polish Jews with Japanese transit visas.[85] Tōgō miscalculated, for the Soviets were willing to facilitate the departure of Polish Jews. But he did not err, since he was obediently following Tokyo's policy.

Only Tōgō and Shigemitsu in London had originally opposed the Axis alliance.[86] When it came to the Jews, Shigemitsu was also ill disposed. At the same time as Tōgō wrote from Moscow, Shigemitsu forwarded a report from Consul General Uchiyama: as England's situation became more dire, prohibitory measures directed towards foreigners were becoming stricter. Although Japanese were not being discriminated against, Jewish German refugees were "making various excuses and requesting visas to come to Japan in order to avoid imprisonment." He was not moved by the May 12 arrests of 26,000 Austrian and German refugees, whom England suspected as Nazis. Shigemitsu affirmed that he was following Tokyo's orders and refraining from issuing visas.[87] He expressed little interest in Jews, despite his history of communicating with N. E. B. Ezra. Rather, he sounded like the senior diplomat that he was—aware of current events and faithful to his post.

Yamaji became active again in July 1940. In an exchange of cables with Tokyo over several weeks, Yamaji questioned whether he should grant a transit visa for a Swiss woman who was not Jewish. She wanted to join her husband, a stateless Jew living in Shanghai. Although she was "Aryan," Yamaji explained, the Vienna authorities would treat her as Jewish. Arita replied that Yamaji could issue a visa and that the wife need not be treated as Jewish if she was traveling without her husband. (Actually, the navy in Shanghai would have regarded the woman as Jewish, in accordance with its restrictions on living in Hongkew.) But this leniency did not matter, because Yamaji posed another question: if the children have "mixed blood," he asked, "do we treat them as Jewish?" Arita's prompt answer was terse and affirmative.

The case should have been closed, but Yamaji returned several days later. Yamaji confirmed that the children needed an entry certificate from the Shanghai consulate, where restrictions were in effect, since they were Jewish. However, the Swiss Consul General in Vienna had entered the argument, asserting that the wife and children all possessed Swiss citizenship and merited transit visas. "If we refuse," wrote Yamaji, "it is not good for Japan-Swiss relations." Arita responded that transit visas could be issued as soon as the family obtained permission to enter Shanghai.[88]

Yamaji revealed how acclimated he was to his environment by wondering whether the Swiss wife should be considered Jewish, employing the term "Aryan," and characterizing the children as "mixed." When the Foreign Ministry responded that that the wife need not be regarded as Jewish, it was admitting that it did differentiate between Jews and others. Whatever claims of "humanitarianism" were uttered by the Japanese authorities in Shanghai, restrictions were intended for Jews and not others. But the equation changed when the Swiss Consul General became involved. The Foreign Ministry showed its susceptibility to the opinions of other nations, whether they favored refugees or not. Between April and December 1940, Yamaji issued more than 500 transit visas, and many of them to Jews.[89] He was simply precise when it came to applying the law.

What about Sugihara's superior, Minister Ōtaka, in Latvia? He issued some visas to Jews, but not many. From the start, he was disinclined to help any Jews. Before Riga he had been stationed in Tsingtao, where he received information on the Far Eastern Jewish Conference. Despite the Conference's three consecutive attempts to welcome Jews into China and Manchukuo, Ōtaka disapproved. Prior to the second conference in 1938 he wrote Arita that Japan should prohibit immigration, since "almost all refugees have no capital" and there could be "possible damage from Communism." "If possible," he asserted, "I recommend measures to refuse immigration as much as possible."[90]

Shortly after the Five Ministers Conference, he forwarded a list of approximately 100 Jewish residents of Tsingtao. The majority were Russian emigrants, but Ōtaka did not fail to be thorough. He even included the name of Samuel Sokobin, who was the American consul there at the time.[91] Ironically, the Jewish community of Kobe characterized Sokobin as "a definite anti-immigrationist" when he served as an acting consul in Japan.[92] By the time Ōtaka reached Riga, the "Pearl of the Baltic," his stand seemed firm, especially since it conformed to Tokyo's instructions. In June 1940, ten German Jews and four Latvian Jews received Japanese transit visas.[93] Between July and November 1940, twenty-two Jewish passengers boarded Nippon Yūsen Kaisha (Japan Mail) steamers in Riga, though this does not necessarily mean that they received visas from the legation.[94] But such small numbers seem paltry when one considers how many applicants there must have been in Latvia. A junior diplomat studying in Riga at the time believes that Jews did not request visas from the legation, but another young diplomat recalls that Latvian Jews with entry visas for other countries received transit visas.[95] Zorach Warhaftig also recalls requests for transit visas from Riga and believes some Poles journeyed to Israel by way of Riga, Stockholm, and Marseille.[96] In general, Polish Jews had difficulty penetrating Latvia's border, but Latvia had 93,000 Jews of its own. Ninety percent died in the Holocaust. Perhaps Latvian Jews did not visit the Japanese legation in Riga because the rumor mill had warned them it was fruitless. Ōtaka was a "strict" man, in the sense that he was serious about his work, according to the young diplomat who did not see many visa applicants.[97] Ōtaka was also a bystander.

As Polish and Lithuanian Jews with transit visas from Sugihara and dubious visas for other places boarded the trans-Siberian railway and embarked on Japanese steamers for Japan, Matsuoka spoke out in early 1941. In a conversation at his home with Lew Zikman, the wealthy businessman from Harbin who had proposed a Jewish settlement, Matsuoka was reported to have said "no racial discrimination or antisemitism can be in japan [sic]." Zikman added that Matsuoka explained, "I concluded an alliance with germany [sic] and italy [sic] but I am sure antisemitism can never take place in japan [sic] and this is not only my idea but it is a part of the great ideal of japan [sic] ever since the empire foundation."[98]

Practicing anti-Semitism and enforcing immigration restrictions were separate issues for Matsuoka. His secretary, Kase Toshikazu, remembers Matsuoka as "a man of rugged honesty and homeliness and possessed of a sterling sense of honor." He was also "dynamic and erratic" and subject to inconsistencies.[99] But the ministry he headed remained consistent in 1941. It became increasingly tough toward the issuing of transit visas.

SUGIHARA'S NEXT STEP

In one of the few interviews Sugihara held before he died in 1986, he wondered about the reaction to his mass issuance of visas. " 'No one ever said anything about it. I remember thinking they probably didn't realize how many I had actually issued."[100] He was correct.

When Sugihara arrived in Berlin from Kaunas, the new ambassador to Germany, Kurusu Saburō, did not comment, which surprised and relieved Sugihara. Mrs. Sugihara ascribed his silence to his sympathy for England and the United States, but it is likely that Kurusu, like the Foreign Ministry in Tokyo, was simply ignorant.[101] If he had known, he may have cautioned Sugihara as he did the ministry when he wrote in December 1940 that there was "every kind of pressure on Germany's Jews, and they are trying to leave Germany in every way." Kurusu concluded, "For us, there is neither a need nor a benefit in sheltering in Asia those who have been driven out of Germany, Italy, Hungary, and various Latin countries. In not stopping the flow now, it will be the root of evil in the future."[102]

Soon after, Sugihara and his family moved to Prague, where he became the acting consul general until the end of February 1941, when he closed the office. Despite any fears he may have entertained in Berlin, he again began issuing visas in September. Between September 13, 1940 and February 28, 1941, he granted sixty-nine visas—almost all were transit visas to German Jews. Many of the recipients recorded their route of Tsuruga, Kobe, and Shanghai on their visa applications.[103] Sugihara noted on some applications in his fluid hand that the applicants were Jewish. Although the applications did not ask whether a person was Jewish or not, the passports announced the fact anyway.

Was his behavior in Prague evidence of what Ervin Staub has called a "continuum of benevolence," in which people who initially agree to help end up contributing significantly over time?[104] The visa recipients were not the kind of people that the Five Ministers Conference had considered. Otto Hahn, opera singer-cum-clerk, and Eliska Singer, pyrotechnics specialist turned housekeeper, would not have dazzled their Japanese hosts with their potential use to the Empire.

Did Sugihara have other motives? Prague had become part of the Reich in March 1939. Sugihara was dangerously close to the Germans at a time when Hitler's policy of emigration had evolved into one of annihilation. He had courage, contacts, or a combination of both. Sugihara continued his relationship with the Polish operatives with whom he had worked in Kaunas. "In that connection with Sugihara, I issued ten to fifteen Manchurian passports for Polish officers from army headquarters," says Kasai Tadakazu of his time at the Manchukuo Affairs Bureau office in Berlin.[105]

Sugihara's next stop was Königsberg in East Prussia, where he once again opened a small office in March 1941. But by December he was gone, after being transferred to the legation in Rumania. Sugihara had been the subject of German surveillance in Kaunas, Prague, and Königsberg. The Germans were suspicious of his interest in German troop movements. They viewed him not as a diplomat, but as a spy and pressured the Foreign Ministry to remove him.[106]

Japan had a small legation in Bucharest, where Sugihara translated Russian documents. It was the largest office in Europe in which Sugihara had worked.[107] His superior, Minister Tsutsui, was no friend of the Jews. In June 1941, the same month that Rumanian troops executed their first major wartime pogrom, Tsutsui advised the Foreign Ministry that Jews are "insects in the bosom of a lion in peacetime, and many are 5th column enemies in wartime."[108] Tsutsui's anti-Semitism worsened as the Holocaust advanced. By July 1942, as deportations to the death camps accelerated, he warned the "Jewish influence that starts in Shanghai and spreads deep roots in every East Asia area must be destroyed."[109] Neither Rumania nor the Japanese legation were an auspicious area for Sugihara to assist Jews. But there was nothing he could do anyway. The Holocaust was in full force. The Sugiharas stayed in Bucharest until the end of the war.

NOTES

1. Masha Leon, unedited interview by Sheryl Narahara for "The Unlikely Liberators" tour, 1.5 hours, 22 September 1994, videocassette.

2. Martin Krygier, "The Making of a Cold Warrior," *Quadrant* (November 1986): 40.

3. Records of United States Department of State Relating to Refugees, "Voluntary Report," by Ray M. Melbourne, 24 May 1941, File 811.111/1536.

4. Lucy S. Dawidowicz, *From That Place and Time* (New York: Bantam Books, 1989), xiii; Martin Gilbert, *Atlas of the Holocaust* (New York: William Morrow, 1988), 67.

5. *Gaimushō shokuin rekinin hyō* (Tokyo: Gaimushō, October 1940), 253.

6. Sugihara Chiune, undated memoir, courtesy of Sugihara Nobuki, Antwerp, Belgium.

7. Toshikazu Kase, *Journey to the Missouri*, ed. David Nelson Rowe (New Haven, CT: Yale University Press, 1950), 157; Ambassador Shigemitsu Akira, interview by author, 29 May 1995, Tokyo, tape recording; Katayama Junnosuke, "Sorenken mitari, kiitari, no shirushi," *Mantetsu kaihō*, no. 167 (1 May 1991): 5.

8. Nakamura Ryūko, interview by author, 6 April 1995, Minokamo, Aichi, tape recording.

9. "Jiyū e no tōsō," *Chūnichi Shimbun*, 3 April 1995, 26.

10. Shimura Giichi, interview.

11. Nakamura Ryūko, interview.

12. Ibid.

13. Bill Craig, "A beacon of humanity in a malevolent world," *Pacific Sunday*, 23 June 1985, 11.

14. Shimura Giichi, interview.

15. Katayama Junnosuke, interview.

16. Ibid.

17. Solly Ganor, *Light One Candle: A Survivor's Tale from Lithuania to Jerusalem* (New York: Kodansha International, 1995), 23.

18. Ibid., 40–41.

19. Ewa Palasz-Rutkowska and Andrzej T. Romer," Polish-Japanese Co-operation during World War II," *Japan Forum* 7 no. 2 (Autumn 1995): 287–97.

20. Telegram from Nomura to Sugihara, #387, 10 January 1940, JPF, folder 9.

21. Telegram from Sugihara to Arita, #50, 21 March 1940, JPF, folder 9.

22. Palasz-Rutkowska, "Polish-Japanese Co-operation," 289–90; "Jiyū e no tōsō," *Chūnichi Shimbun*, 16 April 1995, 30.

23. Sugihara's March 21 cable and this one are both labeled #50. The March one was handwritten and a standard cable, whereas the July 28 one was typed and coded. It is unclear why both cables share the same number. Telegram, from Sugihara to Matsuoka, coded #22785, #50, 28 July 1940, JPF, folder 10.

24. Sugihara Chiune, undated memoir.

25. Records of United States Department of State Relating to the Internal Affairs of Lithuania, 1910–1944, "Enclosure," from American Legation, Kaunas, to Secretary of State, 1 March 1940, File 860m, Despatch 729.

26. Records of U.S. State Department of State: Lithuania, 1910–1944, "From Mr. S. Lozoraitis, Lithuanian Minister to Rome and formerly Minister of Foreign Affairs of Lithuania, to the Lithuanian Legation, Washington," 30 July 1940, File 860m.

27. Sugihara Yukiko, interview by Katori Shunsuke, 1989, Tokyo, tape recording.

28. Sugihara Chiune, undated memoir, courtesy of Sugihara Nobuki, Antwerp, Belgium.

29. Mamoru Shigemitsu, *Japan and Her Destiny*, ed. F. S. G. Piggott, trans. Oswald White (New York: E. P. Dutton, 1958), 197.

30. Abraham Kotsuji, *From Tokyo to Jerusalem* (New York: Bernard Geis Associates, 1964), 143, 159, 160.

31. Shiraishi Masaaki, "Sugihara Chiune to Nihon no tai Yudayajin seisaku," 27 April 1996, Self Defense Agency Research Institute War History Division, Photocopy; telegram from Sugihara to Matsuoka, #24032 abbreviated, #58, 7 August 1940, "Gaikokujin ni taisuru teikoku no ryoken sashō kankei zakken," J230 J/X1; telegram from Matsuoka to Sugihara, abbreviated #26848, #18, 12 August 1940, JPF, folder 10; Sugihara, list of Japanese transit visas. Sugihara asked because Czechoslovakia was already a Reich Protectorate.

32. Telegram from Sugihara to Matsuoka, #24375, #59, 9 August 1940, JPF, folder 10.

33. Telegram from Matsuoka to Sugihara, #27136, #21, 14 August 1940, JPF, folder 10.

34. Sugihara, list of Japanese transit visas. Sugihara's telegram refers to Bergman and the list to Bargman; the difference could be due to pronunciation.

35. Ibid.

36. Telegram from Matsuoka to Sugihara, #27465, #22, 16 August 1940, JPF, folder 10.

37. Ernst L. Presseisen, *Germany and Japan: A Study in Totalitarian Diplomacy: 1933–1941* (The Hague: Martinus Nijhoff, 1958), 255.

38. James William Morley, ed., *Deterrent Diplomacy: Japan, German, and the U.S.S.R., 1935–1940* (New York: Columbia University Press, 1976), 256, 257.

39. Shigemitsu, *Japan and Her Destiny*, 215.

40. Kase Toshikazu, telephone interview by author, 12 June 1995, Tokyo, Japan.

41. Telegram from Sugihara to Matsuoka, #25964, #66, 24 August 1940, JPF, folder 10.

42. Telegram from Matsuoka to Sugihara, #28710, #23, 28 August 1940, JPF, folder 10.

43. Telegram from Sugihara to Matsuoka, #26809, #67, 1 August 1940, JPF, folder 10. The date on this telegram is mistaken, for it refers to Matsuoka's message of August 16. It must therefore be after August 16 and also after August 24, which is the date of Sugihara's message #66. This cable was probably issued between August 25 and September 3. There may have been a typographical error, writing August 1 instead of September 1.

44. "Situation of European Refugees Coming to Japan," 15 April 1941, JPF, folder 11.

45. "Jiyū e no tōsō," *Chūnichi Shimbun*, 8 January 1995, 30.

46. Telegram from Matsuoka to Sugihara, #29345, #24, 3 September 1940, JPF, folder 10.

47. Sugihara, *Rokusen-nin no inochi no visa*, 41.

48. Ibid., 39.

49. Sugihara Chiune, undated memoir.

50. "Minutes, Executive Committee, 5/21/41" AR 33/44, #461: China, General, 1941 January-July, AJJDC Archives.

51. Sugihara, list of Japanese transit visas issued in 1940 by the consulate in Kaunas.

52. Telegram from Acting Consul General Sugihara to Matsuoka, abbreviated #2964, #12, 5 February 1941, JPF, folder 11.

53. Palasz-Rutkowska, "Polish-Japanese Co-operation," 291.

54. Joseph R. Fiszman, discussion regarding "The Quest for Status: Polish-Jewish Refugees in Shanghai, 1941–1949," symposium "Jewish Diasporas in China."

55. Craig, "A beacon of humanity," 13.

56. "Memorandum," 10 September 1940, New York, AR 33/44, #731: Lithuania, General, 1940 June-September, AJJDC Archives.

57. Yad Vashem, *Rescue Attempts during the Holocaust: Proceedings of the Second Yad Vashem International Historical Conference* (Jerusalem: Yad Vashem, 1977), 230.

58. Most accounts highlight the role of Gutwirth in spreading the word. See also, Warhaftig, *Refugee and Survivor: Rescue Efforts during the Holocaust* (Jerusalem: Yad Vashem, 1988), 102, 103, 107.

59. Lieutenant Daszkiewicz, quoted in Palasz-Rutkowska, "Polish-Japanese Co-operation," 290.

60. Records of United States Department of State Relating to Refugees, "Telegram Received," from American Embassy, Moscow, to Secretary of State, 6 October 1940, File 811.111, Despatch 422.

61. Eulogy in memory of Joseph Shimkin, by Rabbi James Lebeau, 26 September 1993, Jewish Community Center, Tokyo, Japan.

62. Sugihara, *Rokusen-nin no inochi no visa*, 35; Sugihara Chiune, undated memoir.

63. Craig, "A beacon of humanity," 13.

64. Warhaftig, *Refugee and Survivor*, 121.

65. Records of United States Department of State Relating to Refugees, "Voluntary Report," by Ray M. Melbourne, 22 May 1941, 10.

66. Telegram from Sugihara to Matsuoka, #28, 28 February 1941, "Gaikokujin ni taisuru zaigai kōkan hakkyū ryoken sashō hōkoku ikken, Ōshū no bu."

67. Letter, from R. L. Zien, Vancouver Jewish Refugee Committee, to Saul Hayes, UJR & WRA, Montreal, AA 33/44, #725: Japan, General, Emigration, 1941 July-December, AJJDC Archives.

68. Hebrew Immigrant Aid Society (HIAS), "Jewish Transients in Japan," by Moise Moiseff, 25 July 1941, Record Group 245.4, series xvb-xvc, HIAS Reports, YIVO.

69. "Survey of Jewish Refugee Immigrants," by Yamaguchi prefecture, July-September 1940, JPF, folder 10.

70. "Incoming Cable," 15 August 1940, AR 33/44, #723: Japan, General, Emigration, 1939–1941 (March), AJJDC Archives.

71. Telegram from *Keihokyoku* to chief of the America Bureau, #89, 13 September 1940, JPF, folder 10.

72. Telegram from Matsuoka to Tōgō, abbreviated #32752, #868, 30 September 1940, JPF, folder 10.

73. "Incoming Cable," 5 October 1940, AR 33/44, #723: Japan, Emigration, 1939–1941 (March), AJJDC Archives.

74. "Extract from a letter from the Jewish Community of Kobe dated Oct. 28th, 1940, translated from Russian," AR 33/44, #723: Japan, Emigration, 1939–1941 (March), AJJDC Archives.

75. Telegram from Matsuoka to embassies and consulates abroad, #1279, 10 October 1940, JPF, folder 10; telegram from the chief of the America Bureau to all shipping companies, #4561, 10 October 1940, JPF, folder 10.

76. Letter (English) from Ernst Baerwald, Relief Aid Committee, Yokohama, to America Bureau, 28 October 1940, JPF, folder 10.

77. Telegram from Toyohara to Umezu, Secret #517, 9 November 1940, JPF, folder 10.

78. "List of Jewish Refugee Immigrants in October from Fukui Prefecture," #1747, 27, November 1940, JPF, folder 10.

79. Telegram from Matsuoka to Sugihara, Prague, abbreviated #3459, #10, 4 February 1941, JPF, folder 11.

80. Report, "Situation of European Refugees Coming to Japan," 15 April 1941, JPF, folder 11.

81. "Chart on Refugee Jews re. Those Who as of February 8 to Present Are Staying in Japan as Refuge," top secret, 14 February 1941, JPF, folder 11.

82. Telegram from Hirata, Stockholm, to Arita, #11014, coded, #253, 25 April 1940, JPF, folder 9.

83. Telegram from Arita to Consul Matsushima, coded #13236, #36, 30 April 1940, JPF, folder 9.

84. Telegram from Kanda to Matsuoka, #51, 10 April 1941, "Gaikokujin ni taisuru zaigai kōkan hakkyū ryoken sashō hōkoku ikken, Ōshū no bu."

85. Telegram from Tōgō to Arita, secret, coded #13936, #665, 20 May 1940, JPF, folder 9.

86. Kase, Journey to the Missouri, 123.

87. Telegram from Shigemitsu to Arita, coded #14220, #840, 22 May 1940, JPF, folder 9.

88. Telegram from Yamaji to Arita, coded #19841, #123, 5 July 1940; telegram from Arita to Yamaji, #22376, #22, 9 July 1940; telegram from Yamaji to Arita, #20335, coded, #127, 9 July 1940; telegram from Arita to Yamaji, #22883, abbreviated, #24, 12 July 1940; telegram from Yamaji to Arita, #21062, coded, #134, 15 July 1940; telegram from Arita to Yamaji, #24706, #26, 23 July 1940, JPF, folder 10.

89. Telegram from Yamaji to Matsuoka, #2, 7 January 1941, "Gaikokujin ni taisuru zaigai kōkan hakkyū ryoken sashō hōkoku ikken, Ōshū no bu."

90. Telegram from Consul General Ōtaka to Arita, coded #34299, #876, 22 November 1938, JPF, folder 4.

91. Telegram from Ōtaka to Arita, #1208, 9 December 1938, JPF, folder 5.

92. HIAS, letter, from J. Epstein, Kobe branch of HICEM to HICEM, Lisbon, 18 August 1941, Record Group 245.4, Series xvb-xvc, HIAS Reports, YIVO.

93. Telegram from Ōtaka to the Foreign Ministry, 2 June 1940, "Gaikokujin ni taisuru zaigai kōkan hakkyū ryoken sashō hōkoku ikken, Ōshū no bu"; telegram from Ōtaka to the Foreign Ministry, 26 June 1940, "Gaikokujin ni taisuru zaigai kōkan hakkyū ryoken sashō hōkoku ikken, Ōshū no bu."

94. Telegram from Matsuoka to offices in North, South, and Central America, #635, top secret, 30 May 1941, JPF, folder 11.

95. Shigemitsu Akira, interview; Katayama Junnosuke, interview.

96. Warhaftig counts some 2,500 Polish Jews who traveled the above route to Israel as well as going via Odessa and Istanbul. He does not provide a more specific breakdown. Warhaftig, 168, 234.

97. Katayama Junnosuke, interview.

98. Cable of Lew Zikman, quoted in letter, from Henry M. Steinfeld (formerly H. Steinfeld, Tokyo) to the American Jewish Joint Distribution Committee, 12 February 1941, San Francisco, AR 33/44, #723: Japan, General, Emigration, 1939–1941 (March), AJJDC, Archives.

99. Kase, *Journey to the Missouri*, 43.

100. Craig, "A beacon of humanity," 13.

101. Sugihara, *Rokusen-nin no inochi no visa*, 43.

102. Telegram from Kurusu to Matsuoka, abbreviated #36932, #1585, secret, 18 December 1940, JPF, folder 10.

103. Telegram from Sugihara to Matsuoka, 18 May 1941, "Gaikokujin ni taisuru zaigai kōkan hakkyū ryoken sashō hōkoku ikken, Ōshū no bu"; Telegram from Sugihara to Matsuoka, #17, 4 February 1941, JPF, folder 11.

104. Ervin Staub, *The Roots of Evil: The Origins of Genocide and Other Group Violence* (Cambridge: Cambridge University Press, 1989), 167.

105. Kasai Tadakazu, interview.

106. "Jiyū e no tōsō," *Chūnichi Shimbun*, 17 April 1995, 26.

107. Sugihara, *Rokusen-nin no inochi no visa*, 88.

108. Telegram from Tsutsui to Matsuoka, coded #15596, #97, 7 June 1941, JPF, folder 11.

109. Telegram from Tsutsui to Tōgō, coded #21011, #122, 31 July 1942, JPF, folder 11.

6

Jewish Refugees in Japan in 1941

"THERE IS NO GOING BACK. WE CAN ONLY GO EAST."[1] Masha Leon captured the sentiments of most Jewish refugees in Lithuania in the summer of 1940. With no other choice, they headed to Japan. Between July
1, 1940, and August 1, 1941, approximately 4,500 Jewish refugees, from
Poland, Germany, and other countries, journeyed to Japan. Three thousand five hundred left by August, among them Susan and Nate Bluman, as well as Masha Leon and Samuil Manski. The remaining 1,000
were transferred to Shanghai in August and September 1941. The
greatest number of arrivals occurred in February and March, with more
than 800 people each month. But in July, when emigration via Siberia
became impossible, only twenty people reached Japan.[2] They had probably been waiting in Vladivostok.

Most people embarked from Lithuania in winter, just as they had
fled Poland one year before. If escaping Poland had been about snow—
crossing frigid streams by crawling over snow-covered logs, pushing
through deep drifts, trying to catch a ride on a sleigh or a wagon full
of hay, leaving Lithuania was about ice. From the window of the trans-
Siberian train, Masha Leon remembers "watching miles and miles and
miles of tundra, frozen white, and white birches—miles and days of
just birches."[3] Once in Vladivostok, refugees boarded Japanese steamers, while icebreakers cleared the harbor. Jerry Milrod recalls dancing
for joy on huge blocks of ice aboard the ship. Everyone continued east.

Although it was winter in Japan too, many refugees most readily
recall the spring. Perhaps their relief at having exited Europe was re-

juvenating. They were indeed fortunate. Not only did they arrive in large numbers, but they also seldom left within the designated two-week period permitted by their visas. Upon arriving in Japan, the local police issued a stamp for a one-month stay. Even this was too short. Refugees remained in Japan for months, until they could find a destination or sail for Shanghai as a last resort. Even those who entered Japan with proper visas had difficulty, as Latin American countries plugged any openings in their immigration policies towards *la raza judia*. Those who believed that the United States was viable watched their hope fade as the immigration law was amended to their regret.

The Japanese did not want the Jews to stay in Japan and tried to prevent them from coming from the Soviet Union. But the Soviets did not want anyone to whom it had issued an exit visa. In the end, the Japanese authorities accepted virtually all those who tried to reach Japan from the Soviet Union with Japanese transit visas, however questionable their status.

Only when Japan seriously began to prepare for war against the United States did the refugees find they could stay no longer. After Pearl Harbor, the Japanese policy towards Jews changed, but the change had no effect on immigration. By then, Europe offered no way out.

A BOTTLENECK IN JAPAN

In 1940, no one in Japan could be expected to remember the ill-fated voyage of the *St. Louis* in May 1939. The unfortunate story took place on different continents with a group of people with whom Japanese rarely dealt. Surely, the story offered no lessons applicable to Japan.

But in July 1940, a message arrived at the third section of the America Bureau from the Japan Tourist Bureau. George McCarthy, the Oriental Passenger Traffic Manager of the American President Line, asked "if the Japanese government is prepared to issue return permits through Japan via Korea and Manchuria to Germany for any German Jewish or other immigrants who have previously arrived in Japan via Siberia and taken steamers to San Francisco."[4] Matsuoka answered without a hint of concern, writing Consul Satō in San Francisco that "They could not obtain transit visas unless they had completed procedures for their destination countries."[5] If the United States were to reject entry, it was an American problem. Little did Matsuoka know that one of his vice consuls was busy stamping transit visas in passports that were missing entry visas. Not much was heard immediately after the American President Line's inquiry, but it was an ominous warning. However isolated politically and geographically it was, Japan was not too distant to develop a refugee problem.

The next warning came in December, and it concerned Palestine. The British ambassador, Robert L. Craigie, notified Matsuoka that immigrants to Palestine who had received immigration permits from the British authorities in Riga and Kaunas were requesting transit visas from Japanese diplomats in the Soviet Union. But Palestine would not permit immigrants without "satisfactory proof of prior identification by a British authority." Craigie wrote, "I feel it desirable to notify Your Excellency at once, so as to avoid the risk of such persons being stranded in Japan."[6]

British permits needed to be verified before they would be accepted; this added another bureaucratic hurdle to the immigration process. The Palestine requirement was not unique; other nations would also require checks. Also, the reference to Kaunas was one of many to come. Those with documents besides Curaçao visas often had incomplete visas or only initial permission from other countries. Although their faulty paperwork had been enough to satisfy Sugihara to issue transit visas, it could only take them so far. Craigie's polite admonition to the Foreign Ministry was the calm before the storm.

On the first of February, news of the gathering storm was picked up in Shanghai. Consul General Horiuchi had heard from the local Jewish relief authorities that 500 Jews were going to Japan from Lithuania. "Although they had visas for Central and South America at first," Horiuchi explained, "they secretly intend to investigate ways to sneak into Shanghai."[7] No one in the foreign concessions was prepared to welcome them.

Soon after, the president of the Kobe Jewish Community told the Foreign Ministry that "a quite new movement of jewish [sic] refugees had started: this time of Polish and Lithuanian jews exoding [sic] from Soviet occupied Poland and Lithuania."[8] By the middle of the month, Mr. Ponevejsky and his community were caring for 800 refugees. He described their destitute condition: "For a year and a half they have been moving from one country to another, so that all their resources, both material and moral, have been exhausted in the struggle to keep alive."[9]

The flow was unstoppable. Ambassador Tatekawa reported from Moscow that 800 Polish refugees in Soviet territory were proceeding towards Palestine and South America with Soviet visas and Japanese visas from Kaunas.[10] Those who arrived in Japan joined those who were already there until they could determine a destination. By the end of March, 1,637 Jewish refugees were stranded in Japan indefinitely.[11]

The Foreign Ministry responded by making it more difficult for Jews still in Europe to obtain Japanese transit visas. Meanwhile, the Hyōgo prefectural authorities were uncomfortable with the visitors to the cosmopolitan port of Kobe. "Six hundred people staying do not stand out, but when there are up to one thousand, first there is the security issue, and when the number rises beyond that, it draws a lot of attention," wrote the manager of the Hyōgo Foreign Affairs Section.[12] One thousand was the Japanese threshold, and it had been reached. How had this happened? The causes of the problem lay in Kaunas, Latin America, and the United States.

LATIN AMERICA REACTS

In February 1941, the CAEJR relief group in Shanghai worried that another *St. Louis* incident was about to occur. A ship transporting 500 emigrants to Haiti was "still floating around somewhere trying to land its human freight" and might end up returning to the port of embarkation in Japan. "We fail to see what can be done in regard to an ultimate destination for the unfortunate beings who are at present roaming the world without an atom of hope," wrote chairman Michael Speelman.[13]

Most Latin American countries had closed their borders in early 1939, but Japanese diplomats did not take notice until the latter half of 1940, when Japan became affected by it. At the same time, some consuls from Latin American nations engaged in selling visas and landing permits, with the encouragement of the Gestapo. No matter how exorbitant the price, Jews were willing to pay.

In September 1940, the consulate in Hamburg became incensed by the fraud committed by Latin consuls and desperate German Jews. Since the consuls were issuing "so-called empty visas," Jews had a tendency to stay in the countries of transit, knowing they would be refused entry at their next stop. Walter Israel Casper, a stateless Jew, held a transit visa from Panama and an entry visa for Haiti, but Consul General Kawamura was determined to reject his application for a Japanese transit visa. "Those being held in 'konzentrations-lager' can be released if they obtain transit or entry visas," he explained. "There are many occasions when relatives have been imploring at our office, but people who are a bother for Germany will be exceedingly bothersome for Japan."[14]

Mr. Yamakawa, another member of the consulate staff, was angry because the Haitian Consul General in Hamburg was known to charge ridiculous prices for entry visas. Jews would pay, because they needed the entry visa specifically to obtain transit visas from Panama, Japan, Manchukuo, and the Soviet Union. Many planned to go to Shanghai. "It is just a matter of time before the Japanese consulate in Hamburg is swindled by fraud and coated with the stigma of corruption from Jews in Shanghai," he wrote. Yamakawa was "indignant since he is sustaining the most damage and if he cannot erase the criticism, he will declare that we should stop issuing visas."[15] The consulate was as concerned about the impact of stateless Jews arriving in Japan as about the damage to the reputation of its office, so much so that it was willing to arbitrarily suspend visa issuance.

Several Japanese diplomats posted to Latin American nations notified the Foreign Ministry about visa scandals, but they did not act until after the communication from Hamburg. Only Ambassador Shiozaki in Chile wrote before that. In July 1940, he reported promptly after the Chilean authorities had notified steamship companies, including Nippon Yūsen Kaisha (Japan Mail), in June that as of April 9 all visas issued before December 6, 1939, were deemed invalid. The reason: some Chilean diplomats abroad had accepted bribes and exceeded their authority in issuing entry visas for Jews.[16]

In December 1940, news began to reach the Foreign Ministry from Panama, which Yamakawa in Hamburg had mentioned three months before. The situation was similar to that of the authorities in Palestine. According to Acting Minister Ōno, without permission from the government of Panama all visas, transit and entry, were void. A major transit point, Panama had found that Haiti, Costa Rica, Santo Domingo, and Honduras were refusing to permit Jewish immigrants and were creating a problem for Panama, where the refugees were delayed.[17]

Matsuoka considered this information significant enough to convey to Japanese offices in Europe two weeks later. He advised that Jews en route to Central and South America from then on should have sufficient funds *and*

1. Permission from their destination country, as well as entry visas.

2. Permission to disembark in Panama, as well as a transit visa from Panama.

"If they don't meet these conditions," stated Matsuoka, "you are not to issue Japanese transit visas."[18] Japan was beginning to react to the policies of other governments, as it realized that repercussions could occur.

Panama refused to permit Jewish refugees to disembark from Japanese ships unless they had received the necessary advance permission from the Panamanian government. When this happened, the ships could not depart for their next port on schedule and ended up taking passengers who also had no place to go. This issue had economic, political, and diplomatic dimensions. It was eerily similar to the *St. Louis* incident, in which the refugees had not been allowed to land in various countries on their transit visas because they did not have permanent visas for their ostensible destination, Cuba. Japanese diplomats in Latin America, however, seemed neither to notice the parallels nor foresee the incidents until they occurred.

Belatedly, the legation in Panama began to gather and communicate relevant information. In early 1941, Acting Minister Nagamine told Tokyo that the Costa Rican ambassador in Panama had confided that Central American countries generally applied the same policy as Costa Rica. Costa Rica had specifically excluded *la raza judia* from eligibility for visas since late 1938. By February 1940, the categorical exception also included Poles.[19]

At least Ambassador Ishii in Rio de Janeiro acted quickly. He notified Tokyo in January that a Brazilian circular dated early that month stated that all visas would be postponed for anyone other than Portuguese, nationals of countries in the Americas, those with employment contracts, and agricultural specialists. "This is to manage as much as possible the increase in illegal entry by European Jews recently."[20]

Jewish refugees could not look to Latin America with much hope. Even Curaçao, an island off the coast of Venezuela, would not welcome them.

CURAÇAO

"It has grown very bad when Polish refugees began to sworm [sic] here, owing to the fact that Curacao [sic] visas didn't entitle people to proceed," wrote J. Epstein, a worker with the international Jewish relief organization HICEM, in Kobe in 1941. To make matters worse, "these were the only visas that Polish refugees held."[21] Curaçao visas were only useful up to a point, and that was Japan.

In 1939, Curaçao's Jewish population consisted of approximately 800 families, 700 of whom were Sephardic. Immediately after the defeat of the Netherlands in May 1940, the Dutch government in exile had interned as enemy aliens all those holding German and Austrian passports.[22] Mr. Is. Jessurun Cardozo of the local Jewish community hastened to differentiate between refugees and internees: "Since the outbreak of war no *refugees* have arrived here. As regards the *internees* I can give the following information," he explained. "At the beginning all [non-Israelites and Israelites] were kept in the same camp, but soon it appeared that this condition could not possibly last." Conditions had "improved" to the point that the "Israelite internees" were permitted to live with other members of their families in a separate camp on the neighboring island of Bonaire and wander freely, rather than be confined to the camp. "The treatment of the internees by our Authorities deserves every praise," commented Mr. Cardozo.[23]

No one wanted to escape Europe safely only to be interned on a small South American island along with Germans and Austrians who might have Nazi allegiances. But in October 1940, no one was aware of this fate. At a meeting held at the Joint's New York office concerning the fate of Lithuanian yeshivoth, Rabbi Teitelbaum hoped that 200 people in Lithuania would obtain American visas after the next presidential election. "If worse comes to worst, they should be brought to Curaçao," while assuring his colleagues that "nobody would be sent to Curacao [sic] without previous consent of the Governor of C."[24]

American Jewish organizations learned in December that Curaçao was not feasible. Irwin Rosen of the Committee on Refugee Aid in Europe reported, "We have received information from Curacao [sic] that persons arriving there with such stamps in their passports will be interned." The refugees faced trouble even before reaching Curaçao. "Recently, as a result of this development, the holders of these so-called Curacao [sic] visas, have been quarantined in Panama and are threatened with deportation."[25] At this time, the refugees had not yet flooded Japan. The problem would only worsen, though some did not give up on Curaçao.

When the Kobe Jewish community found itself caring for 800 refugees in February 1941, it still hoped to send some to Curaçao. Jewcom was worried about the many refugees still in the Soviet Union awaiting Japanese transit visas and believed that these visas would be provided "only in proportion to the departures of those previously arrived here." Although President Ponevejsky defined people without destinations as "so-called hopeless cases," he had heard that the Netherlands colonies, the Dominican Republic, and Bolivia might permit immigrants.[26]

Japanese officials were the last to realize how unrealistic Curaçao was. Joseph Grew relayed to the State Department in April, "The Japanese now know that visas are required For Entry into Dutch colonies and hence it is believed that the Japanese steamship company which provides the only regular passenger facilities between Vladivostok and Tsuruga, Japan, are no longer willing to sell passage to such persons."[27]

The Foreign Ministry finally understood Curaçao visas were not visas at all. Indeed, the Jewish organizations had taken to placing the term "visas" in quotation marks when referring to Curaçao. The Home Ministry, however, placed a different emphasis on the problem when it described the backlog of refugees, approximately 1,321, in Japan in April 1941.[28] "The majority want to go to the Dutch West Indies with Curaçao as a destination, and they have entry visas," the Home Ministry observed. "But in order to enter Curaçao, they must transit through Panama, Chile, or other countries. When the refugees arrive here, they do not have these transit visas and they unavoidably stay here a long time for the procedures."[29] The problem was not Curaçao so much as the other Latin American countries where ships stopped en route there.

Curaçao never materialized as a reasonable destination for the refugees. Perhaps the concept had been ahead of its time. In 1944, when the War Refugee Board actively worked to organize and fund rescue programs, the idea of a "free port" or "temporary haven" was conceived. The community of Oswego, New York, was readied to harbor 1,000 refugees, and 987 arrived. Although the experiment proved more symbolic than successful when it came to integrating the refugees, the War Refugee Board also persuaded Curaçao, the Dutch West Indies, and Surinam to participate.[30] Curaçao became a possibility too late. But, at least, it had served one purpose in helping Jews to flee Europe.

THE UNITED STATES

Most refugees wanted to go to the United States—or rather, America. "America" was a magic word that symbolized possibilities, freedom, and safety. Samuil Manski recalls his mother being rebuffed by officials in Lida. "America is here," they told her. Solly Ganor remembers a Polish Jew angrily telling his family in Kaunas, "You are sitting on a volcano which is about to erupt, and you are all behaving as if you were living in America." Masha Leon's impression is indelible: "All I heard around us was we have got to get to America; we have got to escape."[31]

Thoughts of reaching America propelled the refugees, despite great hurdles. Some of the most formidable were placed before them by American diplomats. The same summer that Sugihara began issuing visas nonstop, Breckinridge Long, chief of the Special War Problems Division of the State Department, advised two State Department officials, "We can delay and effectively stop for a temporary period of indefinite length the number of immigrants into the United States. We could do this simply by advising our consuls to put every obstacle in the way and to resort to various administrative advices which would postpone and postpone the granting of the visas."[32] By and large, American consuls heeded the directives of their superiors and energetically followed their orders.

Even Eleanor Roosevelt had difficulty imposing her indefatigable will on the State Department. Doris Kearns Goodwin describes Mrs. Roosevelt's involvement in helping eighty-three Jewish refugees enter the United States in 1940 as her "sole triumph" in her dogged attempt to stir her husband on refugee issues. Breckinridge Long was furious over her success, which averted another *St. Louis*–like debacle when all the refugees were allowed to disembark from the Portuguese freighter the S.S. *Quanza*.[33] Eighty-three was a small number, and Mrs. Roosevelt was an influential First Lady. What could thousands more refugees who were thousands of miles away expect without such connections?

Rabbi Teitelbaum and his colleagues discovered how difficult it was to bring Europe's revered yeshivoth to the United States. He and Rabbi Wise, among others, met with Breckinridge Long, who asked how many people were on the group's list. Rabbi Teitelbaum answered that 3,800 had been chosen from a total of 10,000 students. Rabbi Wise characterized the reaction of Long as, "If the whole State Department favored the taking of a ship and putting the whole 3,800 men on it, he would manage to have the ship sunk. He is the worst enemy we have."[34]

Meanwhile, in Japan, where some of Rabbi Teitelbaum's beloved students were heading, no one seemed to perceive a problem. To be sure, only 197 refugees had not left Japan by the end of January 1941.[35] Word did come from the embassy in Washington about a seemingly unrelated matter: the United States had rejected France's request to permit German Jews to immigrate from nonoccupied France. The State Department announcement read, "While the United States sympathizes with France's predicament, it has received blows to its social and economic balance, and it cannot help a large number of immigrants."[36]

Little did the Japanese embassy in Washington and the Foreign Ministry in Tokyo realize that the French query and American rejection would affect Japan. But in February, the consulate in Casablanca contacted Tokyo. "There are many Jews from Germany who are trying to move to the United States or Far East, and they are a stampede, rushing in to request Japanese and Shanghai entry visas." The acting consul's response was not so different from his American counterparts: "I am making excuses and completely refuse."[37]

The attitude of the American embassy in Moscow did not help Japan. Ambassador Steinhardt was annoyed when thirty-five refugees visited the embassy in a rush to pick up their visas before catching the next train from Moscow to Vladivostok. The refugees mistakenly believed that their American immigrant visas would be ready and waiting at the embassy, "without due regard to affording the Consular Section of this Embassy sufficient time to entertain their formal applications, much less even a cursory interrogation." Steinhardt did not oblige them; he assumed that the situation could be resolved in Tokyo.[38] This situation happened repeatedly.

Steinhardt did not comprehend the heightened anxiety of Jewish refugees in the Soviet Union. They feared that at any moment they could be arrested, interrogated for days, and summarily deported to Siberia. At some point, their incomplete papers might be discovered, and they might not be able to continue their journey. At all times, they had no idea what awaited them; they only knew that they must keep moving.

As the refugee flow increased, Steinhardt continued to demonstrate little sympathy. His evaluations of refugees became harsher. No longer simply irritated with their demands, he became suspicious of their status. When a refugee revealed that as many as 20 percent of those recommended for visas by the President's Advisory Committee had been recruited by the Soviet Commissariat for Internal Affairs (GPU) to act as agents in the United States, Steinhardt reported the interview in detail. The refugees allegedly complied in order to obtain Soviet exit visas.[39] Several months later, Steinhardt reinforced this point: "It is dangerous, not to say reckless, to continue to grant American visas indiscriminately to applicants recently residing in or who are now residing in the Soviet Union or Soviet-occupied territories."[40]

Steinhardt was a Jew and a diplomat, but he kept these identities separate. In 1941, according to Henry Feingold, Steinhardt opposed refugee advocates and stressed that consuls had the "final word" even when it was obvious that some consuls were anti-Semitic. Not until 1942, when he was transferred to Ankara and he observed what was happening to Jews, did his position change. He became a tireless supporter of various rescue efforts. Unfortunately, Laurence Steinhardt's change of heart came too late for the many refugees who had raced to the embassy from the Moscow railway station in the hope of procuring a visa and departing the Soviet Union in 1941.

Refugees who reached Japan did not necessarily receive much more assistance from the consulates there. In June, Mr. Ponevejsky told the Joint that American consulates were refusing visas to people with relatives in Germany and the Soviet Union.[41] New visa regulations denying visas to immigrants with "close relatives" in occupied Europe did not go into effect until July, but they were already being applied in Kobe. Although this requirement eliminated the majority of refugees, there were still some remaining whose families lived elsewhere or who had no family at all; but it was difficult to convince the consulate when this was the case. Applicants were closely interrogated and told to have any family members appear at the local American consulate, wherever that may be. This process took valuable time.

As time passed, the friction between the United States and Japan diminished the likelihood that many people would be able to wait indefinitely in Japan for American visas to materialize. In March, the Jewish Problem Committee noted "a worst case scenario" that could occur if "transportation in the Pacific were suspended," but it offered no possible solutions to the problem of Jewish refugees in Japan.[42] By the end of July, relations between Japan and the United States had deteriorated. When Japan invaded southern Indochina, the United States, Great Britain, and the Netherlands froze Japanese assets. With the oil embargo of August 1, relations between the two nations were in crisis. It was becoming imperative that all refugees leave Japan and impossible for them to go to the United States.

RECEPTION OF THE REFUGEES IN JAPAN

The international political situation may have been ominous, but when refugees arrived in Japan they saw reason to regain their optimism. For the first time in more than a year, "We did not think about the war," said Masha Leon.[43] Japan delighted the senses and met their profound need for relief. "My first impression was of a fairyland, with small houses, flowers, clean streets, and very polite people," writes Samuil Manski.[44] Fresh fruit, delicious bread, fluffy futons, and luxurious beds were creature comforts they could appreciate after so many deprivations. Japan was a pleasant interlude: it did not matter whether one was bound for the United States, as Masha and Samuil were, or was destined for Shanghai.

Sara Cohen and Hirsh Kupinsky would eventually spend eight years in Shanghai with their parents and uncle. But before that, they spent months in Kobe. Sara's memories are golden—cherry blossoms in bloom and women in colorful kimonos.[45] Her images may resemble those of travel brochures, but she is not alone in remembering the beauty of Japan. She reveled in the freedom that Japan afforded after her family's hasty, hushed flight from Soviet-occupied Poland. Almost fifty years after her stay in Japan, Sara and Hirsh still agree with the words of the president of the Kobe Jewish Community in 1941: "Japan is the first free country they have reached, and its representatives abroad have shown so much humane feeling to our unfortunate fellow-countrymen that we can only express our appreciation."[46]

Even parents, burdened with more concerns than their children could imagine, found Japan a respite. This was partly because of the Jewish Community of Kobe. "Stirred" by the refugees, whose "stories made them loom as miracles of endurance," Jewcom did everything it could to assist them.[47] Jewcom maintained close relations with all the local authorities, including the Tsuruga water police, who inspected the papers of arriving refugees and decided whether to accept them or send them back to Vladivostok. In January 1941, the Joint in New York took Jewcom's relationship for granted when it cabled the organization to negotiate with the police regarding a "CONSIDERABLE NUMBER OF REFUGEES FROM LITHUANIA IN NEAR FUTURE." Indeed, 356 Poles, Germans, and others would arrive in January, a significant increase over the 198 arrivals in December.

Jewcom was successful because it nurtured relations with officials. In a statement of expenses incurred between November 1, 1940, and February 15, 1941, it listed $923.90 for New Year's gifts to officials.[48]

Its costs aroused concern at the Joint, which was coordinating and defraying rescue efforts worldwide. But Jewcom knew what it needed in Japan to be effective. The New Year was the traditional season to express gratitude for favors provided, and admitting Jewish refugees without destinations was most generous.

Officials responded to the climate of cooperation. Alex Treguboff, a former member of Jewcom, recalled that as soon as a ship anchored in Tsuruga he or other representatives would board it to assist the entry process. Although refugees were always advised to state Curaçao as their destination, some inevitably mentioned the United States. Local officials would call Mr. Treguboff over, and he would quietly correct the refugees. "Everyone knew half the visas were false," he said. Some people even came without visas. Mr. Treguboff would quickly issue them, while the Japanese officials waited, watched, and stamped the papers with the "ink still wet."[49]

Some refugees carried identical papers, right down to the name, number, and date. These amateur attempts at fooling the punctilious Japanese officials were the product of the underground stampmaking shops. Yet Itzak Zbarsky, who aided refugees in Kobe, recalled, "The officer would look at it quickly and cover it as quickly because it was so obviously false. This was a very heartbreaking experience."[50]

Once in Japan, the refugees found that they were able to extend their two-week transit visas without any problem. Dr. Abraham Kotsuji assisted the local Jewish community, visiting the Foreign Ministry "almost daily," by his own account. He claimed to have talked with his former boss Matsuoka, who assured him the ministry would not interfere if the prefectural governments agreed to extend visas.[51] A number of former refugees corroborate the help of Kotsuji. While the conversation between Kotsuji and Matsuoka may have occurred, the Foreign Ministry had no reason to interfere in what was the jurisdiction of the prefectural government from the beginning.

Some refugees remained in Japan as long as nine months. During that time, they found that officials were helpful and local citizens were hospitable. The American consulate in Kobe observed, "Notwithstanding Japan's close political relations with Germany, there have been no cases reported of discrimination against Jewish refugees, and newspaper comment has not been unkind."[52] "I think that our treatment in Japan was superb," says Susan Bluman of her time in Kobe. For Samuil Manski, there were only two problems with being a stranger in Kobe: he was always followed when he left his lodgings, and no foreigners were allowed to go near the beautiful, bustling port.[53] But he did not mind being shadowed, because being accompanied meant that he would never become lost. His Japanese hosts, however, did not feel the same way about him.

Refugees were not aware that Japan was preparing for war. They were preoccupied with worrying about relatives they had left behind in Europe and with making the rounds of embassies and aid organizations in the hope of securing destination visas. But in April 1941, the Basic Necessities Control Ordinance resulted in the rationing of rice, fish, vegetables, condiments, and clothing, a move that affected every Japanese household.[54] Individual Japanese continued to treat refugees with kindness; "The Japanese authorities, however, did not seem keen on harboring foreigners in Japan," wrote Zorach Warhaftig.[55]

Those earnest words were an understatement. The Hyōgo prefectural government was anxious about the foreigners. They had so little money that they rarely dined in hotels, preferring to take some bread and vegetables to their rooms. When one person registered at a hotel, many friends would appear—not to visit but to use their friend's bathtub. Moreover, they had a tendency to stain carpets. The prefecture was keeping secret a shelter it had for up to 1,000 people. Its paramount concern was: "How should we make almost two thousand Jews depart?"[56]

The governor of the prefecture advised the Home Ministry and Foreign Ministry on how to handle the unexpected guests. People who contracted illnesses should be treated quickly to prevent the spread of disease; also they should take care not to start fires. They should request special permission from Jewcom on behalf of the prefecture if they intended to travel outside Kobe. They should not loiter, but rather rest at their lodgings. They should not "throng" stores unless they planned to make a purchase, and after paying, they should leave promptly.[57]

Most refugees do not seem to have recognized the discomfort they caused the authorities; they were simply charmed by the small daily gestures of friendship from locals. Even if they felt they were being watched, they were still relatively free. Above all, they felt comparatively safe. However uncertain they were of their next step, the prospect of being shipped to Shanghai was more appealing than that of being sent to Siberia.

THE SOVIET UNION

On January 8, 1941, Paul Baerwald, the chairman of the Joint in New York, and his colleague Bernhard Kahn sent a cable to Henry Monsky in Omaha, Nebraska. One hundred rabbis and students had left Lithuania, they said. However, "TWO HUNDRED MORE MUST LEAVE IMMEDIATELY ELSE WILL BE SENT SIBERIA STOP THEIR EXIT PERMITS EXPIRE JANUARY THIRTEENTH NONRENEWABLE STOP." The Joint officials needed $25,000 from Mr. Monsky's organization to finance the yeshivoth's trip to Japan. Their last words were "TERRIBLE URGENCY."[58]

The Soviets had decreed that refugees must either declare Soviet citizenship or become stateless. In a classic catch-22, those who took Soviet citizenship could not leave Soviet territory, but those who became stateless risked exile to Siberia if they did not use their exit permits in time. As the number of refugees mounted in Japan, Jewish organizations hastened to bring those remaining in Soviet territory there as well.

Japan was being squeezed. It could not force refugees to leave when countries in the Western Hemisphere refused them. The refugees were determined to make it to Japan, and the Soviets stood firm in their insistence that they should. All that Japan could do was try to deter the refugees while they were still in Soviet territory. Once they left Soviet waters and reached the open sea, on cargo ships hastily refitted for passengers, there was no turning back—and the refugees rejoiced.

Acting Consul General Nei in Vladivostok

On February 8, 1941, Acting Consul General Nei wrote from Vladivostok about a new development—that recently every Japanese ship departing Vladivostok for Tsuruga carried 140 to 150 Jews, the majority of whom had received transit visas from the consulate in Kaunas and the remainder from the embassy in Moscow. In addition, the consulate in Vladivostok was receiving cables from sixty to seventy people a day who were in Soviet-occupied territory and in search of transit visas. Nei referred the refugees to the embassy in Moscow, but they would not receive transit visas easily there. Could he issue transit visas?[59] The Foreign Ministry replied two days later and reminded Nei of its regulations and the requirements of Latin American countries and Palestine.[60]

Almost two weeks later, Nei made a terse query. Twenty-two Jews had arrived in Vladivostok "obstinately requesting Japanese transit visas." Once again, he asked what he should do.[61] Nei hesitated to act without the ministry's approval in Tokyo, and he knew that the refugees' papers were not completely in order. But he did not refuse the refugees' requests outright. Tokyo's response was not helpful. "The good services of the Jewish community here still are not successful, and there are approximately twelve hundred refugees congesting Japan at present." The third section of the American Bureau reminded Nei, "Until you confirm destination countries, do not issue visas."[62] In fact, there were approximately 800 refugees in Japan, but the America Bureau may have included recent arrivals with proper papers who would only stay the duration of their transit visa before embarking for their final destinations. In Vladivostok, the refugees waited while Nei struggled with how to handle them.

He was then confronted by a situation that demanded immediate attention. In mid-March, the vessel *Amakusa maru* had returned to Vladivostok from Tsuruga with more than seventy Jews on board.[63] Although they had transit visas courtesy of Sugihara, they did not possess destination visas of any kind; the police in Tsuruga had justified their refusal on the grounds of missing destination visas. Upon the refugees' return to Vladivostok, the Soviet authorities also refused to let them leave the ship. Nei had no choice but to resolve the problem or have a Japanese ship detained and passengers suffer.

It was unusual for so many refugees to be rejected in Tsuruga, where the Tsuruga water police and Jewcom representatives worked hand in hand. "People having the same visas as those that had come to Japan only a month ago—were no more allowed to land here," wrote J. Epstein.[64] The problem was that the number of departures from Japan was not keeping pace with the number of arrivals.

The *Amakusa maru* tried to leave Vladivostok again with the seventy-odd refugees and another group. After completing departure preparations, however, the ship's captain discovered that too many passengers were on board. When he requested passengers to disembark, the Soviets refused on the basis of Soviet law. As the *Amakusa maru* sat in Vladivostok harbor, Nei worried that food would run out on board. Joseph Shimkin, the Joint worker in Lithuania, now on board as a passenger, worried more about the tension between aggravated sailors and anxious refugees. Meanwhile, the captain wanted Nei to certify that the ship carried a temporary excess in passengers, so that it could legally enter Japan.[65]

The Foreign Ministry was not eager to follow the captain's easy solution. Instead, it blamed Central American countries and Palestine for changing their entry regulations after Japan had already issued transit visas, and it immediately tightened its own restrictions. All Japanese visas issued before December 20, 1940, had to be reviewed by the Moscow embassy or Vladivostok consulate to ensure that the papers were in order. Those who passed the check would receive a seal in their passports, which was required to land in Japan. Please explain to the Soviets that this seal is necessary in order for a passenger to board the ship, the ministry advised Nei.[66]

The Soviets were not interested in Japan's new requirements. Most of the refugees on board had received their visas in Kaunas. Since the refugees were not Soviet citizens, there was no reason why the Soviets should be responsible for them. Meanwhile, 150 additional refugees were loitering in Vladivostok with transit visas from the Kaunas consulate and entry visas for Curaçao, the Dutch colonies, and Palestine.[67] Nei realized that the Soviets would not yield, and he sensed that the numbers of refugees would increase. He made his decision and cabled the Foreign Ministry that the *Amakusa maru* would depart with refugees on board whose visas he had not inspected, though there were also some with certificates from his consulate.[68] The next day, he sent details of his conversations with the Soviet authorities. Nei told his superiors in Tokyo that "we are requesting that Intourist take a serious stand when it sells passenger tickets to refugees." Nei was transferring some of the responsibility for the complications to the Soviets.[69]

Did Nei have a choice between following Tokyo's orders or giving in to the Soviets? It was difficult to defy the Soviets, in whose territory he worked. It was more likely that the refugees would be readmitted to Tsuruga, since there were precedents, though such examples were exceptional and in small numbers. Nei did not want to see a Japanese ship become the center of an international incident, with the possible result that other Japanese vessels would not be allowed to use Vladivostok harbor in the future. Yet it is facile to suggest that his decision was easy, since he did take the initiative and disobey Tokyo's orders. Year later, Nei recalled his dilemma: "Should I do it—out of sympathy for others? At the same time, should I wait?" Nei described the latter as "my character," but he chose the former.[70]

Nei's hedge was correct. When the refugees arrived in Tsuruga they did disembark, but only after a farce was played out. A Jewcom representative appeared with Curaçao visas, which the refugees were allowed to use. Although this incident was decisive in alerting the Japanese authorities to the illusion of Curaçao, the water police accepted the visas after Jewcom vowed that the refugees would leave Japan within two weeks.[71] This promise would not be kept.

Nei happened to have been in the class behind Sugihara at the school that later became Harbin Gakuin.[72] Did Nei try to support his older colleague by allowing the visas? Nei did not hesitate to inform Tokyo that the source of the refugees' transit visas was Kaunas; while the ministry already knew this, Nei's steady messages reinforced the point. Yet, he also seemed to sympathize with the refugees. Like Sugihara's cables, Nei's messages displayed a sensitivity that the communications of other diplomats lacked.

At the end of March while the *Amakusa maru* incident was still fresh, Nei reported another hundred refugees delayed in Vladivostok. "Once refugees arrive here, they cannot turn back and they come to our office daily and appeal regarding their distressful situations for transit visas and acceptance seals." Nei promised that he was following orders and had not yet issued one seal. "However," he continued, "those with visas from Japanese consuls are struggling here from afar. If we simply refuse to provide a stamp since they are going to Central America as their destination, this is not good for the credibility of our consulates' visas."[73]

Nei was referring to the last group of Jews to leave Lithuania. If they did not embark for Japan soon, they would exiled to Siberia. "They fear for their lives," wrote the Yokohama Jewish Refugee Assistance Committee. "We would appreciate the Japanese government's magnanimous measures in order to avoid this danger."[74]

Nei could not count on any help from the American consulate in Vladivostok, since it did not issue visas.[75] But he did receive the support of the Japanese embassy in Moscow, where the ambassador had gradually come to realize just how dire the situation was. Tatekawa cabled Tokyo that the people in Vladivostok possessed valid Japanese visas and had gone to Vladivostok without any knowledge of Japan's changes in policy. "They are falling into a predicament," he wrote, "and they repeatedly entreat us to mediate."[76] Eventually, the refugees did depart the Soviet Union for Japan. Unintentionally, they contributed to a change in the approach of the Japanese ambassador to Moscow.

Ambassador Tatekawa in Moscow

It took several months of hundreds of pleading Jews to make Tatekawa consider the problem from the perspective of the refugees. Like Ōshima, Tatekawa was a general by profession. But unlike those of his colleagues in Germany, cables originating from his office suggest a heightened awareness of the Jews and a gradual evolution in attitude.

On March 12, 1941, Tatekawa wrote Tokyo that the acting manager of the consular section had offered an unofficial estimate of 2,000 to 3,000 refugees in Moscow, the majority of whom had visas from the former Kaunas consulate. In addition, more than 300 had applied at the embassy for transit visas. "We are rejecting all according to instructions," he vowed. Indeed, in early February only two people were staying in Japan with transit visas from the embassy in Moscow, whereas 431 had come with transit visas from Kaunas.[77]

The ministry did not care how many refugees were in the Soviet Union, even if they did hold Japanese transit visas that should be guaranteed by the government. It was more concerned with the 1,000 plus Jews in Japan, who could not leave easily. A few days later, the third section of the American Bureau instructed Tatekawa that the Moscow embassy was the only office on the European continent permitted to issue transit visas from then on. In addition, he should cable the destination countries and Tokyo every two weeks with the number of applicable refugees; Tokyo would indicate how many refugees could receive transit visas.[78]

This was a major change in policy and effectively canceled the activities of other Japanese consulates in Europe. People outside Soviet-occupied territory who were able to fulfill all the prescribed conditions of bona fide immigration visas and had sufficient funds would no longer be able to obtain transit visas, because they could not enter the Soviet Union unless they already had a Japanese transit visa. Although no Japanese office had issued as many transit visas as Sugihara's tiny consulate in Kaunas had, the offices in Hamburg, Stockholm, Vienna, Moscow, and Berlin were still active. Between January 1940 and March 1941, 3,377 transit visas were issued by the above diplomatic offices, in comparison to 2,132 issued by the consulate in Kaunas.[79] The data for Kaunas were and are impressive, but every visa from any Japanese office was precious to the refugee who worked to procure it, especially since the other offices rigorously checked all papers.

The directive to Tatekawa was a direct reaction to what was happening before the eyes of the bureaucrats in Tokyo; Jews, Orthodox and otherwise, were wandering the streets of Kobe, Yokohama, and Tokyo. Although the America Bureau requested and received quarterly registers of visas granted by consulates abroad, the sight of foreigners was far more compelling and tangible than pages of lists and applications. Sometimes, the bureau did not even process the lists until after the refugees had arrived in Japan.

Tatekawa accepted the instructions. He was soon flooded with visa requests by mail, but the applications were faulty. "I am at a loss as to the documents of these three hundred, who report that their passports were lost in the mail and other deceitful statements," he began. "Since these are life and death matters for them, they play with very crafty methods." The embassy was granting only one transit visa for every ten applicants who came in person. Since it took more than two weeks to check whether each applicant met Japan's conditions and the Soviets did not allow such a stay, many refugees ended up proceeding to Vladivostok without visas. Tatekawa could do nothing about those with visas from the Kaunas consulate since they bypassed the embassy.[80]

Tatekawa did not trust the applications that were mailed, but many refugees had no choice. They usually did not have the funds for the trip to the Soviet Union until the Joint or another relief organization paid for their journey while their immigration procedures were progressing. In another catch-22, some could not obtain Soviet departure visas without the Japanese transit visa. Neither mail nor travel in the Soviet Union was reliable. Tatekawa believed his treatment of the refugees was "cautious"; for the refugees, it was stringent.

Yet less than two weeks later, he sounded more sympathetic. In early April, Tatekawa expressed his understanding of the refugees' distress when Japan changed its immigration conditions without forewarning. He described the ramifications of the two-week wait (that could extend to more than a month) required while the embassy reviewed visa applications before issuing seals to people who already had visas in the first place. "They have no homes to live in, no places to return to, and they are unable to move. Some people appeal to the insincerity of our replies, and they depart crying on the last day." Tatekawa was resolved: "If there is no fear that they will stay in Japan and cause trouble, suddenly stopping them on the pretense of regulations is too difficult an attitude for our office," he wrote. "I would like you to especially reconsider so that we may issue visas as before to those who do not cause harm and I will notify you every time visas are expected to be issued to up to fifty people."[81]

By this time, refugees were no longer permitted to remain in Vladivostok; the Soviets had applied an April 1 deadline. Moses Beckelman commented, "The Russians have been making deadlines right along and there is nothing that anyone can do about it." When a Joint colleague wondered whether Polish Jews who had already been sent to Siberia might be helped to emigrate, Beckelman referred to a conversation between the American consul in Moscow and a commissar from the Department of the Interior: "Who told you that there are any Poles in Siberia?" asked the commissar.[82]

As Tatekawa and Beckelman indicated, Polish Jews in the Soviet Union risked becoming Soviets in Siberia by default. But that did not mean that Tatekawa had completely turned his back on Japan's interest in stopping the refugee flow; he tried to comply with the ministry's wishes to forward information on visa applications. But he found the system unworkable, given the reality of how difficult it was for applicants to visit the embassy. In addition, "as long as this office cannot permit transit for those with valid Central American, South American, or other authorities' visas, ignoring the applications is a problem for Japan and the Soviet Union." He concluded that he could not cable the ministry regarding applicants.[83] Rejecting requests that were based on genuine documents had diplomatic repercussions.

On the eve of the German invasion of the Soviet Union in June, Tatekawa sent a candid report to Tokyo. "In reference to your inquiry regarding why we have not recently notified you, I believe that you already know my answer as to why it was not possible." He could not blame the refugees for not appearing at the embassy and having trouble with the mail. "In the present war situation, having them mail the passport and necessary documents to us frequently causes them to be lost in the mail, owing to searches. These documents are a matter of life and death for them, and this is impossible." The embassy was still receiving requests from places where Japanese consulates were located, such as Germany, Bulgaria, and Hungary. Tatekawa asked that the Foreign Ministry direct other Japanese offices in Europe to resume immigration procedures.[84]

Over the course of almost three months, Tatekawa's interpretation of Jewish refugees' appeals had altered. But this period was an eternity for refugees caught in German-occupied Europe and the Soviet Union. Less than two weeks after Tatekawa requested that other Japanese consulates be permitted to issue visas, Germany invaded the Soviet Union. Overnight, the eastern escape route vanished. Within days, in Kaunas and Vilna, the killing began.

In Japan, the government remained anxious about the refugees. In June 1941, 1,145 refugees were still in Japan, and the number dropped slightly, to 1,007, in July.[85] United States–Japan relations were spiraling downward. There was no place for Jewish refugees in Japan. The question was not "Where should they go?" but "Where could they be sent?" There was only one answer.

SHANGHAI

Japanese-occupied China continued to be the province of the military, and part of Shanghai continued to be the jurisdiction of the navy. Despite all the visa activity and complications in Europe, restrictions on immigration to the Japanese-occupied sector of Shanghai stayed firmly in place. The authorities seemed oblivious to the tension a short trip away in Japan.

The Home Ministry wanted to send as many as 1,100 refugees to Shanghai. Owing to the heightened political tensions, the sea routes from Japan to North America, South America, India, and Australia had recently been suspended. The ports of Kobe and Shimonoseki were operating under strict antiespionage measures; only the Nippon Yūsen Kaisha (Japan Mail) vessels could transport foreigners to Shanghai. When the United States froze Japanese assets at the end of July, the Joint had stopped remitting funds to the Jewish Community of Kobe.[86]

On August 12, Horiuchi told Foreign Minister Toyota that he was aware that Tokyo wanted 100 rabbis and yeshiva students to move from Kobe to Shanghai. "The Jewish Problem Committee will decide," he wrote. "It would be helpful for you to present the situation to all the Shanghai authorities of the Foreign Ministry, Army, and Navy."[87] Horiuchi did not hesitate to assert the authority of the powers in Shanghai to accept or refuse Tokyo's instructions.

But if the Japanese military in Shanghai had functioned relatively autonomously up until that point, it was no longer true. Tokyo had not bothered to ask Horiuchi's permission when it sent a ship earlier that month with 163 refugees. Horiuchi believed another was due on the 20th with an additional eighty Jews. Horiuchi requested the right to know: "I would like you to contact us in advance regardless of whether they will stay for a long time or are simply in transit," he requested.[88] Tokyo obliged on its own terms. It contacted Horiuchi but only on the day the ship left Kobe. Two hundred and ninety refugees were on board, not eighty as Horiuchi had believed. The ministry mentioned that it needed to send more people to Shanghai quickly.[89]

One day later, Tokyo contacted Shanghai that the Home Ministry would like to send approximately 850 refugees quickly—within a week.[90] Horiuchi's response indicated that Shanghai knew it was useless to claim the right to refuse Tokyo's will, but that the restrictions on residing and conducting business in the Japanese-occupied sector still stood.[91] Tokyo promptly ignored this statement, cabling several days later that 350 refugees would be heading to Shanghai on August 28.[92] The last boat departed Kobe for Shanghai on September 17, and it carried 199 Jews. There were still 128 nurses and patients, infants and companions, and yeshiva students in Japan whom the Hyōgo prefecture hoped to see leave soon.[93] By this point, Japan had made a conditional decision to go to war against the United States should negotiations fail by early October.

In Shanghai, Captain Inuzuka was angry. When a Shanghai relief committee asked the Japanese Naval Landing Party whether the new arrivals could possibly find housing in overcrowded Hongkew, Captain Inuzuka responded the day that the Nippon Yūsen Kaisha (Japan Mail) vessel had departed Japan with the last lot of refugees. He listed six reasons why Japan had no obligation to assist the refugees. Among them was the lack of response to his proposal to "Jewish capitalists" that "steps be taken to create a Real Estate Company under joint Japanese-Jewish capital." This was his settlement scheme. "Although an opportunity to settle the local issue was afforded to influential Jewish individuals in America by the Japanese authorities two years ago by taking the matter up directly with the central Japanese authorities, this chance was ignored by their casual remark that 'though we can readily comprehend Japan's good intentions, we can do nothing about it.' Hence the responsibility of the issue cannot be said to lie only with the Japanese side."[94]

Regardless of Captain Inuzuka's bitterness, his days as a Jewish expert in Shanghai were numbered; in the beginning of 1942, he would be transferred to sea duty. Before then, Japan would alter the Jewish policy it had set at the Five Ministers Conference in December 1938.

PEARL HARBOR AND A REVISED POLICY

By autumn 1941, only several hundred Jews remained in Japan. Most were longtime residents of Japan. A minority were professionals who had escaped Europe but arrived before the refugee influx, such as the musician Joseph Rosenstock, who went to Japan in 1936 and conducted the Nippon Philharmonic Orchestra. Most refugees had found a destination or moved to Shanghai for the duration.[95] "Out of sight, out of mind" applied during the busy months of aborted negotiations and feverish preparation for the attack on Pearl Harbor. Only after Pearl Harbor, when Japan and the United States were at war, did the subject of Jews reappear.

A report was produced in Shanghai in mid-January 1942. The preface explained that the start of the "Greater East Asia War" had eliminated the need to use the Jews to obtain foreign capital and cultivate American relations. Several measures were listed by which the authorities continued to prevent Jews from entering the occupied area, but the report also asserted that some Jews might be aligned with Japanese policy and could be used for the ends of the authorities. Jews from neutral countries could be either helpful or harmful; they should be observed.[96] There was nothing particularly new in this report. The most revealing point, which had been crossed out, concerned the Japanese preoccupation with propaganda. "We need to use our discretion according to citizenship while supporting eight corners under one roof and racial equality on the surface. We do not want propaganda that we are oppressing and driving away Caucasians."[97] If there had been any doubt about the genuine approach of Japanese towards Jews, there was none now. The rhetoric of the "Co-Prosperity Sphere" and "Greater East Asia War" was without substance.

Two days later, on January 17, Foreign Minister Tōgō sent a statement entitled "Emergency Jewish Policy" to the consulates in Manchukuo, Shanghai, Beijing, and Nanking. The policy was an alteration to the decisions of the 1938 Five Ministers Conference and the result of a joint decision by the Foreign Ministry, army, and navy. After an admonition not to allow the enemy to use the instruction as propaganda was issued, it listed three provisions summarized below:

1. Treat German Jews as stateless.
2. Treat favorably those neutral or stateless Jews whom Japan is using or would use in the future. As for others, strictly observe them to eliminate espionage maneuvers.
3. Treat Jews of allied countries whom they would use as nationals of those countries. Treat others according to the latter part of #2.

This was a delusory policy statement; any real prospect that Japan could seriously use the Jews to accomplish its ambitious plans had disappeared. Treating some Jews well was a departure from aspiring to cultivate their friendship and employ their talents. It did not mean much, except that Japan was very different in approach from its Axis partner Nazi Germany. But, then, that had been the case from the beginning.

NOTES

1. Masha Leon, telephone interview, 13 November 1997.

2. "Summary of Important Recent Communications Regarding Overseas Developments," 20 October 1941, AR 33/44, #462: China, General, 1941 August-December. In February 882 arrived, and 805 in March; in April, the figure dropped to 285 and in May to 114. "STATEMENT: June 1st, 1941," AR 33/44, #725: Japan, General, Emigration, 1941 July-December; "STATEMENT for the month of July 1941," AR 33/44, #725: Japan, General, Emigration, 1941 July-December; Letter from Eastern Jewish Central Information Bureau for Emigrants to AJJDC, 9 July 1941, AR 33/44, #488: China, General, Emigration, 1941 May-December, all in AJJDC Archives.

3. Masha Leon, unedited interview by Sheryl Narahara for "The Unlikely Liberators" tour, 1.5 hours, 22 September 1994, videocassette.

4. Telegram from Japan Tourist Bureau to M. Maki, third section chief of America Bureau, 19 July 1940, JPF, folder 10.

5. Telegram from Matsuoka to Satō, #25076, #28, 26 July 1940, JPF, folder 10.

6. Letter (English) from R. H. Craigie, British Embassy, to Matsuoka, 27 December 1940, JPF, folder 10.

7. Telegram from Horiuchi to Matsuoka, coded #50702, #146, Part 1, 1 February 1941, JPF, folder 11.

8. Letter (English) from A. Ponevejsky to the Foreign Ministry, 9 February 1941, JPF, folder 11.

9. Letter from A. Ponevejsky to the Joint, 18 February 1941, AR 33/44, #723: Japan, General, Emigration, 1939–1941 (March), AJJDC Archives.

10. Telegram from Tatekawa to Matsuoka, coded #2774, #149 secret, 3 February 1941, JPF, folder 11.

11. Jewcom Kobe, "Census of Jewish Refugees entering and leaving Kobe from 7/1/40–2/28/41" and "For 3/41," JPF, folder 11.

12. Telegram from Nippon Yūsen Kaisha (Japan Mail) Kobe branch chief to President (Passenger Section), 9 April 1941, JPF, folder 11.

13. Letter No. 67 from the M. Speelman, CAEJR, 7 February 1941, AR 33/44, #461: China, General, 1941 January-July, AJJDC Archives.

14. Telegram from Kawamura to Matsuoka, top secret #71, 12 September 1940, JPF, folder 10.

15. Telegram from Yamakawa, Hamburg Consulate General, to Ambassador Kurusu, Berlin, top secret #21, 12 December 1940, JPF, folder 10.

16. Telegram from Shiozaki to Matsuoka, top secret, 25 July 1940, JPF, folder 10.

17. Telegram from Ōno to Matsuoka, #36106, abbreviated, #211, 7 December 1940; ministry memo, JPF, 9 December 1940, JPF folder 10.

18. Telegram from Matsuoka to Kurusu, Germany, and Tatekawa, Moscow, abbreviated #41,000–41,001, #2669, 20 December 1941, JPF, folder 10.

19. Note: enclosures are in Spanish. Telegram from Nagamine to Matsuoka, #5, 7 January 1941, JPF, folder 11.

20. Telegram from Ishii to Matsuoka, coded #1298, secret #11, 18 January 1941, JPF, folder 11.

21. Letter from J. Epstein, Kobe branch of HICEM, to HICEM, Lisbon, 18 August 1941, HIAS Reports.

22. It is not clear whether the Jews who were interned were recent arrivals or long-term residents of Curaçao. *Annotated Catalogue*, "Archives of the American Joint Distribution Committee 1933–1944," AJJDC Archives, 201.

23. Emphasis in original document. Letter from Is. Jessurun Cardozo, Mikve Israel, to the Joint, 18 November 1941, AR 33/44, #533: Curaçao, AJJDC Archives.

24. "Meeting of Finance Committee on Lithuanian Yeshivoth," 21 October 1940, AR 33/44, #738: Lithuania, Emigration, 1940–1941 (January), AJJDC Archives.

25. Letter from Irwin Rosen to Isaac L. Asofsky, HIAS, 17 December 1940, AR 33/44, #533: Curaçao, AJJDC Archives.

26. Letter from A. Ponevejsky to the Joint, 18 February 1941.

27. Records of United States Department of State Relating to Refugees, "Telegram Received," by Ambassador Grew, 7 April 1941, File 811.111/1242.

28. "STATEMENT: June 1st, 1941," File #725, Japan File, AJJDC Archives.

29. Telegram from Home Ministry *Keihokyoku* to chief of America Bureau, #32, 14 April 1941, JPF, folder 11.

30. Feingold, *The Politics of Rescue*, 263.

31. Samuil Manski, *With God's Help* (Madison, WI: Charles F. Manski, 1990), 33; Solly Ganor, *Light One Candle: A Survivor's Tale from Lithuania to Jerusalem* (New York: Kodansha International, 1995), 37; Masha Leon, unedited interview by Sheryl Narahara.

32. Breckinridge Long, Long MSS, Long memo to Adolf A. Berle, Jr., and James C. Dunn, 26 June 1940, quoted in Feingold, *The Politics of Rescue: The Roosevelt Administration and the Holocaust, 1938–1945* (New Brunswick, NJ: Rutgers University Press, 1970), 142.

33. Doris Kearns Goodwin, *No Ordinary Time: Franklin and Eleanor Roosevelt: The Home Front in World War II* (New York: Touchstone, 1994), 174.

34. "Meeting of Finance Committee on Lithuanian Yeshivoth," 26 December 1940.

35. "STATEMENT: June 1st, 1941," AR 33/44, #725: Japan, General, Emigration, 1941 July-December, AJJDC Archives.

36. Telegram from Washington to the Foreign Ministry, #131, 10 January 1941, JPF, folder 11.

37. Telegram from Acting Consul Iida to Matsuoka, secret #31, 24 February 1941, JPF, folder 11.

38. Records of United States Department of State Relating to Refugees, "Telegram Received," by Ambassador Steinhardt, 6 October 1940, File 811.111 Refugees/422.

39. Department of State, "The Ambassador in the Soviet Union (Steinhardt) to the Secretary of State," 9 January 1941, Despatch 801, 811.111 Refugees, *Foreign Relations of the United States: Diplomatic Papers*, 1941, vol. 1, *General and the Soviet Union*, 598.

40. Department of State, "The Ambassador in the Soviet Union (Steinhardt) to the Secretary of State," 30 May 1941, Despatch 1456, 811.111 Refugees, *Foreign Relations of the United States: Diplomatic Papers*, 1941, vol. 1, *General and the Soviet Union*, 619.

41. Letter from Moses W. Beckelman to Moses A. Leavitt, 3 June 1941, AR 33/44, #724: Japan, General, Emigration, 1941 April-June, AJJDC Archives.

42. "Report on the Problem of Jewish Refugees," Summary of explanation by the Jewish Problem Committee, 24 March 1941, JPF, folder 11.

43. Masha Leon, telephone interview, 13 November 1997.

44. Samuil Manski, *With God's Help*, 45.

45. Sara Cohen, interview by author, December 25, 1993, Toronto, notes.

46. Hirsh Kupinsky, interview by author, December 15, 1993, Toronto, notes; Letter from A. Ponevejsky to the Joint, 18 February 1941.

47. "Jewish Transients in Japan," by Moise Moiseff, 25 July 1941, Record Group 245.4, series xvb-xvc, HIAS Reports, YIVO.

48. "Outgoing Cable," 13 January 1941, AR 33/44, #723: Japan, General, Emigration, 1939–1941 (March); "STATEMENT: June 1st, 1941," AR 33/44, #725: Japan, General, Emigration, 1941 July-December; "Spent for Relief," by the Jewish Community of Kobe, 15 February 1941, #723, Japan, AJJDC Archives, New York.

49. *Escape to the Rising Sun* (Belgium: Diane Perelsztejn, 1990), film.

50. Cheryl A. Silverman, "Jewish Emigres and Popular Images of Jews in Japan," Ph.D. diss., Columbia University, 1989.

51. Abraham Kotsuji, *From Tokyo to Jerusalem* (New York: Bernard Geis Associates, 1964), 162, 163.

52. Records of United States Department of State Relating to Refugees, "Voluntary Report," by Ray M. Melbourne, 24 May 1941, File 811.111/1536.

53. Susan Bluman, interview; Samuil Manski, interview.

54. Saburō Ienaga, *The Pacific War, 1931–1945* (New York: Pantheon Books, 1968), 193.

55. Zorach Warhaftig, *Refugee and Survivor: Rescue Efforts during the Holocaust* (Jerusalem: Yad Vashem, 1988), 155.

56. Telegram from Nippon Yūsen Kaisha (Japan Mail) Kobe branch chief to President (Passenger Section), 9 April 1941.

57. Report from Hyōgo Prefecture Governor to the Home Ministry, Acting Foreign Minister Konoe, various prefectures and police, etc., 18 April 1941, JPF, folder 11.

58. Cable from Paul Baerwald and Bernhard Kahn to Henry Monsky, Omaha, 8 January 1941, AR 33/44, #738: Lithuania, Emigration, 1940–1941 (January), AJJDC Archives.

59. Telegram from Nei to Matsuoka, abbreviated #3252, #50, JPF, folder 11.

60. Telegram from Matsuoka to Nei, abbreviated, secret #4162, #38, 10 February 1941, JPF, folder 11.

61. Telegram from Nei to Matsuoka, coded #4421, #69, 21 February 1941, JPF, folder 11.

62. Telegram from Matsuoka to Nei, coded #6067, #53, 25 February 1941, JPF, folder 11.

63. Note that accounts range from seventy-two, to seventy-four, to eighty persons, depending on the source. The March dates range from March 13, 14, and 16. The story, however, is the same.

64. Letter from J. Epstein, Kobe branch of HICEM, to HICEM, Lisbon, 18 August 1941.

65. Telegram from Nei to Konoe, coded #7168, #94, 19 March 1941, JPF, folder 11.

66. Telegram from Konoe to Nei, coded #8992, #69, secret, 19 March 1941, JPF, folder 11.

67. Telegram from Nei to Konoe, coded #7274, #96, 20 March 1941, JPF, folder 11.

68. Telegram from Nei to Konoe, coded #7278, #99, 20 March 1941, JPF, folder 11.

69. Telegram from Nei to Konoe, coded #7412, #100, 21 March 1941, JPF, folder 11.

70. Nei Saburō, interviewed in "Yudayajin o sukutta 1500-mai no visa," NHK radio drama, 45 min., 1989, tape.

71. Undated newspaper article, JPF, folder 11; letter Kobe branch of HICEM, to HICEM, Lisbon, 25 June 1941, HIAS Reports.

72. Sugihara Yukiko, Rokusen-nin no inochi no visa (Tokyo: Asahi Sonorama, 1990), 184.

73. Telegram from Nei to Konoe, coded #8372, #109, 30 March 1941, JPF, folder 11.

74. Letter from Yokohama Jewish Refugee Assistance Committee to the Foreign Ministry, 27 March 1941, JPF, folder 11.

75. "Memorandum of Telephone Conversation with Mr. M. W. Beckelman, Saturday, March 29, 1941—8 P.M.," AR 33/44, #461: China, General, 1941 January-July, AJJDC Archives.

76. Telegram from Tatekawa to Konoe, coded #8684, #385, 2 April 1941, JPF, folder 11.

77. Telegram from Tatekawa to Matsuoka, coded #6561, #292, 12 March 1941, JPF, folder 11. "Chart on Refugee Jews Regarding Those Who as of 2/8 to Present Are Staying in Japan as Refuge," top secret, 14 February 1941, JPF, folder 11.

78. Telegram from the Foreign Ministry (Third Section of the America Bureau), coded #8764, secret #283, 17 March 1941, JPF, folder 11.

79. "The Number of Transit Visas Issued to European Refugees," undated (precedes 10 March 1941 document), JPF, folder 11.

80. Telegram from Tatekawa to Konoe, coded #7495, #334, 21 March 1941, JPF, folder 11.

81. Telegram from Tatekawa to Konoe, coded #8733, #386, 2 April 1941, JPF, folder 11.

82. "Memorandum of Telephone Conversation with Mr. M. W. Beckelman, Saturday, March 29, 1941—8 P.M.," AR 33/44, #461: China, General, 1941 January-July, AJJDC Archives.

83. Telegram from Tatekawa to Konoe, coded #10613, #491, 19 April 1941, JPF, folder 11.

84. Telegram from Tatekawa to Matsuoka, #185, 10 June 1941, JPF, folder 11.

85. "STATEMENT for the month of JUNE 1941"; "STATEMENT for the month of JULY 1941," AR 33/44, #725: Japan, General, Emigration, 1941 July-December, AJJDC Archives.

86. Report from the Governor of Hyōgo Prefecture to the Home Minister, Foreign Minister, Communications Minister, Police Headquarters, various prefectural offices, etc., 30 August 1941, JPF, folder 11.

87. Telegram from Horiuchi to Toyota, coded #55848, #1505, 12 August 1941, JPF, folder 11.

88. Telegram from Horiuchi to Toyota, coded #55876, #1510, 13 August 1941, JPF, folder 11.

89. Telegram from Toyota to Horiuchi, coded #32493, top secret, #852, 20 August 1941, JPF, folder 11.

90. Telegram from Toyota to Horiuchi, coded #32628, top secret, #857, 21 August 1941, JPF, folder 11.

91. Telegram from Horiuchi to Toyota, coded #56132, #1563, 22 August 1941, JPF, folder 11.

92. Telegram from Toyota to Horiuchi, coded #33211, top secret, #882, 26 August 1941, JPF, folder 11.

93. Telegram from the Governor of Hyōgo Prefecture to the Home Minister, Foreign Minister, Communications Minister, Police Headquarters, various prefectural offices, etc., 21 September 1941, JPF, folder 11.

94. "Memorandum," from Inuzuka, handed to Captain Herzberg, 17 September 1941, AR 33/44, #462: China, General, 1941 August-December, AJJDC Archives.

95. Ben-Ami Shillony, *Politics and Culture in Wartime Japan* (Oxford: Clarendon Press, 1981), 165.

96. Report, "Treatment and Policy Proposal for Jews in Our Military-Occupied Area," 15 January 1942, JPF, folder 11.

97. Ibid.

98. "Emergency Jewish Policy," from Tōgō to Ambassador Umezu, Consul General Horiuchi, Counselor Tsuchida, Beijing, Ambassador Shigemitsu, Nanking, top secret, 17 January 1942, JPF, folder 11.

7

Conclusion

MAY WAS THE LAST FULL MONTH for Jews to escape Europe before the German forces invaded the Soviet Union on June 22, 1941. The Jews were frantic to leave, but their options were few. Even those who had crossed the Baltic Sea to neutral Sweden anticipated going elsewhere. They were waiting to go to Japan. "As long as the Far East is quiet," wrote Ernst Baerwald to the Joint in early May, "there is still a possibility to have in Japan an outlet for the many German Refugees who are waiting in Germany and Sweden and Norway for their Japanese Transit Visa." As optimistic as Mr. Baerwald sounded, he also mentioned in the letter the possibility of a "break in the American Japanese relations."[1] Time was closing in, and the wave of war was about to overtake the refugees. These refugees wavered on the crest, just before the European war spread and months before the Pacific War erupted.

Neither international political conditions nor the internal discussions within the Foreign Ministry favored Mr. Baerwald's refugees in Germany and northern Europe. It is doubtful whether they made it to Japan; by this date the Foreign Ministry was determined to prevent all refugee arrivals in Japan. The ministry was most concerned with why over 1,600 refugees were staying in Japan at the end of March.[2]

In mid-April, several weeks before Mr. Baerwald's hopeful letter, the ministry produced a report on the "Situation of European Refugees Coming to Japan." Stamped by the chiefs of the first and third sections of the America Bureau as well as the Bureau head, it enumerated eleven dates on which consuls had been instructed to follow ministry directives.[3] The report spanned the history of European emigration to China and Japan from 1938 to 1941. It began in October 1938, when consuls were advised to avoid entry visas and issue transit visas; it ended in March 1941, when the embassy in Moscow was appointed the sole distributor of transit visas in Europe and both the offices in Vladivostok and Moscow were instructed to review all transit visas before issuing a stamp of approval. What the report demonstrated, above all, was a gradual tightening of the application of Japanese immigration regulations as the refugee flow began, increased, and overflowed into an unprepared Japan.

Japan had never expected Jewish refugees to reach its shores. To be sure, there had been small Jewish communities in Japan, but they were too tiny to notice. Manchukuo, however, was different. A thriving Jewish community had preceded the Japanese to Harbin. When the Japanese created the puppet state of Manchukuo in 1932, the Harbin Jews could only hope that Japanese actions would realize the espoused ideals of a state embracing all races. Unfortunately, the advocacy and practice with respect to racial equality were distinct, and the Jewish community found itself under siege by anti-Semitic White Russians, with Japanese complicity. Dr. Kaufman, the leader of the Harbin Jewish community, found that one means to stop the harassment and persecution was to warn that the news of it would spread worldwide.

One of the themes of Japanese contact with the Jews was the underlying concern with negative publicity, especially in the United States. While Dr. Kaufman's admonition was correct, the Japanese fear that bad press would adversely affect United States–Japan relations was not. Japanese officials overestimated the influence that American Jews held in the United States. The Far Eastern Jewish Conferences, held from 1937 until 1939, were exercises in propaganda that were supposed to impress American Jews and American public opinion, but any goodwill generated was confined to Manchukuo.

Japanese diplomats in the United States reported on the dissemination of news about Jews in Asia. Although they were superbly trained to recognize and communicate trends, they underestimated or ignored the divisions within the American Jewish community and the nonpartisan attitude of the Jewish organizations. While there was an anti-Semitic element in the ministry in Tokyo, most diplomats abroad did not persecute Jews. Instead, they obediently followed instructions from Tokyo, including those concerning Japanese immigration.

The Japanese immigration law was vague but useful; when Japan desired to refuse entry or transit, the lack of detailed provisions made it easy. But it had never been tested by a large number of refugees. Although the governor of each prefecture had the right to accept or refuse entry, in reality it was difficult to reject people who held Japanese visas. The key was to obtain a visa in the first place. Visa inquiries from consuls abroad were processed by the third section of the America Bureau, which treated them as routine until the refugee flow began in earnest.

When refugees began departing Austria and Germany in 1938, primarily for Manchukuo and China, they caused consternation in Vienna, Tokyo, and Harbin. Japan was surprised by Nazi Germany's attitude towards the Jews and did not anticipate its repercussions in the Far East. Yamaji in Vienna signaled the beginning of the exodus, requested precise instructions, and suggested that the Japanese immigration law was not enough to deter refugees. Tokyo listened to Yamaji but refused to prohibit immigration and transit completely. The ministry, however, demonstrated a low threshold of tolerance when fifty-five Jews were reported to be heading to Japan in November 1938. Nor was the Kwantung Army excited about the prospects of refugees in Manchukuo or North China; indeed, it was frustrated by Soviet encouragement of Jewish emigration from European countries to Manchukuo.

On December 6, 1938, just before the refugee flow to Shanghai began to increase dramatically, the government determined its basic policy towards Jews at the Five Ministers Conference. It vowed to treat Jews according to the existing immigration law, except for those who could be useful, such as businessmen and technicians. The policy statement of the Five Minister Conference resulted from consensus among the most influential members of the cabinet. While some of the military's Jewish experts may have been behind the provision inviting those with money and skills to Japan, the Foreign Ministry drafted the statement that was sent to its consuls abroad.

How important was the conference in the end? The 1941 report "Situation of European Refugees Coming to Japan" does not even mention it. Instead, it refers to a December 7 postconference telegram sent to all consuls abroad as a repetition of one in October after Yamaji's inquiry provoked alarm in Tokyo. Further, if there was any question that the policy would result in a link between refugees, rescue, and settlements in China, the report belies it: all subsequent moves had everything to do with restricting refugees and nothing to do with rescue or settlements.

Ultimately, the Five Ministers Conference statement was a guideline set by ministers concerned with such larger issues as protecting Japan-German relations while not injuring further Japan-American relations. A balancing act was an idea that cabinet ministers could ponder and on which they could pontificate. But diplomats in the field were confronted by reality, such as how to handle Walter Israel Casper, a stateless Jew in Germany with a suspicious Haitian entry visa and a Panamanian transit visa. Diplomats lived by detailed directives. The policy of the Five Ministers Conference was anything but precise, and diplomats frequently required instructions following it. The directions they received were clear—discourage refugees from going to Japan or Japanese-occupied territory.

Although eight foreign ministers were appointed between *Kristall-nacht* and Pearl Harbor, none of them demonstrated substantial leadership regarding the refugees. Addressing the House of Peers in 1939, Arita announced that Japan would not discriminate against the Jews. Meeting privately with the Harbin industrial Lew Zikman in December 1940, Matsuoka promised the same thing. The two had different politics, which greatly affected the stance of the ministry when it faced overriding issues such as the course of the war in China and the merits of the Tripartite Pact, but the switch from one charismatic minister to another had little impact on policy toward the refugees.

It is not clear how much the foreign ministers knew about the refugees. Kase Toshikazu recalled in an interview that he could not recall dealing with the refugees when he was secretary to Matsuoka. He did not even remember any comments in 1941, when more than a thousand were still in Japan and bound for Shanghai, two regions where they could not be missed.

Several months after the Five Ministers Conference, there were several thousand refugees in Shanghai. The Consular Body discussed ways to stem the tide, but its suggestions were ineffective. Italy and Germany claimed that it was impossible to stop refugees from going to Shanghai, and diplomats from other nations claimed that the problem was outside their jurisdiction. No single diplomat initiated a discussion about the moral issue of challenging persecution.

Victor Sassoon, a Jewish tycoon in Shanghai, defied any notions that funds for Japan would be forthcoming from wealthy Shanghai Jews, when he traveled about North America criticizing the Japanese army. Captain Inuzuka, the navy's Jewish expert, was angered, but the diplomats who reported on Sassoon's comments to the American and Canadian press were quiet. As always, they were faithful messengers of news, but not necessarily analysts.

Whatever visions Captain Inuzuka and others may have had of employing Jewish wealth to create settlements for Jewish refugees and generate investment capital for Japan were secondary to the restrictive action taken in Shanghai in summer 1939. The Japanese sought to stop all new refugee arrivals, and the International Settlement and French Concession quickly followed. Despite protestations to the contrary, the Japanese move targeted Jews. They were, after all, the only refugees heading to Shanghai. The navy was clearly in charge; at the official press conference announcing the restrictions, a navy spokesman appeared. Diplomats at the consulate were left to notify other diplomats of the move, in the most circumspect language. Whatever language was employed and justifications offered, the Japanese action was disastrous for Jews still in Austria and Germany. By autumn 1939 and early 1940, the refugee flow was reduced to a trickle.

Meanwhile, the authorities in Manchukuo demonstrated little interest in settlement schemes. Some plans were conceived by Jewish financiers, and others by such Manchukuo players as Ayukawa Yoshisuke of Manchukuo Heavy Industries Development Corporation and the Manchurian Southern Railway research section. The military, however, did not agree, and it was the ultimate power. Indeed, the commander of the Kwantung Army concurrently held the post of Japan's ambassador to Manchukuo. All of Tamura Kōzō's shuttling between Japanese officials and Jewish leaders in the United States amounted to little, because he could not convince the Americans of his sincerity and backing, and the military did not wholeheartedly seek a settlement in the first place. Dr. Kaufman had been lucky to venture that 150 people a year ought to be permitted into Manchukuo.

While diplomats deferred to the military in China, in Japan the ministry bureaucrats deferred to the Home Ministry. The third section of the America Bureau forwarded all inquiries for entry and transit visas to the Home Ministry, which invariably rejected adults but permitted children to join their families in Japan. The stories behind these rejected applications are heartbreaking. They also lay to rest any theory that the Japanese government actively implemented the clause of the Five Ministers Conference regarding special consideration for capitalists and technicians, for there were applicants who might have allowed a little exploitation in exchange for a visa. But that did not happen.

Applicants in Europe needed the assistance of the Kobe Jewish Community, which had cultivated local officials to permit the entry of refugees who otherwise might have been refused. All of the community's skills were summoned when refugees with curious Curaçao visas began arriving in late 1940. Sometimes, like Susan and Nate Bluman, they had no entry visas at all. But they did possess transit visas from the consulate in Kaunas.

Not surprisingly, the 1941 report recounting the ministry's dates of important communications referred to admonishing the Kaunas consulate for issuing visas to people without destinations and sufficient funds. Who was Sugihara Chiune, and what drove him to issue so many transit visas? He produced more than 2,000 visas in summer 1940, which represented more than a third of the total number of transit visas issued by all the Japanese consulates in Europe between January 1940 and March 1941.

In the "Situation of European Refugees Coming to Japan," there is a section concerning the reasons that so many refugees were stranded in

Japan in mid-April 1941. "According to the Home Ministry, from March 20th to the present, there are seventeen hundred refugees staying here who should not be if their visas are according to instructions." Four reasons followed. One concerned the unilateral moves by Central American countries and Palestine to change entry procedures, another was the expiration of valid destination visas after the refugees obtained Japanese transit visas, and another was that some refugees were simply waiting for ships. Only one point concerned the conduct of a Japanese consulate. The Kaunas consulate was the only place from which refugees—2,132 of them—had left with transit visas, although not all possessed the necessary destination visas.

Although the motivations of Sugihara Chiune are intriguing and important, they are shrouded by dissenting opinions. Former refugees are forever grateful and speak glowingly of a kind man. Relatives are determined to burnish his reputation. He also has his detractors, who knew him in Europe and Japan and doubt his character and his benevolence towards the Jews. Part of the ambiguity of Sugihara concerns his postwar life. The Sugiharas returned to Japan from Europe in 1947 and were shocked by the devastated country they called home. Within three months Sugihara was summoned to the Foreign Ministry, where Vice-Minister Okazaki instructed him that there was no longer a post available. Chiune resigned without comment. Yukiko believes that her husband was dismissed because of his aid to the Jews. Chiune's sister Ryūko recalls being "treated like a stranger" when she approached one of her brother's former bosses after the war.[4]

The Foreign Ministry takes a different stand. It has officially stated that between 1946 and 1947, the ministry staff was reduced by one third. The Occupation was in force, and little diplomacy was being conducted by Japan at the time. Former diplomats concur, adding that the ministry required America specialists possessing fluency in English; few opportunities existed for those with expertise in Russian. He was also not on the elite track. Finally, Sugihara was old; in 1947, he was forty-seven, and the ministry's retirement age was fifty.

The truth may lie somewhere between Yukiko's opinion and the ministry's explanation. Only Sugihara and Okazaki know what transpired the day Sugihara left the ministry forever.

Whatever feelings Sugihara had regarding his actions in Kaunas and resignation in Tokyo, he kept to himself. Once he did reveal in a brief, unpublished memoir that "[he] did not pay any attention and just acted according to [his] sense of human justice, out of love for mankind." But he also avoided conveying the depths of his emotions, claiming that he never tried to learn about the refugees' experiences in Japan, for "after the war I did my best to forget the past."[5]

Like the renowned Oscar Schindler, Sugihara Chiune was a complex man. His time in Kaunas showed him to be a diplomat, humanitarian, and intelligence agent. Did his involvement with spies detract from his assistance to Jews? Even if Sugihara had made an agreement with Polish intelligence contacts, the number of visas he issued attracted too much attention, and their recipients were clearly not Polish soldiers but civilians. Was he also a bitter man, disappointed with his noncareer status and willing to risk the little he had on desperate refugees? A positive answer would not mean that he was any less humanitarian. Were rewards promised for issuing visas from either the refugees or the Polish operatives with whom he worked? An affirmative answer would affect his status as one of the "Righteous Among the Nations of the World" at Yad Vashem. These questions are valid, but some may never be adequately answered, partly because Sugihara was so consistently silent regarding this episode in his life. Ultimately, the data on the number of transit visas issued by Japanese consulates in Europe were explanatory. Sugihara was, above all, exceptional.

Much of the laudatory press regarding Sugihara has mentioned his defiance of government orders. To be sure, he ignored repeated requests from Tokyo to verify that refugees had destinations. Curaçao did the trick, but its effectiveness only lasted until the refugees reached Japan, from which they could not proceed with such as insubstantial "visa." Sugihara knew how suspect the Curaçao visas were and how unlikely it was that suddenly thousands of people should proceed there. But technically, Japanese immigration regulations were fulfilled by the Curaçao visas, and the necessary funds for the refugees' living expenses and travel were provided by Jewish charities.

As forced a solution Curaçao may have appeared to be, it was not beyond the bounds of possibility. In the late 1930s and early 1940s, nations worldwide contemplated settlements for refugees in the most exotic places. In addition, all other nations' consulates had withdrawn from their Kaunas offices by August 25, 1940—the Soviet deadline— and Sugihara did not have many colleagues with whom to confer. Finally, was Curaçao any stranger than Shanghai as an unexpected haven for European Jews? No one knew for certain whether Jewish refugees would be interned there until December 1940, long after Sugihara had left Kaunas.

Tokyo did not pick up on Sugihara's activity until months later. There were early signs in late summer and autumn 1940 as a few arrived or were reported to be heading to Japan, but the source of their visas was not clear for months. By then, hundreds were embarking from Vladivostok for Tsuruga monthly and "congesting" Japan, to the ministry's regret.

When compared with the activity and comments of other diplomats in Europe, Sugihara stands out. Not many of the personalities of Japanese diplomats emerge strongly in the pages of the Jewish Problem File. Those that do leave an impression were insistent and persistent, whether they were like the precise Yamaji in Vienna alerting the ministry to every implication of policy, or the opinionated Tsutsui voicing the virulent anti-Semitism that echoed that of his host country, Rumania. Few voiced sympathy for the Jews. The majority, whatever their feelings, strictly enforced Japanese immigration regulations.

Until the end of 1940, most Jews who passed through Japan left within the duration of their transit visas. Even the majority of those who came in 1941 moved on, because they had shown bona fide entry visas to Japanese diplomats in European capitals in order to obtain transit visas. Some of the recipients of Sugihara visas, such as Susan and Nate Bluman and Samuil Manski, obtained immigration visas once in Japan.

Yet, only Sugihara had issued visas to refugees whose papers were incomplete, and they represented approximately 2,000 of approximately 4,500 who arrived in Japan between July 1940 and May 1941.[6] Although the late 1930s and 1940s were a period when countries could and did cancel their own visas without shame, Japan never did, even upon realizing that only those from Kaunas were a problem. The Foreign Ministry believed that keeping its visas credible meant honoring them, even when there was little hope that many of the refugees who desired to emigrate to the United States would actually be able to.

As a result, groups of refugees roved in Kobe, where they attracted local attention and reveled in the relative freedom of Japan and kind hospitality of the Japanese. The Hyōgo prefectural authorities, however, were watchful and worried. They wanted the refugees to leave as soon as possible.

The Soviets felt the same way toward those who had exit visas. When Japanese diplomats in Moscow and Vladivostok tried to prevent more refugees from going to Japan, as their ministry advised, the Soviets refused to let the refugees stay. In the end, Nei backed down and sent on their way refugees delayed in Vladivostok—before notifying the ministry. The ministry backpedaled, trying to determine why so many refugees were in Japan. It produced the April report, after introducing tighter restrictions in the Soviet Union. Meanwhile, Tatekawa, Nei's superior in Moscow, grew more sensitive to the appeals of refugees for transit visas, and more frustrated by the ministry's unworkable restrictions. By then, however, it was almost too late. It was June.

The story in Europe may have ended by June 1941, but there were over 1,000 refugees still in Japan at that time. By mid-September, they were shipped to Shanghai as Japan prepared for war against the United States. The Japanese authorities in Shanghai were given no choice but to concede to the wishes of the Foreign and Home ministries.

Finally, with the attack on Pearl Harbor, any notion of cultivating the Jews as a means of altering the course of United States–Japan relations was abandoned. The Japanese wished to avoid the appearance of discriminating against the refugees and professed an interest in treating well those whom it could use, but any special interest in the Jews was over. All along, the Japanese stereotype of the wealthy, dangerous Jew had been incompatible with the reality of impoverished, desperate refugees fleeing persecution. The Foreign Ministry may have toyed with the former idea, but it tolerated the latter.

The policy of the Ministry of Foreign Affairs toward the Jews was a case of reacting to events rather than predicting or influencing them. The ministry failed to foresee not only the import of Hitler's racial policies but also the impact in Latin America and North America, where no one desired the Jews. Only when a Japanese steamer was inconvenienced in Panama owing to its Jewish passengers, and hundreds of Jews arrived in Japan every month in early 1941, did the ministry become alert to how difficult it would be to emigrate to Central and South America.

Once provoked, the ministry was specific about discouraging refugees from coming to Japan. But as long as transit remained possible, refugees would try to travel there, especially as other escape routes disappeared. As long as Tokyo instructed its diplomats to reject gently, refugees believed that Japan was possible, especially since other countries were not so discreet. Consistently, Japanese diplomats employed euphemisms and refused verbally—without a written, unmistakable rejection—in order to soften the blow to refugees' hopes. When a Manchukuo diplomat wrote that he was "answering verbally and refusing euphemistically," he captured the essence of the Japanese diplomatic style.

The ministry was intent on not arousing the wrath of its unsuitable partner Germany and its future enemy the United States. Nor did it wish to anger the Jews. When Arita instructed Ōshima to conduct quiet negotiations with the German foreign office to stop refugees from going to Shanghai in August 1939, he was determined that the issue not be used as propaganda damaging to Japanese-Jewish and Japanese-German relations. Jews in Europe and Jews in the United States would have been surprised to learn that there was such a relationship with the Japanese. The Germans did not care whether Japan became involved with the Jews, because ridding Europe of the Jews was their priority.

The ministry was clearly concerned about the nature of Japan's relations with the rest of the world. But how concerned was it with guiding values? To be sure, references were often made in reports to racial equality and racial harmony, but this rhetoric was representative of

Japan's imperialist ambitions. The majority of cables from diplomats abroad who witnessed the troubles Jews encountered were devoid of any moral discussion about persecution and human rights. But then, these are modern terms that postdate World War II. Indeed, a *Jerusalem Report* journalist has written, "Before the Second World War, anti-Semitism was defined more narrowly as wanting to harm Jews. In the postwar era, it was broadened to include prejudice that might lead one to wish Jews harm. More recently, it's come to mean any stereotype—or disagreement—with the Jewish community."[7] It is worth remembering historian Henry Feingold's admonition that emphasizing the rescue theme lends it an importance that that few decision makers were willing to give it during the war.[8] His statement applies to diplomats from every country.

When Japan is evaluated in terms of the behavior of other countries, it measures up. On numerous occasions, diplomats intervened to prevent yet another tragic *St. Louis*–style incident. They did not want ships traveling to Shanghai or from Japan to circle needlessly. Refugees en route to Shanghai who arrived after the August 21 deadline were not turned back. Jewish passengers who wanted to disembark in Lisbon in February 1940 were assisted by the Japanese ambassador. Others in trouble in Panama were helped by diplomats in December 1940. To be sure, the ships were Japanese vessels, and revenue and national pride were at stake. But another tragedy could have happened so easily.

What if Japan had refused to accept transit visas issued by the consulate in Kaunas? It could have avoided harboring over a thousand refugees who had no prospects elsewhere, and no other nation would have cared if it disavowed the actions of one of its minor diplomats in an insignificant location. But Japan never considered such an action. Initially, it accepted refugees by accident—before it knew that their visas were suspect. Later, it accepted them by default—after it realized that the Soviets would not negotiate. But accept them it did. In the end, more than 24,000 people—those who emigrated successfully before Pearl Harbor and those who endured the war in Shanghai—thankfully lived to share their stories of how they escaped the Holocaust through the aid of an Axis ally in Asia.

NOTES

1. Letter from Ernst Baerwald, Berkeley, to Moses A. Leavitt, New York, 5 May 1941, AR 33/44, #724: Japan, General, Emigration, 1941 April-June, AJJDC Archives.

2. "JewCom Kobe 'Census of Jewish Refugees Entering and Leaving Kobe,' For 3/41," JPF, folder 11.

3. Report, "Situation of European Refugees Coming to Japan," 15 April 1941, JPF, folder 11.

4. Nakamura Ryūko, interview by author, 6 April 1995, Minakamo, Aichi, tape recording.

5. Sugihara Chiune, undated memoir, courtesy of Sugihara Nobuki, Antwerp, Belgium.

6. I am relying on two documents, to which I have referred in chapters 1 and 7. (1) Between July 1, 1940, and May 31, 1941, 4,664 Jewish refugees arrived in Japan. HIAS, "Jewish Transients in Japan," by Moise Moiseff, 25 July 1941, Record Group 245.4, series xvb-xvc, HIAS Reports, File MKM 15.57, folder xvc-7, YIVO. (2) Between July 1, 1940, and August 1, 1941, 4,500 Jewish refugees arrived in Japan. "Summary of Important Recent Communications Regarding Overseas Developments," 20 October 1941, AR 33/44, #462: China, General, 1941 August-December, AJJDC Archives.

7. J. J. Goldberg, "Overanxious about Anti-Semitism," *The New Republic*, in *Globe and Mail* (Toronto), 24 May 1993, 9(A).

8. Henry L. Feingold, *The Politics of Rescue: The Roosevelt Administration and the Holocaust 1938–1945* (New Brunswick, NJ: Rutgers University Press, 1970), xii.

Bibliography

PRIMARY SOURCES

Unpublished International Organization Documents

Records of the American Jewish Joint Distribution Committee. "China, Japan, Lithuania, and Caraçao Files, 1933–1944." AJJDC Archives, New York.

Records of the Hebrew Immigrant Aid Society (HIAS). Record Group 245.4, Series XVB–XVC. "HIAS Reports." YIVO Institute for Jewish Research, New York.

Records of the Hebrew Immigrant Aid Society. Record Group 245.4. Series I–XI. YIVO Institute for Jewish Research, New York.

Records of the "Shanghai Collection, 1926–1948." Record Group 243. YIVO Institute for Jewish Research, New York.

Records of Stephen S. Wise. American Jewish Historical Society, Waltham, Massachusetts.

Unpublished and Published Japanese Government Documents

Ministry of Foreign Affairs. "America ni okeru Yudayajin mondai." File Chōsa 2–44. Diplomatic Records Office, Ministry of Foreign Affairs, Tokyo.

———. "Gaikokujin ni taisuru teikoku no ryoken sashō kankei zakken." File J 2.3.0. J/X1. Diplomatic Records Office, Ministry of Foreign Affairs, Tokyo.

———. "Gaikokujin ni taisuru zaigai kōkan hakkyū ryoken sashō hōkoku ikken, Ōshū no bu." File J 2.3.0 J/X 2–6. Diplomatic Records Office, Ministry of Foreign Affairs, Tokyo.

———. *Gaimushō kikō hensen zu*, Gaimu Daijin Kanbō Sōmu Sanjikan Shitsu, October 1971.

———. *Gaimushō nenkan ni*. Gaimu Daijin Kanbō Jinji Ka, October 1942.

———. *Gaimushō nenkan ni*. Gaimu Daijin Kanbo Jinji Ka, February 1953.

———. *Gaimushō shokuin rekinin hyō*. October 1940.

———. *Gaimushō shokuin ryakureki*. 1977.

———. *Gaimushō shokuinroku*. 1942.

———. "Kaku koku taizai teikoku ryōji ninmen kankei zakken 'Kaunas' no bu." File M 2.1.0. 10–92. Diplomatic Records Office, Ministry of Foreign Affairs, Tokyo.

———. "Minzoku mondai kankei zakken: Yudayajin mondai." File I 4.6.0.1–2. Diplomatic Records Office, Ministry of Foreign Affairs, Tokyo. Files 3–11, 13.

———. "Minzoku mondai kankei zakken: Yudayajin mondai kyokutō Yudaya minzoku taikai kankei." File I 4.6.0. 1–2. Diplomatic Records Office, Ministry of Foreign Affairs, Tokyo.

Published United States Government Documents

Department of State. *Foreign Relations of the United States: Diplomatic Papers*. Washington, DC: Government Printing Office, 1936–1945.

Unpublished United States Government Documents

Records of Former German and Japanese Embassies and Consulates, 1890–1945. File T-179. National Archives, Washington, DC.

Records of the Department of State Relating to the Internal Affairs of China, 1930–1939. File 893. National Archives, Washington, DC.

Records of the Department of State Relating to the Internal Affairs of China, 1940–1944. File 893. National Archives, Washington, DC.

Records of the Department of State Relating to the Internal Affairs of Japan, 1930–1939. File 894. National Archives, Washington, DC.

Records of the Department of State Relating to the Internal Affairs of Japan, 1940–1944. File 894. National Archives, Washington, DC.

Records of the Department of State Relating to the Internal Affairs of Lithuania, 1910–1944. File 860m. National Archives, Washington, DC.

Interviews

Bluman, Susan. Interview by author, 21 November 1994, Vancouver. Tape recording.

Cohen, Sarah. Interview by author, 25 December 1993, Toronto. Tape recording.

Glaser, Julious. Phone interview by author, 13 December 1992, Brookline, MA. Notes.

Iwai, Jōei. Interview by author, 8 April 1995, Yaotsu, Japan. Tape recording.

Iwai, Seinosuke. Phone interview by author, 4 April 1994, Tokyo. Notes.

Kasai, Tadakazu. Interview by author, 7 April 1995, Gifu, Japan. Tape recording.

Kase, Toshikazu. Phone interview by author, 21 June 1995, Tokyo. Notes.

Katayama, Junnosuke. Interview by author, 31 August 1995, Tokyo. Tape recording; 24 November 1996, Tokyo. Notes.

Konuma, Hiko. Interview by Shino Teruhisa, 12 March 1996, Morioka, Japan. Tape recording.

Kupinsky, Hirsh. Interview by author, 15 December 1993, Toronto. Notes.

Leon, Masha. Phone Interview by author, 13 November 1997, Tokyo. Notes.

———. Interview by Sheryl Narahara for "The Unlikely Liberators" tour, 22 September 1994. Videocassette.

Manabe, Ryōichi. Interview by author, 25 May 1995, Tokyo. Tape recording.

Manski, Samuil. Interview by author, 6 October 1995, Newton, Massachusetts. Tape recording.

Nakamura, Ryūko. Interview by author, 8 April 1995, Minokamo, Japan. Tape recording.

Shigemitsu, Akira. Interview by author, 29 May 1995, Tokyo. Tape recording.

Shigemitsu, Ayako. Interview by author, 29 May 1995, Tokyo. Tape recording.

Shimkin, Joseph. Interview by Katori Shunsuke for NHK radio drama "Yudayajin o sukutta 1500-mai no visa," courtesy of Katori Shunsuke.

Shimkin, Sumiko. Interview by author, 20 December 1994, Tokyo. Tape recording.

Shimura, Giichi. Interview by author, 19 April 1995, Tokyo. Tape recording.

Sugihara, Nobuki. Phone interview by author, 9 August 1996, Tokyo. Notes.

Sugihara, Yukiko. Interview by author, 24 September 1992, Kamakura. Tape recording.

———. Interview by Katori Shunsuke for NHK radio drama "Yudayajin o sukutta 1500-mai no visa," courtesy of Katori Shunsuke.

Takechi, Rikako. Phone interview by author, 11 June 1995, Tokyo. Notes.

Takechi, Yūji. Phone interview by author, 24 May 1998, Tokyo. Notes.

Takeuchi, Harumi. Interview by author, 1 February 1995, Tokyo. Tape recording.

Tokura, Eiji. Interview by author, 10 February 1995, Tokyo. Tape recording.

Letters

Sugihara Chiune. Undated memoir courtesy of Sugihara Nobuki. Antwerp, Belgium.

SECONDARY SOURCES

Books

Agar, Herbert. *The Saving Remnant*. New York: Viking Press, 1960.

Arendt, Hannah. *Eichmann in Jerusalem: A Report on the Banality of Evil*. New York: Viking Press, 1963.

————. *The Origins of Totalitarianism*. New York: Harcourt, Brace, 1951.

Ayukawa Yoshisuke Sensei Tsuisōroku. *Ayukawa Yoshisuke sensei tsuisōroku*. Tokyo: Hensan Kankokai, 1968.

Bauer, Yehuda. *My Brother's Keeper: A History of the American Jewish Joint Distribution Committee 1929–1939*. Philadelphia: Jewish Publication Society of America, 1974.

————. "Rescue Operations through Vilna." In *Yad Vashem Studies on the European Jewish Catastrophe and Resistance*, ed. Livia Rothkirchen. Jerusalem: Yad Vashem, 1973.

Behr, Edward. *Hirohito: Behind the Myth*. New York: Villard Books, 1989.

Ben-Eliezer, Judith. *Shanghai Lost, Jerusalem Regained*. Tel Aviv: Steimatzky, 1985.

Borg, Dorothy, and Shumpei Okamoto. *Pearl Harbor as History: Japan-American Relations 1931–1941*. New York: Columbia University Press, 1973.

Brackman, Arnold C. *The Other Nuremberg*. New York: William Morrow, 1987.

Buruma, Ian. *The Wages of Guilt*. New York: Meridian Books, 1995.

Chūnichi Shimbunsha, ed. *Jiyū E No Tōsō: Sugihara Visa to Yudayajin*. Tokyo: Tokyo Shimbun Shuppan Kyoku, 1995.

Cohn, Norman. *Warrant for Genocide*. Chico, CA: Scholars Press, 1981.

Cook, Haruko Taya, and Theodore F. Cook. *Japan at War: An Oral History*. New York: The New Press, 1992.

Crowley, James B. *Japan's Quest for Autonomy: National Security and Foreign Policy: 1930–1938*. Princeton, NJ: Princeton University Press, 1966.

Dawidowicz, Lucy S. *From That Place and Time*. New York: Bantam Books, 1989.

————. *The War against the Jews, 1933–1945*. New York: Holt, Rinehart and Winston, 1985.

Delisle, Esther. *The Traitor and the Jew*. Montreal: Robert Davies Publishing, 1993.

Dicker, Herman. *Wanderers and Settlers in the Far East: A Century of Jewish Life in China and Japan*. New York: Twayne Publishers, 1962.

Dower, John W. *War without Mercy*. New York: Pantheon Books, 1986.

Emiot, Israel. *The Birobidzhan Affair*. Translated by Max Rosenfeld. Philadelphia: The Jewish Publication Society of America, 1981.

Fairbank, John King. *The United States & China*. Cambridge: Harvard University Press, 1981.

Feingold, Henry L. *The Politics of Rescue: The Roosevelt Administration and the Holocaust, 1938–1945*. New Brunswick, NJ: Rutgers University Press, 1970.

Fogelman, Eva. *Conscience & Courage: Rescuers of Jews during the Holocaust*. New York: Doubleday, 1994.

Ganor, Solly. *Light One Candle: A Survivor's Tale from Lithuania to Jerusalem*. New York: Kodansha International, 1995.

Gilbert, Martin. *Atlas of the Holocaust*. New York: William Morrow, 1988.

Goodman, David G., and Masanori Miyazawa. *Jews in the Japanese Mind*. New York: The Free Press, 1995.

Goodwin, Doris Kearns. *No Ordinary Time: Franklin and Eleanor Roosevelt: The Home Front in World War II*. New York: Touchstone, 1994.

Grew, Joseph C. *Report from Tokyo: A Message to the American People*. New York: Simon & Schuster, 1942.

———. *Ten Years in Japan*. New York: Simon and Schuster, 1944.

———. *Turbulent Era: A Diplomatic Record of Forty Years, 1904–45*: Edited by Walter Johnson. Boston: Houghton Mifflin, 1952.

Hata, Ikuhiko. *Shōwashi no nazo o ou*. Tokyo: Bungei Shunjū, 1993.

Hautzig, Esther. *Remember Who You Are: Stories about Being Jewish*. New York: Crown Publishers, 1990.

Heppner, Ernest G. *Shanghai Refuge: A Memoir of the World War II Jewish Ghetto*. Lincoln: University of Nebraska Press, 1993.

Higuchi, Kiichiro. *Atsu Kiska gunshireikan no kaisōroku*. Tokyo: Fuyō Shobō, 1971.

Hilberg, Raul. *The Destruction of the European Jews*. Vols. 1–3. New York and London: Holmes and Meier, 1985.

Holocaust Oral History Project and Unlikely Liberators Project, ed. *Igai na kaihōsha*. Tokyo: Jōhō Center Shuppan Kyoku, 1995.

Ienaga, Saburō. *The Pacific War, 1931–1945*. New York: Pantheon Books, 1978.

Inuzuka, Kyoko. *Yudaya mondai to nihon no kōsaku*. Tokyo: Nihon Kōgyō Shimbunsha, 1982.

Itō, Takeo. *Life along the South Manchurian Railway*. Translated by Joshua A. Fogel. Armonk, NY: M. E. Sharpe, 1988.

Kase, Toshikazu. *Gaikōkan*. Tokyo: Kodansha, 1957.

———. *Journey to the Missouri*. Edited by David Nelson Rowe. New Haven, CT: Yale University Press, 1950.

———. *Watakushi no gendai gaikōshi*. Tokyo: Kodansha, 1971.

Katori, Shunsuke. *Mō hitotsu no Shōwa*. Tokyo: Kodansha, 1994.

Keneally, Thomas. *Schindler's List*. New York: Simon and Schuster, 1982.

Kotsuji, Abraham. *From Tokyo to Jerusalem*. New York: Bernard Geis Associates, 1964.

Kranzler, David. *Japanese, Nazis and Jews*. Hoboken, NJ: Ktav Publishing House, 1976.

Krasno, Rena. *Strangers Always: A Jewish Family in Wartime Shanghai*. Berkeley, CA: Pacific View Press, 1992.

Langer, Lawrence L. *Versions of Survival: The Holocaust and the Human Spirit*. Albany: State University of New York Press, 1982.

Lattimore, Owen. *Manchuria: Cradle of Conflict*. New York: Macmillan, 1932.

Leitner, Yecheskel. *Operation: Torah Rescue*. Jerusalem and New York: Feldheim Publishers, 1987.

Levine, Hillel. *In Search of Sugihara*. New York: The Free Press, 1996.

Lipschitz, Chaim U. *The Shanghai Collection*. Edited by Sonia Winter, Hallie Cantor, Judy Bendet. New York: Maznaim Publishing, 1988.

Manski, Samuil. *With God's Help*. Madison, WI: Charles F. Manski, 1990.

Marrus, Michael R. *The Holocaust in History*. London: Penguin Books, 1987.

Marton, Kati. *Wallenberg*. New York: Random House, 1982.

Maxon, Yale Candee. *Control of Japanese Foreign Policy: A Study of Civil-Military Rivalry, 1930–1945*. Westport, CT: Greenwood Press, 1973.

Meskill, Johanna Menzel. *Hitler & Japan: The Hollow Alliance*. New York: Atherton Press, 1966.

Miyazawa, Masanori. *Nihon ni okeru Yudaya Israel rongi bunken mokuroku—1877–1988*. Tokyo: Shinsensha, 1990.

———. *Yudayajin ronkō: Nihon ni okeru rongi no tsuiseki*. Tokyo: Shinsensha, 1982.

Morley, James William, ed. *Deterrent Diplomacy: Japan, Germany, and the U.S.S.R., 1935–1940*. New York: Columbia University Press, 1976.

———. *The China Quagmire: Japan's Expansion on the Asian Continent, 1933–1941*. New York: Columbia University Press, 1983.

Neu, Charles E. *The Troubled Encounter: The United States and Japan*. New York: John Wiley & Sons, 1975.

Nicolson, Harold. *Diplomacy*. London: Oxford University Press, 1963.

Nussbaum, Chaim. *Chaplain on the River Kwai*. New York: Shapolsky Publishing, 1988.

Oliner, Samuel P., and Pearl M. Oliner. *The Altruistic Personality: Rescuers of Jews in Nazi Europe*. New York: The Free Press, 1988.

Patent, Gregory. *Shanghai Passage*. New York: Clarion Books, 1990.

Peattie, Mark R. *Ishiwara Kanji and Japan's Confrontation with the West*. Princeton, NJ: Princeton University Press, 1975.

Perry, John Curtis. *Facing West*. Westport, CT: Praeger, 1994.

Presseisen, Ernst L. *Germany and Japan: A Study in Totalitarian Diplomacy: 1933–1941*. The Hague: Martinus Nijhoff, 1958.

Rittner, Carol, and Sondra Myers, eds. *The Courage to Care: Rescuers of Jews during the Holocaust*. New York: New York University Press, 1986.

Ross, James R. *Escape to Shanghai: A Jewish Community in China*. New York: The Free Press, 1994.

Rubin, Evelyn Pike. *Ghetto Shanghai*. New York: Shengold Publishers, Inc., 1993.

Shigemitsu, Akira. *Roshiajin no omoide*. Tokyo: by the author, 1993.

Shigemitsu, Mamoru. *Japan and Her Destiny: My Struggle for Peace*. Edited by F.S.G. Piggott. Translated by Oswald White. New York: E. P. Dutton, 1958.

Shillony, Ben-Ami. *Politics and Culture in Wartime Japan*. Oxford: Clarendon Press, 1981.

———. *The Jews and the Japanese: The Successful Outsiders*. Rutland, VT and Tokyo: Charles E. Tuttle Company, 1991.

Shino, Teruhisa. *Yakusoku no kuni e no nagai tabi*. Tokyo: Librio Shuppan, 1988.

Sloves, Henri. *L'État Juif de L'Union Sovietique*. Paris: Les Presses d'Aujourd'hui, 1982.

Staub, Ervin. *The Roots of Evil: The Origins of Genocide and Other Group Violence*. Cambridge: Cambridge University Press, 1989.

Stoessinger, John G. *Night Journey: A Story of Survival and Deliverance*. Chicago: Playboy Press, 1978.

———. *The Refugee and the World Community*. Minneapolis: University of Minnesota Press, 1956.

Sugihara, Yukiko. *Rokusen-nin no inochi no visa*. Tokyo: Asahi Sonorama, 1990.

Sugita, Rokuichi. *Higashi Asia e kita Yudayajin*. Tokyo: Otowa Shobō, 1967.

Sugiyama, Hajime. *Sugiyama Memo*. Tokyo: Hara Shobō, 1989.

Theroux, Paul. *Riding the Iron Rooster: By Train through China*. London: Penguin Books, 1988.

Tokayer, Marvin, and Mary Swartz. *The Fugu Plan: The Untold Story of the Japanese and the Jews during World War II*. New York: Paddington Press, 1979.

Tokyo Metropolitan Museum of Photography. *The Founding and Development of Modern Photography in Japan*. Tokyo: Tokyo Metropolitan Culture Foundation, 1995.

Warhaftig, Zorach. *Refugee and Survivor: Rescue Efforts during the Holocaust*. Jerusalem: Yad Vashem, 1988.

Wilson, George M., ed. *Crisis Politics in Prewar Japan*. Tokyo: Voyagers' Press, 1970.

Yad Vashem. *Rescue Attempts during the Holocaust*. Jerusalem: Yad Vashem, 1977.

Yasue, Hirō. *Dairen tokumu kikan to maboroshi no Yudaya kokka*. Tokyo: Yawata Press, 1989.

Journals and Magazines

"A Conversation with . . . Historian Gerhard Weinberg Discussed the War's Consequences With Chairman Sheldon Hackney." *Humanities*. March/April 1995, 5–9, 49–53.

"Ai no ketsudan." *Budō-ki* 444 February 1993: 1–4.

Alter, Jonathan. "After the Survivors." *Newsweek*, 20 December 1993, 116–120.

Bernstein, Jeremy. "In Many Tongues." *Atlantic Monthly*, October 1993, 92–102.

Blumenthal, W. Michael. "Shanghai: The Persistence of Interest." *Points East* 10, no. 1 (March 1996): 1, 3, 4.

Craig, Bill. "A beacon of humanity in a malevolent world." *Pacific Sunday*, 23 June 1985, 11–14.

Dickey, Christopher. "France's Guerrilla Doctor." *Vanity Fair*, April 1993, 92–111.

Gorman, Christine. "A Conspiracy of Goodness." *Time*, 16 March 1992, 67, 69.

Golub, Jennifer. "Japanese Attitudes Toward Jews." Pacific Rim Institute of the American Jewish Committee. Los Angeles: American Jewish Committee, 1992.

Guang, Pan. "Shanghai's Case in the Annals of Jewish Diaspora: An Appreciation." *Points East* 9, no. 2 (August 1994): 1, 7–8.

Heuberger, Ruth Eva. "The Jewish Community of Japan and the Citrins—Founding Members." *Points East* 8, no. 1 (February 1993): 22–24.

"How the Swiss Betrayed Germany's Fleeing Jews." *The Guardian*. Quoted in *Tokyo Jewish News* 17, no. 3 (February–March 1995): 10.

Ishii, Shinpei. "A Return to Wartime Manchuria: The Travel Journal of a Postwar Japanese." Translated by Michael S. Molasky. *Chūō Kōron*, September 1991, 212–220.

Kase, Hideaki. "Nihon no naka no Yudayajin." *Chūō Kōron*. May 1971, 234–247.

Katayama, Junnosuke. "Sorenken mitari, kiitari, no shirushi." *Mantetsu kaihō*, no. 167 (1 May 1991): 5–9.

Krasno, Rena. "Russian Jews in Shanghai." *Points East* 9, no. 2 (August 1994): 1, 4–6.

Krygier, Richard. "The Making of a Cold Warrior: The Prehistory of the Australian Association." *Quadrant*, November 1986, 38–43.

Lavender, Emerson, and Norman Sheffe. "Escape along the Comet Line," *This Country Canada* (Autumn 1993): 21–31.

Maruyama, Naoki. "Asia taiheiyō chiiki ni okeru Yudayajin shakai." In *Pacific Basin Project* 7, Center for Japan-US Relations, International University. Japan: International University, 1986.

———. "1930 nendai ni okeru Nihon no hanyudayashugi." *Kokusai daigaku chūtō kenkyūjo kiyō*. 1987–1988, 411–438.

Miyazawa, Masanori. "Daseba best seller Nihonzin wa naze 'Yudaya imbō' setsu o konomu no ka." *Sapio*. 23 March 1995, 14–15.

———. "Japanese Anti-Semitism in the Thirties." *Midstream* 33 (March 1987): 23–27.

———. "Nichi-Yu dosoron to koshi koden." *Koshi koden ronsō* (August 1993): 164–171.

———. "Schindler's List o megutte." *Gekkan Chapel Hour*. 12 December 1994, 32–37.

———. "Shōwa zenki ni okeru Nihon no tai Yudaya seisaku." In *Social Science Research*, Waseda University Social Science Research Institute, 1994.

Ōno, Masami. "Haran no jigyōka kyū-Manshū de bōryaku." *Aera*. 7 August 1995, 58–60.

Palasz-Rutkowska, Ewa, and Andrzej T. Romer. "Polish-Japanese Co-operation during World War II." *Japan Forum* 7, no. 2 (Autumn 1995): 286–314.

Ryback, Timothy W. "Evidence of Evil." *New Yorker*, 15 November 1993, 68–81.

Shapiro, Laura. "Denying the Holocaust." *Newsweek*, 20 December 1993, 120.

Shatzkes, Pamela. "Kobe: A Japanese Haven for Jewish Refugees, 1940–1941." *Points East* 8, no. 1 (February 1993): 10–16.

Shirokura, Yoshimitsu, and Hiroshi Yuasa. "Nihon no Schindler' Yudayajin rokusen-nin o sukutta Sugihara Chiune no itoku o yogosu izoku no 'gyōjō.'" *Sunday Mainichi*, 19 June 1994, 26–30.

Tracey, David. "Visas for Life." *Reader's Digest*, January 1994, 69–74.

Woodward, Kenneth L. "We Are Witnesses." *Newsweek*, 26 April 1993, 48–51.

Encyclopedias

Encyclopedia Americana, 1969 ed. S.v. "Passport."

Encyclopedia Britannica, 1965 ed. S.v. "Passport."

Encyclopedia Judaica. Jerusalem: Keter Publishing, 1971. S.v. "Japan," by H. Kublin and s.v. "Refugees (1933–1949)," by A. Tartakower.

Japan Biographical Encyclopedia and Who's Who. 3rd Edition. Tokyo: Rengo Press, 1964–1965.
Ministry of Foreign Affairs, Diplomatic Records Office. *Nihon gaikōshi jiten.* Tokyo: Yamagawa Shuppansha, 1991.

Newspapers

Abella, Irving. "Shalom." *Toronto Star,* 3 December 1992, 1(H) and 2(H).
Ain, Meryl. "Remembering a 'miracle.' " *The Jewish Week, Inc.,* 19–25 April 1991, 4 and 43.
Berghahn, V. R. "Revisionism in Germany," review of *Forever in the Shadow of Hitler,* translated by James Knowlton and Truett Cates, and *The Path to Genocide,* by Christopher R. Browning, *New York Times Book Review,* 18 April 1993, 3 and 33.
Browning, Christopher R. "He Outfought the Holocaust," review of *A Surplus of Memory,* by Yitzhak Zuckerman, *New York Times Book Review,* 23 May 1993, 22–23.
"Chūtō koensaku to Nihonjin no kokusai kankaku." *New York Nichibei,* 21 March 1991, 2.
"Daisenzen 5000-nin no Yudayajin ni visa hakkyū." *Yomiuri America,* 26 April 1991.
Draper, Paula. "The Internees." *Toronto Star,* 3 December 1992, 13(H).
Goldberg, Carey. "The Honors Come Late for a Japanese Schindler." *New York Times,* 8 November 1995, 1(B) and 3(B).
Goldberg, J. J. "Overanxious about Anti-Semitism." *Globe and Mail,* 24 May 1993, 9(A).
Goldman, Ari L. "A Yeshiva Honors Japanese Protector." *New York Times,* 21 April 1991, 32.
Goleman, Daniel. "How to be your brother's keeper." *Globe and Mail,* 28 June 1993, 11(A).
"Hautzig attends dedication of 'Hill of Humanity' in Japan." *Chatham Courier,* 27 August 1992, 1(B).
"How U.S. Interned Nikkei of Peru." *Nikkei Voice,* Toronto, August 1993, 1 and 8.
Ihara, Keiko. "A widow's tale." *Japan Times Weekly,* 17 December 1994, 11.
———. "Swindler's List." *Japan Times Weekly,* 17 December 1994, 11.
"Japan apologises to Righteous Gentile." *The Australian Jewish News,* 13 December 1991.
"Japanese Diplomat Honoured Posthumously." *CJST News,* Summer 1993, 2.
"Jiyū e no tōsō." *Chūnichi Shimbun.* 1, 2, 3, 5, 6, 7, 8, 9, 10, 11, 12, 13, 14, 15, 16, 17, 22, 23, 24, 25, 26, 27 January; 27, 28, 29, 30 March; 2, 3, 4, 5, 6, 7, 8, 9, 14, 15, 16, 17, 18, 19, 20, 21 April 1995.
Kahn, Joseph. "Jews Revisit a City That Offered Refuge Far from Europe." *Wall Street Journal,* 9 May 1994.
Kalmanowitz, Moses. "Japan Gave Refuge to a Polish Yeshiva." *New York Times,* 20 March 1991, 28(A).
Katz, Kuniko. "Sugihara ryōji ni tasukerare Nihon o tsuka shita hitori Yudayajin Leo Lanchart-san." *OCS News,* 24 February 1992, 6–7.

Keeler, Bob. "The Good Consul." *Newsday*, 22 September 1994, 4(B) and 5(B).

"Ko Sugihara Sempo-shi no kōseki ni hikari." *Nikkei Shimbun*, 3 December 1991.

Kominik, Anna. " 'An Honest, Good Man Who Saved Our Lives.' " *New York Post*, 8 November 1995, 17.

———. " 'Japanese Schindler' to Get His Due." *New York Post*, 8 November 1995, 17.

Langer, Lawrence L. "Zion's Response to the Holocaust," review of *The Seventh Million*, by Tom Segev, *New York Times Book Review*, 18 April 1993, 3 and 37.

Lee, Stacy. "Mission to Japan: The Unlikely Liberators." *Hawaii Herald*, 7 October 1994, 1(A) and 9(A).

Lehmann, Manfred R. "Japan Remembers Rabbi Kalmanowitz, of Blessed Memory." *Algemeiner Journal*, 12 April 1991, 21.

Levine, Hillel. "Sugihara's List." *New York Times*, 20 September 1994.

"Manshū Yudaya dasshutsu-yuki." *Hokkaido Shimbun*, 17, 18, 19, 21, 22, 23, 24, 25, 26, 27, 28, 29, 30, 31 August 1994.

"Ministry Admits to Pearl Harbor Error." *Asahi Evening News*, 21 November 1994, 1.

Moosa, Eugene. "Jewish refugee here to honor diplomat who saved thousands." *Japan Times*, 18 September 1992, 3.

"Nihon no Schindler shinobi." *Yomiuri Shimbun*, 20 September 1995.

Paris, Erna. Review of *Conscience & Courage: Rescuers of Jews during the Holocaust* by Eva Fogelman, *Globe and Mail*, 7 May 1994, 23(C).

Stoddard, Ed. "Lithuania Honors Its 'Schindler.' " *Baltic Observer*, 29 June–5 July 1995, 5.

"Sugihara aided officers from Poland during war." *Japan Times*, 15 March 1995, 2.

"Surviving a POW camp in Fredericton." *Globe and Mail*, 29 September 1993, 5(C).

"Survivors left stunned by Holocaust survey." *Globe and Mail*, 20 April 1993, 13(A).

Tabata, Masanori. "Mystery behind the myth." *Japan Times Weekly*, 17 December 1994, 6–7.

———. "Manchuria, the Japanese and the Jews." *Japan Times Weekly*, 17 December 1994, 8–10.

Tsukiyama, Ted T. "Chiune (Sempo) Sugihara." *Hawaii Herald*, 7 October 1994, 1(A) and 10(A) and 11(A).

"Wasei Schindler Sugihara List." *Ehime Newspaper*, 26 August 1994.

Watanabe, Teresa. "An Unsung 'Schindler' from Japan." *Los Angeles Times*, 20 March 1994, 1(A) and 8(A).

"Yudayakei beijin to Nikkei heishi ga rainichi." *Nihon Keizai Shimbun*, 21 September 1994.

"Yudaya nanmin sukutta Higuchi Route." *Hokkaido Shimbun*, 14 August 1994, 1.

"Zaibei Yudayajin kanshajō." *Kyōdō*, 22 April 1991.

UNPUBLISHED MATERIALS

Catalogues

Harvard University Library. *China and the Jews*. Cambridge: Harvard University, 1992.

Dissertation

Silverman, Cheryl A. "Jewish Emigres and Popular Images of Jews in Japan." Ph.D. diss., Columbia University, 1989.

Films and Radio

Acts of Faith. Film and discussion regarding Denmark's response to the Holocaust at St. Ansfar Lutheran Church, Toronto, Canada, November 16, 1993. 13th Annual Holocaust Education Week coordinated by Holocaust Education Sub-Committee of Jewish Federation of Greater Toronto.
Escape to the Rising Sun. By Diane Perelsztejn. 1 hour. 1990.
Rokusen-nin no inochi no visa. FMK radio interview. 30 min. 1992. Tape.
Rokusen-nin no Yudaya nanmin o sukutta visa. Film produced by Naofumi Otani for TV Tokyo. 1 hour. Eiko Co., Ltd., 1994. Videocassette.
Yudayajin o sukutta 1500-mai no visa. NHK radio drama. 45 min. 1989. Tape.

Programs

The Mirrer Yeshiva Tribute Dinner, in New York on 21 April 1991.
"Senpo Sugihara" theater program, Gekidan Dora, in Tokyo from May 28–31, 1992.

"Reports and Proceedings"

Bresler, Boris. "Harbin Jewish Community (1898–1958): Politics, Prosperity, Adversity." Paper presented as part of the symposium "Jewish Diasporas in China: Comparative and Historical Perspectives" at Harvard University John K. Fairbank Center for East Asian Research, Cambridge, 16–18 August 1992.
Fiszman, Joseph R. "The Quest for Status: Polish-Jewish Refugees in Shanghai, 1941–1949." Paper presented as part of the symposium "Jewish Diasporas in China: Comparative and Historical Perspectives" at Harvard University John K. Fairbank Center for East Asian Research, Cambridge, 16–18 August 1992.
Maruyama, Naoki. "The Shanghai Zionist Association and Japan." Paper presented as part of the symposium "Jewish Diasporas in China: Comparative and Historical Perspectives" at Harvard University John K.

Fairbank Center for East Asian Research, Cambridge, 16–18 August 1992.

Ristaino, Marcia R. "Response to Ernest G. Heppner's comments on my paper: New Information on Shanghai Jewish Refugees: The Evidence of the Shanghai Municipal Police Files, National Archives, Washington, D.C." Paper presented as part of the symposium "Jewish Diasporas in China: Comparative and Historical Perspectives," Harvard University John K. Fairbank Center for East Asian Research, Cambridge, 16–18 August 1992.

Shiraishi, Masaaki. "Sugihara Chiune to Nihon No Tai Yudayajin Seisaku." Tokyo: Self-Defense Agency Research Institute War History Division, 27 April 1996. Photocopy.

Speeches

Remarks by Ambassador Masamichi Hanabusa, Consul General of Japan at the Mirrer Yeshiva Central Institute Dinner, 21 April, 1991.

Speech by Dr. Samuel P. Oliner, at Beth Tzedec Congregation, Toronto, Canada, 4 November, 1993. 13th Annual Holocaust Education Week coordinated by Holocaust Education Sub-Committee of Jewish Federation of Greater Toronto.

Speech by Dr. Ewa Palasz-Rutkowska, at the Asiatic Society of Japan, OAG Haus, Tokyo, 13 March, 1995.

Speech by Dr. Marion Pritchard, at Pride of Israel Synagogue, Toronto, Canada, 10 November, 1993. 13th Annual Holocaust Education Week coordinated by Holocaust Education Sub-Committee of Jewish Federation of Greater Toronto.

Speech by Dr. Ervin Staub, at Beth David B'nai Israel Beth Am Synagogue, Toronto, Canada, 15 November, 1993. 13th Annual Holocaust Education Week coordinated by Holocaust Education Sub-Committee of Jewish Federation of Greater Toronto.

Transcripts

Interview of Ambassador Masamichi Hanabusa and Mirrer Yeshiva representatives. News 4 New York, WNBC-Channel 4. 13 February 1991.

Index

About the Author

PAMELA ROTNER SAKAMOTO lives and writes in Tokyo. She has been a lecturer at Doshisha University and Baika Junior College, and her articles have appeared in *Points East* and *The Fletcher Forum*. She is presently working as an expert consultant for the United States Holocaust Memorial Museum, which is preparing a special exhibition in 2000 concerning the flight of Polish Jews to Japan and Asia in 1940 and 1941.